The Bedside Rambler

Also by Christopher Somerville

The Bedside Rambler

A Tour Through Country Writers' Britain

CHRISTOPHER SOMERVILLE

HarperCollins

An Imprint of HarperCollins*Publishers*

First published in 1991
by HarperCollins Publishers,
77–85 Fulham Palace Road,
Hammersmith, London W6 8JB

9   8   7   6   5   4   3   2   1

BRITISH LIBRARY CATALOGUING IN PUBLICATION DATA
The Bedside rambler
1. Great Britain. Countryside
I. Somerville, Christopher 1949–
941.009734

ISBN 0 00 215486 2

Typeset in Linotype Pilgrim by
The Spartan Press Ltd, Lymington, Hants.
Printed and bound in Great Britain by
Hartnolls Limited, Bodmin, Cornwall

To Kathleen and Matthew Rasell –
a little taste of home

CONTENTS

INTRODUCTION

There is a wonderful assortment of landscape packed into the narrow confines of Britain. No other country of comparable size can show quite such a spread of mountain and moorland, forest and farmland, hill and valley, downland and dell, marsh, cliff and sandy shore. The character of the British countryside is enormously diverse, too – the bleakness of an Essex saltmarsh, the sweeping flow of the chalk downs of Sussex, the lush richness of Somerset grazing meadows, the drama of water-sculpted limestone ledges of the Yorkshire Dales and the hard beauty of the Welsh and Scottish mountains. These great variations in the mood and appearance of the landscape have inspired writing of equal variety all down the ages, by ploughmen and poets, dons and dunces, all fired by the same desire to catch and set down the flavour of their particular patch of Britain.

The rural writers of these islands have not all been rosy-cheeked scribblers on the hillside, bursting with love for nature, God and man. Some of those with the keenest insight into their local countryside and its communities have turned out to be sad people: poor John Skinner, the rector of the North Somerset coal-mining village of Camerton, for example, who at the end of a long life of misery walked into the woods behind his house and shot himself. Others, like Henry Williamson and Richard Jefferies, felt more at ease the further away they were from their fellow men. Yet Mary Russell Mitford, on her nutting expedition at Three Mile Cross in Berkshire, glows with bonhomie as she writes of her 'dear companion, active and eager and delighted as a boy'.

The quality of the country writers' work is as varied as their personalities, from the poetical fluency of a Laurie Lee or a Neil Gunn to the stumbling, misspelt reminiscences of the King of the Norfolk Poachers, Frederick Rolfe.

What all the pieces included in *The Bedside Rambler* have in common is a vivid sense of the countryside as vibrantly alive, in its appearance, its moods, its customs, people and wildlife. Not all the writing is fine. But each piece shines a revealing light on a chosen place; a light which reflects back to illuminate the writers themselves.

To show how Britain's countryside slips from one aspect to another, blends one set of characteristics with the next, this collection of country writing takes the form of a journey from Land's End in westernmost Cornwall to John o'Groats at the furthest northern outpost of Scotland. We visit fifteen separate regions as we go, each one linked to the next by a description of my own travels as I wandered through the land on foot, by train and by car, joining up the different sections of the long trail through Britain. The trail winds around each region, stopping at selected places to view them through the eyes of individual writers. There is no chronological shape to the journey – you'll find yourself in Dorset, for example, in the company of the very twentieth-century Ken Allsop at one stopping place, then with Thomas Hardy a few miles and a hundred years away. You'll see the Lake District in 1800 through Dorothy Wordsworth's romantically focused eyes, contrasted with the level and practical stare of Celia Fiennes a century earlier. Evocative country writing knows no bounds of time, nor of type. There are diarists here such as Parson Woodforde in Norfolk and curate Kilvert on the Welsh borders; novelists like Charles Dickens in the Kentish marshes and R. L. Stevenson on Rannoch Moor; the naturalists Gilbert White at Selborne in Hampshire, and Richard Mabey in north Norfolk. Quirky travellers take us a step of the way with them – George Borrow self-satisfied in Wild Wales, Dr Samuel Johnson grumbling in Glenelg. The poets who write of their countryside range from William Barnes and his Dorset in dialect to Phoebe Hesketh's crystal-clear pictures of the Lancashire moors and Robbie Burns's mixture of fun and polemic along the Scottish rivers.

10

Certain writers make more than one appearance along the way. Here I admit to having been less than adamantine of will – I found that I just couldn't keep them out. H. V. Morton forces his way into the foreground in several places through sheer *brio* and enthusiasm. The beautiful writing of Edward Thomas, whether in prose or in poetry, illuminates every place he chooses to describe. The same applies to Richard Jefferies, in either pastoral or mystical mood, and to Francis Kilvert, enhanced by his love of life in all its manifestations. The most faithful of all our companions, though, is John Hillaby, pursuing on foot his own *Journey Through Britain*. He is there to start us off at Land's End, and turns up again to welcome us at John o'Groats, having popped up at our elbow in several places along the way.

These writers with their multiple entries have undoubtedly denied others what I'm sure many readers will see as their rightful places in this collection. But the ones that got away are every anthologist's apology. If you regret the absence of your personal favourite – a writer who has shone a special light on your own treasured piece of Britain – then all I can say is that your regret is fully shared by me, having had to lay aside so many writers I badly wanted to include. This book could have been ten times as long, and still there would have been room for more. I had enormous fun putting it together, travelling the length and breadth of Britain. I revelled in the company of old friends among the country writers and met many new ones, both famous and obscure. I hope that as you take this journey you, too, will be inspired to read more of their writings, and to visit the places that they celebrated.

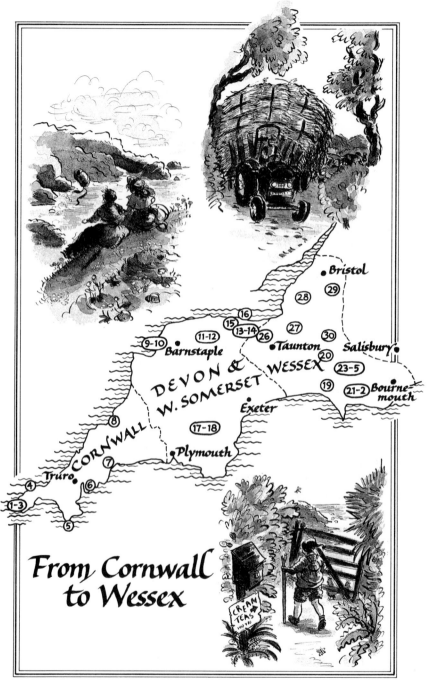

From Cornwall to Wessex

I

From Cornwall

Down the years writers have made the long journey through Cornwall, south and west until they can go no further, to hone their literary blades on the rocks and cliffs of Land's End. Around this spiky toe of Britain, poking into the Atlantic, romance and realism intertwine: treacherous waters that hide the legendary land of Lyonesse, black stacks of rock, shipwrecks and smugglers, the petering out of the land at its furthermost point. Diarists, novelists, travel writers, naturalists, all have responded to the urge to see what lay at the end of the road. Their accounts of what they found there are often far from ecstatic – too many other visitors, too many shoddy shacks. For better or worse, though, there's no other place to start our journey through Britain, travelling along the bare, shoulder-like granite coastline that Cornwall turns to the sea.

Four of the writers represented here will enliven this collection in other parts of Britain – the American-born naturalist W. H. Hudson, writing around the turn of the twentieth century; the romantic, opinionated H. V. Morton from the 1920s; Francis Kilvert, the diarist curate of Clyro half a century before; and the great modern long-distance walker John Hillaby, creator of a rich stew of country writing that we will dip into again and again along our way. Three of these writers on Cornwall – Kilvert, John Skinner and C. A. Johns – are clerics on holiday, always a sharp-eyed species of country writer. Daphne du Maurier, with Cornwall in her blood and bone, finds beauty in the most industrial of landscapes. And Sir John Betjeman sums up what Cornwall means to millions – the safe childhood adventure of the family seaside holiday.

LAND'S END

1. John Hillaby, *Journey Through Britain* (1968)

I left at seven o'clock in the morning and I have been asked to say that my wife was there to see me off. There isn't, in fact, much else that I can say. It was misty. I couldn't see much. I could hear nothing except the twittering of invisible larks. I felt dizzy, not from the height of the clifftops, nor elation at the start. The feeling came from an unfamiliar breakfast of cold roast fowl and champagne. And that soon wore off.

2. W. H. Hudson, *The Land's End* (1908)

Although the vague image of an imagined Land's End fades from the mind and is perhaps lost when the reality is known, the ancient associations of the place remain, and, if a visit be rightly timed, they may invest it with a sublimity and fascination not its own. I loitered many days near that spot in mid-winter, in the worst possible weather, but even when pining for a change to blue skies and genial sunshine I blessed the daily furious winds which served to keep the pilgrims away, and to half blot out the vulgar modern buildings with rain and mist from the Atlantic. At dark I would fight my way against the wind to the cliff, and down by the sloping narrow neck of land to the masses of loosely piled rocks at its extremity. It was a very solitary place at that hour, where one feared not to be intruded on by any other night-wanderer in human shape. The raving of the wind among the rocks; the dark ocean – exceedingly dark except when the flying clouds were broken and the stars shining in the clear spaces touched the big black incoming waves with a steely-grey light; the jagged isolated rocks, on which so many ships have been shattered, rising in awful blackness from the spectral

foam that appeared and vanished and appeared again;
the multitudinous hoarse sounds of the sea, with
throbbing and hollow booming noises in the caverns
beneath – all together served to bring back something of
the old vanished picture or vision of Bolerium as we first
imagine it. The glare from the various lighthouses
visible at this point only served to heighten the inex-
pressibly sombre effect, since shining from a distance
they made the gloomy world appear vaster. Down in the
south, twenty-five miles away, the low clouds were lit
up at short intervals by wide white flashes as of sheet
lightning from the Lizard lights, the most powerful of
all lights, the reflection of which may be seen at a
distance of sixty or seventy miles at sea. In front of the
Land's End promontory, within five miles of it, was the
angry red glare from the Longships tower, and further
away to the left the white revolving light of the Wolf
lighthouse.

It was perhaps on some tempestuous winter night at
the Land's End that the fancy, told as a legend or
superstitious belief in J. H. Pearce's *Cornish Drolls*,
occurred to him or to someone, that the Wolf Rock was
the habitation of a great black dog, a terrible supernatural beast that preys on the souls of the dead. For the rock
lies directly in the route of those who die on the
mainland and journey over the sea to their ultimate
abode, the Scilly Isles: and when the wind blows hard
against them and they are beaten down like migrating
birds and fly close to the surface, he is able as they come
over the rock to capture and devour them.

3. John Skinner, *Diary* (1797)

Having explored all that was worthy of notice at
St Just, we proceed under the direction of our guide to
Land's End, about six miles distant. This is the most
westerly promontory in England, and exhibits a mass of
rock rising majestically from the waves. The strata of
these rocks run so even that you may almost fancy they
are indebted to the chissel for their smooth surface, and
that they were piled one on the other by the gigantic

efforts of human architects. The sea view from this rocky promontory is very grand, and the eye reposes with pleasure on the lighthouse, built on some detached rocks out at Sea, called the Long Ships, to warn off sailors from this dangerous shore.

Having taken a rough sketch, we remounted our horses, bestowing a trifle on some youngsters who had nearly ran a mile to hold them, and trotted on.

GURNARD'S HEAD

4. Francis Kilvert, *Diary* (1870)

Friday, 29 July 1870

Oh that sunny happy evening gathering ferns among the Cliffs. *Asplenium Marinum*, with its bright glossy green leaves, hiding itself so provokingly in the narrowest crevices of the rocks. I wandered round the cliffs to the broken rocks at the furthest point of Gurnard's Head, and sat alone amongst the wilderness of broken shattered tumbled cliffs, listening to the booming and breaking of the waves below and watching the flying skirts of the showers of spray. Perfect solitude. The rest of the party were climbing about in the rocks somewhere overhead, but not a voice or sound was to be heard except the boom of the sea and the crying of the white-winged gulls. Not a sign or vestige of any other living thing.

A scramble up among the rocks to search for ferns for Mrs H. Not very successful, and H. had got her some much finer ones, but she did not despise mine, though they were very poor little ones in comparison.

The rest of the party had come down from a scrambling like goats and conies in the high rocks, the ladies having had to mount by means of the gentlemen's backs and knees.

We returned by Penzance hearing it was a better road, and we did not repent of it.

THE LIZARD

5. Rev. C. A. Johns, *A Week at the Lizard* (1848)

All along this part of the coast, the rocks assume more of
the character of the trappean formation, than is apparent elsewhere, especially if they are beheld from the sea.
They do not readily decompose from exposure to the
air, nor has the sea worn away the base, consequently they present neither a slanting nor perpendicular
continuous surface, but consist of huge weather-beaten
blocks and slabs, piled together in wild grandeur.
The next point is usually marked in the maps 'the
Beast Point'; the fishermen call it 'the Base', a corrup-
tion perhaps of Bass, from the fish of that name, which
abounds here; and just beyond this is the Hot Point. By
dint of a little scrambling one may here descend to the
water's edge and attain a favourite fishing spot, where
the tide sweeps by the feet like a rapid river. Following
the safer course, the path brings us to a shed, on the
brow of the cliff, used by fishermen when on the
look-out for pilchards. Here an exceedingly beautiful
prospect suddenly opens on the view; a noble bay about
five miles across, formed by picturesque cliffs, broken
into an undulating line by a succession of picturesque
valleys; a flag-staff on one of the highest of these, and
two or three white cottages peeping out from between
the headlands, point out the locality of the fishing
village and coast guard station, Cadgwith.

Someway beyond this the land sinks; and here a
narrow yellow line indicates a sandy beach, known by
the name of Kennack Sands. The opposite boundary of
the bay is formed by a bold, bluff, head-land, the
Black-head, a most appropriate name, for the whole
face of the cliff, with the exception of one narrow
perpendicular strip, called Sparnick, is of a remarkably
dingy hue. In the distance, the Deadman Point is
distinctly visible, with a vessel or two entering or
quitting Falmouth Harbour, which lies between; and if
the weather be very clear, the Rame Head, the most
easterly head-land in the country, may be descried

stretching out a long way on the horizon, as unsubstantial in appearance as a fog-bank. One or two lobster catchers are creeping along under the cliffs in their tiny vessels, and a few fishing boats of a larger size are making for the offing, there to set their drift-nets, as soon as night sets in; just beneath us, on a projecting ledge of rock, lie the whitening bones of a lamb, killed and devoured by ravens, before it was strong enough to seek safety by flight; and the deep croak of the same bird, or the shrill note of the jackdaw, divides with the dashing of the sea below us and its murmuring roll beyond the whole empire of sound.

Glorious as this scene is by day, it becomes sublime under the influence of a summer or autumn moonlight. The single broad path of glory emblazoned by a cloudless moon on the sea, at all times one of the most striking objects in nature, is here infinitely finer, and more calculated to produce a spirit of devotion, than I have ever seen it elsewhere. It is, I think, impossible for the eye to rest on that bright path, terminating as it does in a circle of mild brilliancy, without exciting the mind, the devotional mind at least, to meditate on the bright way which leads from the dark boundaries of this world to the centre of all Light and Goodness . . .

The guides at Kynance will ascend the Gull Rock with ease, nay, rapidity, and for a trifling remuneration bring back eggs or young birds for any one who will employ them. If the following anecdote be, as I am assured it is, true, one scarcely knows whether the imprudence or presence of mind of these men is most to be wondered at.

A gentleman wished to have in his possession a living specimen of the chough, or Cornish crow, a bird which is now becoming rare, and which always builds in the precipitous sides of the cliffs. Two brothers engaged to furnish him with young birds from the nest. They accordingly provided themselves with a rope, and proceeded to a place which they knew to be frequented by these birds. One of them tied an end of the rope round his waist, and his brother lowered him over the edge of the cliff, *holding the rope in his hand*. When he had arrived opposite the nests, he found that they were built under an overhanging rock, so as to be beyond his reach. Nothing daunted, he set the rope a-swinging until he was carried into the hollow, when he held fast by the rock; but finding the rope too short to allow him to gain the nest, he untied it from his waist, climbed into the cavity, and secured his prize, which he stored away in his bosom. Meanwhile the rope had swung back to the perpendicular, and was resting motionless. Without hesitation he called out to his brother above, 'Stand by the rope! I'm going to leap to it!' He did so; but the rope, as might have been expected, slipped through his hands, and he fell into the sea. The brother felt the jerk, and looking out over the edge of the cliff, saw him neither dashed in pieces nor drowned, but rubbing the water from his face, and exclaiming, 'Carry my shoes round to the cove, brother John, I'll be round as soon as thee wast!' And so he was, and moreover bringing his birds safe with him. This perilous adventure is said to have happened in the parish of Breage.

St Just-in-Roseland

6. H. V. Morton, *In Search of England* (1927)

I have blundered into a Garden of Eden that cannot be described in pen or paint. There is a degree of beauty that flies so high that no net of words or no snare of colour can hope to capture it, and of this order is the beauty of St Just in Roseland, the companion village to St Anthony.

There are a few cottages lost in trees, a vicarage with two old cannon balls propping open the garden gate, and a church. The church is grey and small and, as a church, not worth notice; but it stands in a churchyard which is one of the little-known glories of Cornwall. I would like to know if there is in the whole of England a churchyard more beautiful than this. There is hardly a level yard in it. You stand at the lych-gate, and look down into a green cup filled with flowers and arched by great trees. In the dip is the little church, its tower level with you as you stand above. The white gravestones rise up from ferns and flowers.

Beyond the church a screen of trees forms a tracery of leaves through which, shining white in the sun, you see the ground sloping steeply towards the creek beyond which is that strong arm of the sea, Carrick Roads. Over the roof of the church blue water gleams; above it rise the distant fields of the opposite bank. This churchyard is drowsy with the bee and rich with a leafy pungency. There is also a tropic smell in it, a smell of palms and foreign trees.

An elderly clergyman was training a plant over a wall. He looked up and smiled.

'Yes, I am the vicar. Which do you prefer – those wine-dark rhododendrons or the pink? And do you notice that rather subtle shade in between? I like that, don't you?'

'Who was St Just, sir?' I asked.

'St Just was,' he replied, taking off his broad black hat and smoothing his silver hair, 'St Just was – I want you to admire those pansies! Now look at this. Isn't it beautiful?'

He bent down and, taking a deep velvet flower between two fingers, turned its head gently towards me.

'You were saying that St Just was—'

'Ah, yes, forgive me! St Just – oh, the trouble I've had with those japonicas.'

He shook his head.

'St Just?' I murmured hopefully.

'That tall tree over there came from Australia,' he remarked proudly. 'By the way, I have a tropical garden behind the church which you must see.'

I abandoned the saint.

'You have made this garden?'

'With my own hands I have made it,' he replied lovingly. 'It took a long time.' Here he straightened his spare figure and cast a look round over the indescribable tangle of loveliness. 'But it was worth it.'

He smiled at me, and quoted Isaiah:

'"Instead of the thorn shall come up the fig tree, and instead of the briar shall come up the myrtle tree; and it shall be to the Lord for a name, for an everlasting sign that shall not be cut off."'

'CORNISH ALPS', HENSBARROW DOWNS

7. Daphne du Maurier, *Vanishing Cornwall* (1967)

The interest to the layman, and to the casual wanderer who finds himself by chance or intention in the china-clay country, is the strange, almost fantastic beauty of the landscape, where spoil-heaps of waste matter shaped like pyramids point to the sky, great quarries formed about their base descending into pits filled with water, icy green like arctic pools. The pyramids are generally highest, and the pools deepest, on land which is no longer used; the spoil-heaps sprout grass-seed, even gorse, upon the pumice-stone quality of their surface, and the water in the pits, deeper far than Dozmare, is there because the clay has been sucked off and work begun again on virgin ground.

These clay-heaps, with their attendant lakes and disused quarries, have the same grandeur as tin mines in decay but in a wilder and more magical sense, for they are not sentinels of stone or brick constructed to house engines but mountains formed out of the rocky soil itself, and the pools, man-made, are augmented by water seeping from underground sources and by the winter rains. Sites in full production may work close at hand, cranes swing wide, trolley-buckets climb to the summit of a waste-heap, looking at a distance as small as a child's toy, before unloading and returning to base, lorries pass in and out of entrances to the road, the precincts barred by wire and DANGER notices; but the discarded pyramids and pools seem as remote from the industry near by as any lonely tor upon the moors.

Wild flowers straggle across the waste, seeds flourish

into nameless plants, wandering birds from the moorland skim the lakes or dabble at the water's edge.
Seagulls, flying inland, hover above the surface. There
is nothing ugly here. Cornishmen are wresting a living
from the granite as they have done through countless
generations, leaving nature to deal in her own fashion
with forgotten ground, which, being prodigal of hand,
she has done with a lavish and a careless grace.

The highest point in this lunar landscape is the
1027-foot beacon on Hensbarrow Downs, from where
the whole fantastic conical chain can be seen spreading
west towards St Dennis and Nanpean, or splayed out
fanwise to north and south in indiscriminate heaps.
Beside the beacon are ancient barrows, communal
burial-places of those who settled here in prehistoric
times, and the beacon itself was once the site of a
watchhouse, like others on high points, where a man
would lodge himself to watch for the approach of
enemies on sea or land, and, if he sighted them, kindle a
fire to warn his fellows.

A stranger set down upon this spot today, or closer
still amongst the slag and shale, white hills on either
side of him, would think himself a thousand miles from
Cornwall, in the canyons of Colorado, perhaps, or the
volcanic craters on the moon.

DAYMER BAY

8. John Betjeman, *Summoned By Bells* (1960)

> . . . Then before breakfast down toward the sea
> I ran alone, monarch of miles of sand,
> Its shining stretches satin-smooth and vein'd.
> I felt beneath bare feet the lugworm casts
> And walked where only gulls and oyster-catchers
> Had stepped before me to the water's edge.
> The morning tide flowed in to welcome me,
> The fan-shaped scallop shells, the backs of crabs,
> The bits of driftwood worn to reptile shapes,

The heaps of bladder-wrack the tide had left
(Which, lifted up, sent sandhoppers to leap
In hundreds round me) answered 'Welcome back!'
Along the links and under cold Bray Hill
Fresh water pattered from an iris marsh
And drowned the golf-balls on its stealthy way
Over the slates in which the elvers hid,
And spread across the beach.

To Devon and West Somerset

The North Cornwall Railway that once brought the young John Betjeman from London to 'far Trebetherick' has lost its rails, its signals, its trains and passengers. Leaving Cornwall for North Devon as a gorse-smothered, flower-filled, bird-haunted green corridor in the countryside, it bends and straightens, bends and straightens for fifty miles through moor and farmland, a haven for wildlife and walkers, the least frequented footpath in all the county.

From Daymer Bay I walked at low tide along the sands of the Camel estuary, to bob across the river on the little ferry into Padstow's crooked old waterfront. At the end of the quay behind the fish dock stands the square station building where the track of the disused North Cornwall Railway began. It wound along the estuary for five miles inland to Wadebridge, following every curve of the River Camel, before striking out across many lonely miles of northern Cornwall's bleakest farmland. There is nothing cosy about this landscape of moor and boggy valleys. But the old railway's succession of deep cuttings gives shelter from the eternally blowing sea wind; and where sunlight penetrates deeply enough, the gorse patches and buddleia bushes that have colonized the ballast of the abandoned trackbed are thronged with butterflies. Emerging from these cuttings, the views suddenly broaden over miles of upland and distant sea vistas under wide skies.

The decommissioned stations of the North Cornwall Railway still stand on their platforms, exposed to wind and weather – St Kew Highway, Port Isaac Road, Delabole, Camelford, Otterham. Some of them are sadly derelict and crumbledown. Others have been lovingly converted into neat houses in well-scrubbed gardens, decorated with old railway benches and gas-lamps. Fashioning a comfortable house out of an old railway station is a labour of love if ever there was one. Damp and draughts are endemic in their poky, dark rooms. But they are steeped in nostalgia. Decaying or restored, the stations carry a whiff of train-smoke and a whisper of romance.

At Launceston the Norman castle on its green mound over the town marks a transition in the landscape. Behind are the cold moors of north Cornwall; in front, as the old railway slips ever northwards, lie the steeper valleys, the woods and streams of Devon. For fourteen long miles up a narrow valley beside the River Carey I trudged the old track as it clung to the river, squeezing along under farms perched up high on the hill slopes. Sycamores and hazels growing in the trackbed block out all far views, concentrating the gaze on what is near at hand – limestone chunks of ballast, coarse grass, clumps of rosebay willowherb, finches and thrushes in the bushes, caterpillars on the yellow ragwort – all enclosed in a tunnel of trees. Slogging up the valley, I came at last to Halwill Junction where four lines of railway once met at the grim little station on its windy ridge. Now the four disused tracks sprouted green grass whiskers, and the circle of the goods yard turntable was full of purple clover. No more southbound trains to Padstow; no more slow locals to Bude in the west or Okehampton in the east. None northward, either, to Torrington and on to Barnstaple on the Two Rivers estuary.

Next morning I left Halwill Junction and headed north into the moors along the track of a short branch line with a long name – the North Devon and Cornwall Junction Light Railway. From the moors of Merton and Marland ball clay was dug and sent along the rails of the ND&CJLR to Barnstaple and the wider world. And from those moors we enter the country of the Two Rivers, Taw and Torridge.

Henry Williamson arrived in North Devon in 1921, a twenty-six-year-old ex-soldier with a compulsion to write, nursing a spirit wounded beyond healing during three years' Great War service. His first few years in the country of the Two Rivers, a countryside then virtually untouched by the motor car and by tourism, brought him some peace of mind as he roamed the lanes, fields and rivers between Exmoor and the Atlantic coast. Awkwardness, prickliness and suspicion were soon to sour the rest of his long life – he died in 1977 – but for this short time his senses were at their acutest pitch, feeding his pen constantly. Countless hours spent painstakingly observing and recording nature in all its operations bore fruit in the writing of *Tarka the Otter* (1927), by far his most famous work.

We follow the old railway track beside the River Torridge, now a footpath known as the Tarka Trail, down to cross the wide estuary where Torridge meets Taw. Here was one of Williamson's favourite walks, from his cottage at Georgeham along the sand dunes of Braunton Burrows. There follows a description of the climax of a deer hunt on Exmoor in the 1880s, written by Richard Jefferies, one of the finest country writers ever to put pen to paper. Jefferies, born in Wiltshire, was only thirty-eight when he died of the wasting disease fibroid phthisis in 1887, but his output of country writing – mostly short pieces for newspapers and weekly magazines – was prodigious. Henry Williamson acknowledged Jefferies as his master and inspiration. Both writers possessed a rare insight into animal life, and the fluency of expression to share it with their readers, as well as the equally rare capacity to stand and sit absolutely still for hours on end, melting into the background and reducing themselves to a pair of all-seeing eyes and a meticulously recording brain.

From the centre of Exmoor we move on, by way of the deep combes of Lorna Doone country and a comic episode on Porlock Hill with H. V. Morton, to re-encounter Jefferies and Williamson at Cloutsham Farm under the northern slope of Exmoor's highest peak, Dunkery Beacon. Then our journey goes south to the opposite end of Devon, leaving the warm red sandstone and green trees of Exmoor for the dark grey granite and chill bogs of Dartmoor. Sabine Baring-Gould (1834–1924), rector and squire of Lew Trenchard on the western side of Dartmoor, wrote hundreds of other and better things than 'Onward, Christian Soldiers', for which he is best remembered today. I have let Baring-Gould stand alone on Dartmoor, giving his scholarship full play over various aspects of the scene in his *Book of Dartmoor* (1900) – though John Hillaby ends this selection, manfully, by marching full tilt into a bog.

BRAUNTON BURROWS, NORTH DEVON

9. Henry Williamson, *Tarka the Otter* (1927)

The otters were alarmed by the coming of the man, and that night they left the headland, returning to the Burrows, and hunting rabbits in the great warren of the sandhills. A cold mist lay on the plains and in the hollows, riming the marram grasses and the withered stems of thistle and mullein, so that in the morning mildew and fungi in strange plant forms seemed to have grown out of the sand. On the coarser hairs of the otters' coats the hoar remained white, but on the shorter and softer hairs it melted into little balls of water. Everything except the otters and birds and bullocks was white. The sedges and reeds of the duckponds were white, so was the rigging of the ketches in the pill. The hoof-holes of cattle were filmed with brittle ice. In the cold windless air came distinct the quacking of ducks and the whistling of drakes as the wild-fowl flighted from the ponds and saltings in the sea, where they slept by day.

The otters lay up near a cattle shippen, among reeds with white feathery tops. A dull red sun, without heat or rays, moved over them, sinking slowly down the sky. For two days and two nights the frosty vapour lay over the Burrows, and then came a north wind which poured like liquid glass from Exmoor and made all things distinct. The wind made whips of the dwarf willows, and hissed through clumps of the great sea-rushes. The spines of the marram grasses scratched wildly at the rushing air, which passed over the hollows where larks and linnets crouched with puffed feathers. Like a spirit freed by the sun's ruin and levelling all things before a new creation, the wind drove grains of sand against the legs and ruffled feathers of the little birds, as though it would breathe annihilation upon them, strip their frail bones of skin and flesh, and grind them until they became again that which was before the earth's old travail. Vainly the sharp and hard points of the marram grasses drew their circles on the sand: the Icicle Spirit was coming, and no terrestrial power could exorcize it.

The north wind carried a strange thickset bird which drifted without feather sound over the dry bracken of Ferny Hill, where Tarka and Greymuzzle had gone for warmth. Its plumage was white-barred and spotted with dark brown. Its fierce eyes were ringed with yellow, the colour of the lichens on the stone shippens. Mile after mile its soft and silent wings had carried it, from a frozen land where the Northern Lights stared in stark perpetuity upon the ice-fields. The thickset bird was an Arctic Owl, and its name was Bubu, which means Terrible. It quartered the mires and the burrows, and the grip of its feathered feet was death to many ducks and rabbits.

10. Henry Williamson, *Tales of Moorland and Estuary* (1953)

It was a steady pull up the lane, but at the top there was bright reward. I stood in the clear air of morning gazing over hundreds of square miles of land and sea. Far below, spread out like a model contour map, were the sandhills of the Burrows, blown by the sea-winds into a desert extending behind a shallow shore. A long headland enclosed the southern ocean, ending at Harty Point. There, across the steely-blue sea, on the horizon of sky and ocean, was Lundy, standing high; its cliffs, like those of the promontory, seen in clear detail in the low rays of the eastern sun. My watch said seven o'clock, but the world had been fresh and bright for over two hours. Across the Burrows I saw the white stalk of the lighthouse, among sandhills this side of the estuary of the Two Rivers: and across the water, the village which was my destination, built around the base of a green hill.

Usually I walked between twelve and fifteen miles every day. The thought of being indoors was unbearable. With happy anticipation I gazed at the route before me, of the miles along broad sands in which the ribs of wooden ships were embedded.

Descending the hill, I crossed the sandhills, and soon was walking in the spindrift at the edge of the sea. For a change, I traversed the sands, with their shells of razorfish and cockle, and walked along the upper-tide-lines among the corks and feathers and notched skeletons of birds struck down and plucked by the peregrine falcons. There were pink crab shells and sand-blasted bottles, dry seaweed thongs and barnacle-riddled driftwood, among which ran the ring-plovers upon stone and shell, piping their frail cries as they arose in flight before one; and after a swift wing-jerking circular flight they would glide to their feet again, to stand as still as the stones and watch the stranger whose bare feet were purring in the dry sand above the tide-line, where they were dreaming of laying their eggs.

Beyond the wrack-strewn hollows in the breaches of the sandhills lay the estuary, with waves breaking white on the submerged shoal called the South Tail. As I strode along the shore, still carrying my shoes, I saw oyster-catchers on a shingle bank; and rounding Aery Point, was soon trudging on wet loose gravel to the lighthouse, and thence upon the lower rocks, among pools where crabs hurried from my shadow, and strange small fish, locked in by the lapsed tide, reamed into the dark, seaweed-haunted depths. I was making for the middle ridge from where a waved handkerchief would bring a boat from the far shore, to row the traveller across the estuary for a shilling.

Such is a walk on a spring morning, when a man is free and facing life with zest: a timeless walk, every moment lived in peace; a walk that seems to go on for ever, and then it is all behind one, but living in the mind, timelessly.

EXMOOR

11. Richard Jefferies, *Red Deer* (1884)

No more able to run, the hunted stag stands at bay in the river, choosing a place so deep that the hounds must swim to reach him, while he is firm on his feet. Though they swarm about him, if the water is deep enough he can keep them at bay with his antlers for a time; but they are too numerous. His strength decreases as their eagerness increases, for they attack him for his flesh; they hunt not only for the joy of the chase, but the savage flavour of blood. Hounds that have not before seen a stag at bay rush in, and are received on the terrible brow-points.

After delivering a blow with his antlers, the stag holds his head high up, his large eyes straining down on the hounds, and his mouth shut. They swarm upon him, and weary him out, pulling him down at last by his legs, and he falls with his legs under him as a bullock lies. The hounds are whipped off, or they would tear him to pieces – their teeth marks are generally left in the skin – and the huntsman comes to kill him. But first, even now, his antlers must be secured, for they turn furiously towards all who approach, and he can kick as hard as a pony. There is a lasso, or headline, kept for the purpose, and supposed to be carried with the hunt; but it often happens that it is not at hand when wanted. One or two of the most experienced present run in, the thong of a whip is twisted round the antlers, and the head drawn back as far as possible, so as to stretch and expose the neck.

Instantly the huntsman thrusts his knife with a quick deep stab – the deer gives a convulsive throb and start, and dies instantaneously. The neck of a stag is covered for some way down from the head with rougher, shaggier hair than the rest of the skin. It is just where this rough hair ceases that the stab is given. Until within the last few years the huntsman used to cut the throat across, high up under the chin, when there was much blood, which the present way does not cause. If any fresh sportsman is in at the death his face is 'blooded', and there is often a scramble for trophies, as the slot, or hoofs, tufts of hair torn from the skin, or the tusks. The teeth polish well, and are set in scarfpins; the slots are often silver-mounted as the base of candlesticks.

12. Hope Bourne, *Wild Harvest* (1978)

Outside rain lashes out of the blackness of night and a rising storm shakes the trees and sends its roaring voice across the moor and down the combe. All around, mile upon mile of hill and bog, field and wood and stream-filled valley lie in the dark, hidden from me but felt intensely like a Presence. Far-off, each a mile or so in distance at the nearest, lie hill farms, islands of light and life in the immensity of winter night, and each is a neighbour, unseen now but known.

Beyond the gates the lane begins, starting on its outward journey to civilization – or what passes for that in these parts. Rough and stony and grass-matted in the middle, pooled with mud in parts, it goes down a quarter-mile to a gate and little bridge over a rushing moorland stream. Thence it debouches onto the open moor for a mile, becoming a track amongst bracken and rushes, rainwashed and rutty. Eventually it reaches a tarmaced road and ends thereat, having made contact with the twentieth century.

CLOUTSHAM, WEST SOMERSET

13. Henry Williamson, *The Old Stag and Other Hunting Stories* (1932)

Stumberleap Farm was a long stone building roofed with slate. Bright yellow lichens spread in patches over the walls and roof. Starlings sang upon the great square chimney tuns, in the cracks of which grew ferns of wall-rue and hart's tongue. On the top of each tun two slabs of shale were mortared in the form of a triangle, to cut the winds which in winter would pour down the chimneys. Beeches and pines surrounded the cluster of house, barns, and shippen. One of the beech trees was hollow and had held the nest of a brown owl every spring for half a century. On a thick branch parallel with the ground a rope swing was tied, and the farm children played here, swinging from the same branch from which their great-great-great-great-grandfather had hung after a raid by the robbers of Hoccombe-goyal.

At half-past ten, the time of the meet, over a hundred people had come to the farm. Hunters neighed, men and women smiled and chatted, moved about greeting friends; pink and grey and tweed coats made gay colour in the field behind the farm. The sun of a fair September morning dropped its gold into the dewy freshness of the valley. In blinding spikes and splashes of light it moved up the southern sky, above the sombre moor whose summit undulated with the four curves of Dunkery's cloud-high crest. Seen from the Ball, the moor's outline against blue space was like the back of a monster petrified in the fires of earth's creation, showing black bristles singed almost to the roots; westwards the last paw-stroke of the dying monster had made claw-rips in the steep slope of Lucott Ridge.

14. Richard Jefferies, *Red Deer* (1884)

Across a deep valley – a rifle-shot distant – rises a steep slope covered with oak. Openings in the oaks are green with brake, and where the fern has not grown the reddish hue of the loose stones is visible. The slope is far higher than the hill on which I stand, and extends right and left, surrounding me. To the left it is all woods! woods! woods! – a valley of woods, interminable oak, under which hundreds of deer might hide. On the right it is heather – thousands of acres of heather – gradually expanding into the mountainous breadth of Dunkery Beacon.

Now in June the heather is dark, yet beneath the darkness there are faint shades of purple and green; it looks dry and heated under the sunshine. Dunkery towers over as if the green (Cloutsham) Ball were a molehill. I can see now that a great trench – a natural fosse – surrounds me on every side, except where a neck of land like a drawbridge gives access to the mount . . .

It is a great natural stage erected in the centre of a circular theatre of moor and forest, and the spectator has only to face in different directions to watch the hunt travel round him. While the hunt has to go miles, he has but to stroll a few hundred yards; presently the deer, breaking cover, comes up over the summit of the Ball by one of its scarcely visible paths, and crosses it in front of him within a stone's throw. If an army had cast up a rocky stand for a Xerxes to view the sport, they could not have done it more effectually . . .

Cloutsham Farm stands where the neck of land connects the round green mount with the general level of the moors. The old thatched house – it is one of Sir Thomas Acland's thatched houses – has a hearth as wide as that of a hunting lodge should be, and an arched inner doorway of oak. A rude massiveness characterizes the place. A balcony on the first floor overlooks the steepest part of the vast natural fosse surrounding the mount, and the mountainous breadth of Dunkery Beacon rises exactly opposite, shutting out the lower half of the sky.

Something is now moving among the heather near the summit, so distant and so dim that it is difficult to distinguish what it is. But the sheep yonder are white and these three animals are dark, a little inclined to redness. They move quickly in line, and are larger than sheep; they must be hinds. It is only when endeavouring to determine what any particular object is, that you recognize the breadth and height of the Beacon side.

DOONE VALLEY

15. R. D. Blackmore, *Lorna Doone* (1869)

Mother had done a most wondrous thing, which made all the neighbours say that she must be mad, at least. Upon the Monday morning, while her husband lay unburied, she cast a white hood over her hair, and gathered a black cloak round her, and, taking counsel of no one, set off on foot for the Doone-gate.

In the early afternoon she came to the hollow and barren entrance; where in truth there was no gate, only darkness to go through. If I get on with this story, I shall have to tell of it by and by, as I saw it afterwards; and will not dwell there now. Enough that no gun was fired at her, only her eyes were covered over, and somebody led her by the hand, without any wish to hurt her.

A very rough and headstrong road was all that she remembered, for she could not think as she wished to do, with the cold iron pushed against her. At the end of this road they delivered her eyes, and she could scarce believe them.

For she stood at the head of a deep green valley, carved from out the mountains in a perfect oval, with a fence of sheer rock standing round it, eighty feet or a hundred high; from whose brink black wooded hills swept up to the sky-line. By her side a little river glided out from underground with a soft dark babble, un-awares of daylight; then growing brighter, lapsed away, and fell into the valley. There, as it ran down the meadow, alders stood on either marge, and grass was blading out upon it, and yellow tufts of rushes gathered, looking at the hurry. But further down, on either bank, were covered houses, built of stone, square and roughly cornered, set as if the brook were meant to be the street between them. Only one room high they were, and not placed opposite each other, but in and out as skittles are; only that the first of all, which proved to be the captain's, was a sort of double house, or rather two houses joined together by a plank-bridge over the river.

Fourteen cots my mother counted, all very much of a pattern, and nothing to choose between them, unless it were the captain's. Deep in the quiet valley there, away from noise, and violence, and brawl, save that of the rivulet, any man would have deemed them homes of simple mind and innocence. Yet not a single house stood there but was the home of murder.

PORLOCK HILL

16. H. V. Morton, *In Search of England* (1927)

Should I descend the old hill that slips away into the valley like a toboggan slide, or should I pay one-and-six and take the new toll road? Considering the average price for switchbacks at fairs and exhibitions, I considered one and sixpence almost a bargain.

I notice that they wisely collect it before you begin the descent, and not at the other end.

I went on steadily down the one-in-four gradient, the hind wheel in the air and the bonnet to the earth. As I was taking a bend in a most workman-like manner, and wondering about the humorist who had put up at a corner a red DANGEROUS, a motor-cycle and a side-car came warily towards me round a bend, making a noise like a machine-gun corps showing off to a general. On the motor-cycle was an earnest young man; in the side-car was a girl.

'Love,' I thought, 'conquereth all things.'

I proceeded sentimentally for the next half mile, admiring the red gravel of the road, the rich red sandstone banks, the yellow cubes of sunlight falling through the lace of leaves, when suddenly . . .

I pulled up on the edge of a suit-case that lay, looking most out of place, in the centre of the road.

I imagine that Porlock Hill shakes off more luggage than any hill in England. There lay the suit-case upside-down! When I picked it up the clasps sprang back and the contents lurched heavily into the lid. I clumsily patted them back, and as I did so it was not possible to be unaware of a pink silk night-dress nestling in a most affectionate manner between a man's tweed waistcoat and his jacket. One other thing I saw – a small blue crescent of confetti clung like a burr in the tweed.

Well, what was a man to do?

I stood midway on Porlock Hill. The birds sang as, I suppose, they sang in Eden, the leaves moved and flittered as they did in the first garden, and somewhere along that steep road Adam and Eve were exploding towards their honeymoon; and in my arms their trousseaux!

Dartmoor

17. Sabine Baring-Gould, *A Book of Dartmoor* (1900)

Let it not be supposed that in winter Dartmoor is a desolation and a horror. It is by no means an unpleasant place for a sojourn then. When below are mud and mist, aloft on the moor the ground is hard with frost and the air crisp and clear. Down below we are oppressed with the fall of the leaf, affecting us, if inclined to asthma and bronchitis; and in the short, dull days of December and January our spirits wax dark amidst naked trees and when our ankles are deep in mud. There are no trees on Dartmoor to expose their naked limbs, and tell us that vegetation is dead. The shoulders of down are draped in brown sealskin mantles – the ling and heather, as lovely in its sleep as in its waking state; the mosses, touched by frost, turn to rainbow hues. For colour effects give me Dartmoor in winter.

And then the peat fires! What fires can surpass them? They do not flame, but they glow, and diffuse an aroma that fills the lungs with balm. The turf-cutting is one of the annual labours on the moor. Every farm has its peat-bog, and in the proper season a sufficiency of fuel is cut, then carried and stacked for winter use. I may be mistaken, but it seems to me that cooking done over a peat fire surpasses cooking at the best club in London. But it may be that on the moor one relishes a meal in a manner impossible elsewhere . . .

What all are welcome to go after is that which is abundant on every moorside – but nowhere finer than on such as have not been subjected to periodical 'swaling' or burning. I refer to the whortleberry. This delicious fruit, eaten with Devonshire cream, is indeed a delicacy. A gentleman from London was visiting me one day. As he was fond of good things, I gave him whortleberry and cream. He ate it in dead silence, then leaned back in his chair, looked at me with eyes full of feeling, and said, 'I am thankful that I have lived to this day . . .'

On the hillsides, and in the bottoms, quaking-bogs may be lighted upon or tumbled into. To light upon them is easy enough, to get out of one if tumbled into is a difficult matter. They are happily small, and can be at once recognized by the vivid green pillow of moss that overlies them. This pillow is sufficiently close in texture and buoyant to support a man's weight, but it has a mischievous habit of thinning around the edge, and if the water be stepped into where this fringe is, it is quite possible for the inexperienced to go under, and be enabled at his leisure to investigate the lower surface of the covering *duvet* of porous moss. Whether he will be able to give to the world the benefit of his observations may be open to question.

The thing to be done by anyone who gets into such a bog is to spread his arms out – this will prevent his sinking – and if he cannot struggle out, to wait, cooling his toes in bog water, till assistance comes. It is a difficult matter to extricate horses when they flounder in, as is not infrequently the case in hunting; every plunge sends the poor beasts in deeper.

One afternoon, in the year 1851, I was in the Walkham valley above Merrivale Bridge digging into what at the time I fondly believed was a tumulus, but which I subsequently discovered to be a mound thrown up for the accommodation of rabbits, when a warren was contemplated on the slope of Mis Tor.

Towards evening I was startled to see a most extraordinary object approach me – a man in a draggled, dingy, and disconsolate condition, hardly able to crawl along. When he came up to me he burst into tears, and it was some time before I could get his story from him. He was a tailor of Plymouth, who had left his home to attend the funeral of a cousin at Sampford Spiney or Walkhampton, I forget which. At that time there was no railway between Tavistock and Launceston; communication was by coach.

When the tailor, on the coach, reached Roborough Down, ''Ere you are!' said the driver. 'You go along there, and you can't miss it!' indicating a direction with his whip.

So the tailor, in his glossy black suit, and with his box-hat set jauntily on his head, descended from the coach, leaped into the road, his umbrella, also black, under his arm, and with a composed countenance started along the road that had been pointed out.

Where and how he missed his way he could not explain, nor can I guess, but instead of finding himself at the house of mourning, and partaking there of cake and gin, and dropping a sympathetic tear, he got up on to Dartmoor, and got – with considerable dexterity – away from all roads.

He wandered on and on, becoming hungry, feeling the gloss go out of his new black suit, and raws develop upon his top-hat as it got knocked against rocks in some of his falls.

Night set in, and, as Homer says, 'all the paths were darkened' – but where the tailor found himself there were no paths to become obscured. He lay in a bog for some time, unable to extricate himself. He lost his umbrella, and finally lost his hat. His imagination conjured up frightful objects; if he did not lose his courage, it was because, as a tailor, he had none to lose.

He told me incredible tales of the large, glaring-eyed monsters that had stared at him as he lay in the bog. They were probably sheep, but as nine tailors fled when a snail put out its horns, no wonder that this solitary member of the profession was scared at a sheep.

The poor wretch had eaten nothing since the morning of the preceding day. Happily I had half a Cornish pasty with me, and I gave it him. He fell on it ravenously.

Then I showed him the way to the little inn at Merrivale Bridge, and advised him to hire a trap there and get back to Plymouth as quickly as might be.

'I solemnly swear to you, sir,' said he, 'nothing will ever induce me to set foot on Dartmoor again. If I chance to see it from the Hoe, sir, I'll avert my eyes. How can people think to come here for pleasure – for pleasure, sir! But there, Chinamen eat birds'-nests. There are depraved appetites among human beings, and only unwholesome-minded individuals can love Dartmoor.'

18. John Hillaby, *Journey Through Britain* (1965)

The marvel is that in the mist I got anywhere. It hung about all day, sometimes so thickly that I couldn't see for more than a few paces. When that happened I hung about, wriggling my toes and stamping my feet like a restive horse. But for most of the time the visibility veered between twenty and forty yards. During what can be euphemistically described as bright intervals, I moved on as fast as I could on a bearing of seventy degrees.

To do this I took a sight on the most distant object I could see, usually a tuft of grass or a vaguely distinguishable hunk of peat, and made for it, counting the paces on the way. The counting didn't amount to much, navigation-wise, but it gave me something to do. All this became a childish ritual, like hopping over paving-stones, sloping arms, or taking part in a square dance.

One, two, three, four . . . keeping my eyes on the

marker tuft, with only an occasional glance down to avoid the worst of the wet patches, I muttered the numbers aloud . . . *seven, eight, nine, ten* . . . who cared a damn about the big bad mist? Play it cool, man. Nobody who tackles a problem scientifically gets hurt . . . kids' stuff, this . . . *thirteen, fourteen, fifteen* . . . seemed to be getting brighter. A lot brighter. I could see beyond the tuft. Maybe twenty yards . . . *seventeen, eighteen, nineteen* . . . and then a splosh as I went into two feet of water.

Optimism vanished as I looked round for something more substantial to walk on. Couldn't see the marker when I got going again. Chose something else in what I took to be the right direction . . . *twenty-two, twenty-three, twenty-four* . . . only a few paces to go. Mental censor asked if I wasn't feeling *just* a bit tired? Nonsense! Never felt better in my life. Mist is good for you. Like Guinness. But it really wasn't. I knew it wasn't . . . *twenty-nine, thirty*.

In thirty sodden steps, in fifty seconds, in less time than it takes to relate this, I usually swung, unpredictably, between elation and depression. Little fantasies, some comforting, some frightful, flickered on and off like a series of projected slides, leaving only for the most part that feeling of damp, rather miserable ordinariness. In this way I suppose I must have covered several miles. In the scenic, the seeing-something-ahead, sense I saw very little.

Towards noon I hustled down a long slope and, at a point where the murk seemed unusually thick, I went in up to the bottom of my jacket. Done for, I thought. I got out by leaning backwards and lifting one foot out slowly, and then the other, and then looked around. Nothing comforting. The bog stretched out as far as I could see. In the cold air, the surface steamed slightly, like a pudding. I chucked a piece of turf in. It quivered. From the map it looked as if I had walked into Cranmere Pool.

To Wessex

The village of Chagford, into which John Hillaby staggered late that night after his misadventures on Dartmoor, lies under the eastern edge of the moor – almost literally under. The moor rears up at the back of Chagford, a brown ridge halfway up the sky. The village itself, full of old-fashioned dark shops and tight streets between sparkling granite walls, is surrounded by the greenest of green landscapes. Long, sweeping hillsides rise and fall between steep green valleys. There are plenty of trees – oak, ash, beech – and hilly pasture fields of cows and sheep. But Dartmoor's bleak face looks over these rolling shoulders whenever you glance up and west. Tin from the moor made Chagford prosperous in medieval days; and sheep from the pastures did the same for Moretonhampstead four miles eastward. From Moreton-hampstead's narrow, climbing streets the green combe sides are seen blocking in the spaces between the houses, rising higher as you descend from the little town to the valley bottom. But this is still a hard, granite landscape where boulders lie naked on the fields and the roadside banks are of granite blocks. That familiar and well-loved Devonian softness of red earth and sandstone makes no inroads into the stern Dartmoor influence on the landscape until you are well on the way to Exeter.

Two roads connect Dartmoor with Dorset – the B3212 which straggles some forty miles across the middle of Dartmoor and away east to Exeter, and the A3052 which takes up the journey and carries it on for nearly another thirty miles, all the way through east Devon until it hands

over the reins to the A35 just inside the Dorset border at
Lyme Regis. They are both rather outmoded roads, the B3212
particularly so: a real snaking, writhing West Country minor
road, gnashingly frustrating for those in a hurry and stuck
behind a tractor, blissfully enticing for anyone with time
to saunter those long switchback miles from the granite into the sandstone, the hard into the soft. The road plunges
into each combe by zigzags, bends sharply over a little bridge
and shallow stream at the bottom, winds laboriously up
again to the next ridge. At Dunsford, where the church
stands up prettily against high green fields, the moorland
wildness is finally tamed into farmland lushness. At Long-
down there is the first wide panorama over the city of Exeter,
sprawling across its plain, backed by the blue, far-off Black-
down hills. And then there is the crawl into, through or
around the city, a red sandstone fullstop to the B3212.

At Clyst St Mary, having shaken off the last of Exeter's
outskirts, the dramas of Dartmoor and its eastward combes
are behind you; those of the swooping Dorset cliffs of greensand, chalk and clay some miles still in front. The fields roll
flatly, a gentle pastoral lowland landscape until the three
main rivers of east Devon begin to mould some more excitement into the scene. Otter and Axe come grandly south down
their respective valleys to empty into Lyme Bay from wide
mouths; Sid runs a more modest course, slipping down to the
sea through the streets of Sidmouth. All three rivers have
carved deeply into the chalk and greensand over the millennia, as have other springs and streams. These cliffs look solid,
but they are tottering section by section into the sea. There is a
constant trickle of clay and pebbles on to the east Devon and
Dorset beaches from the cliffs, which now and then – usually
after an especially heavy rainstorm – vomit hundreds of tons
of material from their unsettled bellies. They are crammed
with fossils, too, beach treasure for those prepared to risk
bombardment from the crumbling cliff faces above.

Over the cliffs and down across the river valleys runs the
A3052, more of a tourist road than Dartmoor's B3212, but
still an old-fangled, single-carriageway affair of brake-
groaning descents and second-gear climbs. This is the locals'
own holiday road, shuttling Devon and Dorset families at

weekends east and west to minor roads that thread away and down to Salcombe Regis, Branscombe, Beer or Seaton. Branscombe above all is the place to go – out of season. In high summer you will be just one of a thousand 'grockles' (the West Country name for tourists) jamming the narrow lane from the A3052, but from autumn to spring Branscombe is largely unvisited. The bowed old houses, white and cream lumpy walls under thatch, fall steeply with the lane and green combe sides past the twelfth-century church of St Winifred to the old thatched forge at the valley bottom. The smith is kept busy making lanterns, gates, weather vanes and other fancy ironwork for the local trade at his blackened furnace in the dusty, dark smithy where tools and bars of iron hang and lie in every cobwebbed corner. A twisting mile more and the lane ends on the shore between towering chalk cliffs at Branscombe Mouth.

Far above on the crest of the hills, the A3052 undulates eastwards into the wide green plain of the River Axe at Seaton, and climbs again to its final, superb high view over Lyme Regis and the Dorset cliffs beyond as they march away into the distance around the curve of Lyme Bay. Their green and gold caps dominate the little resort tucked away at the meeting place of steep roads from west, north and east. Into Lyme you plunge with a view over the Cobb, the town's ancient, curved breakwater and quay; down Broad Street, over medieval Buddle Bridge above the beach, and up again. Above Black Ven cliff, where in 1811 Mary Anning and her brother made the first discovery of the prehistoric fish lizard Ichthyosaurus, you leave the A3052 at the end of its long trek from Exeter and join an altogether more modern and fast-running road, the A35. The speed increases, and the inland views into wide valleys flash by. The valley sides rise to wooded tops, their green slopes softly indented with the characteristic elasticity of the underlying chalks and sands. The granite hardness of Dartmoor seems a world away as the road dips through villages whose houses glow in golden hamstone.

This exhilarating fast run comes to an end in the wide street of Bridport with its tall, plain-fronted houses, shops and inns. Here you strike off into a tangle of narrow lanes that lead north and west into the heart of Thomas Hardy's Wessex countryside. Rounded ridges tower over the lanes, pressing ever closer above the valleys. Long views and wide horizons play no part at this end of the journey. The focus narrows and foreshortens to a steep hillside, a hairpin bend in the lane, a barn outlined against the sky hundreds of feet above. The sensation here is of worming one's way deep into secret country – warm and welcoming when the sun lights up those slopes, dank and ominous when rain darkens them. Twisting and turning, forcing you down through the gears to a slow crawl, the lane at last brings you through the trees to West Milton and the old mill by the stream.

The mill house at West Milton became a green retreat for Kenneth Allsop, who in the 1960s found success and national fame as a television presenter after years as a writer of books and articles. Allsop was also a dedicated naturalist and keenly involved in the infant conservation movement. Though overshadowed by his late television fame, writing was always an essential part of his life, very often defending the countryside he loved.

Here in the heart of Dorset though, all literary knees bend to Thomas Hardy, creator of the 'Wessex' through which a vast Victorian reading public came to know this part of the world. We travel through the landscape of *Tess of the d'Urbervilles*, north to her home countryside in the 'Vale of Little Dairies', Blackmoor Vale; then south to the Frome Valley (the 'Valley of the Great Dairies') where Tess met Angel Clare at Talbothays Dairy. From there north again into the lush Stour valley, to find Francis Kilvert of Clyro paying a call on William Barnes, the Dorset dialect poet. Then, with a long northern leap, we land in a deep combe in the Quantock hills, where Richard Jefferies is lazing – with his eyes, as usual, very wide open. Now we cross the flat peat moors of the Somerset Levels and go up again into the limestone Mendip hills where Rev. John Skinner of Camerton, nearly thirty years older than his jaunty self at Land's End, wiser and sadder too, gets provoked into a brawl in the cornfield. Parson Woodforde would never have allowed himself to lash out like Skinner, though in his later years in Norfolk (where we shall meet him further on in our travels), he certainly received provocation enough. Here at Ansford, the end of our journeying through the West Country, Woodforde is a young man not yet thirty years old, faithfully logging – as he continued to do all through his life – the little pains and pleasures of each day.

WEST MILTON, DORSET

19. Kenneth Allsop, *In the Country* (1972)

You can tell it's spring. From the cap of Round Knoll I look upon the April sun, bright as the celandines, glinting with crescendoing power upon scattered farm buildings – every tin inch of them.

Doing a rough sum I calculate that it can't take more than another twenty-five years to rebuild Wessex entirely with corrugated iron.

Primroses cluster around rusty sheets of it rammed in the hedge of Larchcombe Lane. Simpler, isn't it, than filling gaps with thorn slips or by laying the old boughs?

In the next village the mossy thatch was rotting off a cottage. It has been replaced by that asbestos composition like an elephant's wrinkled hide. Of course thatchers are scarce and tiling would probably cost ten times what the whole cottage did originally.

Between there and my mill two sunken rutted lanes cross at an askew swastika junction. It is called Bellbakery. There was once a bit of a village there, gone now but for one cottage, which was the bakehouse and pub. It is the loneliest of spots. At least, it was lonely. I often came that way when homeward bound near dusk.

In the meadows partridges skreaked like rusty hinges on doors parting to let in the dark. From its telegraph post podium a yellowhammer's asthmatic little-bit-of-bread-and-no-cheese trill promulgated its ownership of a patch of furze.

It was at this hour that the barn owls flapped to the ivied rim of the tumbledown lime kiln, blearily peered about through heart-shaped facial feathers, then spread their wings for the night's hunting.

If I leaned quietly at the five-barred gate, they came floating past within feet, thistledown-soft and silent, cream and golden footpads prowling down the fence for a vole or shrew.

That's how it was. The owls and yellowhammers and partridges are still around, but it's hardly the same secluded valley. Now it's the site of a pig farm. And why indeed shouldn't this parcel of land provide bacon for us as well as meat for owls? But need it be so shriekingly ugly? The sties, barns, hutments and food stores, plonked smack dab in the middle, are metal down to the last rivet.

Buildings put up by earlier farmers were like out-crops of the surrounding earth, harmonious, organic, as fitting as the field oaks and the kingcups. Stone was carted from the great Purbeck quarries to construct the grand houses and the splendid church towers in the fifteenth-century perpendicular style. But most of the humbler buildings on the chalk were made either from cob faced with flint and roofed with wheat-straw thatch, although some were put up with bricks available from the belt of London clay, and roofed with healens, or flagstones, by squires of the more prosperous Georgian period.

Most in my village and around were made of blocks of sandstone cut from the hillsides west of Emminster. (When I was picking some stone to repair a derelict wall, Daniel, who was giving me a hand, said that piece was 'too beefy'. It looked just the opposite to me: too crumbly. And indeed that was what he meant, I discovered. Porous limestone interlayered with shale is called 'beef' hereabouts.) The honey-coloured stone soaked up the sun like flesh and had a rosy afterglow in the half light.

The new structures, like Manned Spacecraft Centres, don't. Their angular hardness provides no texture for lichens and mosses; no swallows or robins can find nesting places in the pre-fab hangars. Alien and raw, these rootless mass-production units can never become part of the contour of the country.

So the tinscape spreads. Why not use stone and slate and straw? It 'isn't worth it' – meaning that it's cheaper to bolt together the gawky components.

Hovering around these rustic shantytowns, of course, are bodies entitled Rural District Planning Committees. What consideration do they give to standards which are seemly and appropriate to the areas they oversee? Cheapness is all.

BLACKMOOR VALE

20. Thomas Hardy, *Tess of the d'Urbervilles* (1891)

The village of Marlott lay amid the north-eastern undulations of the beautiful Vale of Blakemore or Blackmoor aforesaid, an engirdled and secluded region, for the most part untrodden as yet by tourist or landscape-painter, though within a four hours' journey from London.

It is a vale whose acquaintance is best made by viewing it from the summits of the hills that surround it – except perhaps during the droughts of summer. An unguided ramble into its recesses in bad weather is apt to engender dissatisfaction with its narrow, tortuous, and miry ways.

This fertile and sheltered tract of country, in which the fields are never brown and the springs never dry, is bounded on the south by the bold chalk ridge that embraces the prominences of Hambledon Hill, Bulbarrow, Nettlecombe-Tout, Dogbury, High Stoy, and Bubb Down. The traveller from the coast, who, after plodding northward for a score of miles over calcareous downs and corn-lands, suddenly reaches the verge of one of these escarpments, is surprised and delighted to behold, extended like a map beneath him, a country differing absolutely from that which he has passed through. Behind him the hills are open, the sun blazes down upon fields so large as to give an unenclosed character to the landscape, the lanes are white, the hedges low and plashed, the atmosphere colourless. Here, in the valley, the world seems to be constructed upon a smaller and more delicate scale; the fields are mere paddocks, so reduced that from this height their hedgerows appear a network of dark green threads overspreading the paler green of the grass. The atmosphere beneath is languorous, and is so tinged with azure that what artists call the middle distance partakes also of that hue, while the horizon beyond is of the deepest ultramarine. Arable lands are few and limited; with but slight exceptions the prospect is a broad rich mass of grass and trees, mantling minor hills and dales within the major. Such is the Vale of Blackmoor.

FROME VALLEY

21. Thomas Hardy, *Tess of the d'Urbervilles* (1891)

Tess found herself on a summit commanding the long-sought-for vale, the Valley of the Great Dairies, the valley in which milk and butter grew to rankness, and were produced more profusely, if less delicately, than at her home – the verdant plain so well watered by the river Var or Froom.

It was intrinsically different from the Vale of Little Dairies, Blackmoor Vale, which, save during her disastrous sojourn at Trantridge, she had exclusively known till now. The world was drawn to a larger pattern here. The enclosures numbered fifty acres instead of ten, the farmsteads were more extended, the groups of cattle formed tribes hereabout; there only families. These myriads of cows stretching under her eyes from the far east to the far west outnumbered any she had ever seen at one glance before. The green lea was speckled as thickly with them as a canvas by Van Alsloot or Sallaert with burghers. The ripe hues of the red and dun kine absorbed the evening sunlight, which the white-coated animals returned to the eye in rays almost dazzling, even at the distant elevation on which she stood.

The bird's-eye perspective before her was not so luxuriantly beautiful, perhaps, as that other one which she knew so well; yet it was more cheering. It lacked the intensely blue atmosphere of the rival vale, and its heavy soils and scents; the new air was clear, bracing, ethereal. The river itself, which nourished the grass and cows of these renowned dairies, flowed not like the streams in Blackmoor. Those were slow, silent, often turbid; flowing over beds of mud into which the incautious wader might sink and vanish unawares. The Froom waters were clear as the pure River of Life shown to the Evangelist, rapid as the shadow of a cloud, with pebbly shallows that prattled to the sky all day long. There the water-flower was the lily: the crowfoot here.

22. Thomas Hardy, 'Weathers'

I

This is the weather the cuckoo likes,
    And so do I;
When showers betumble the chestnut spikes,
    And nestlings fly:
And the little brown nightingale bills his best,
And they sit outside at 'The Travellers' Rest,'
And maids come forth sprig-muslin drest,
And citizens dream of the south and west,
    And so do I.

II

This is the weather the shepherd shuns,
    And so do I;
When beeches drip in browns and duns,
    And thresh, and ply;
And hill-hid tides throb, throe on throe,
And meadow rivulets overflow,
And drops on gate-bars hang in a row,
And rooks in families homeward go,
    And so do I.

STOUR VALLEY

23. Francis Kilvert, *Diary* (1870)

Thursday, May Eve, 1874

We walked together to the Poet's [William Barnes's] house, Winterbourne Came Rectory, about a mile from Fordington. The house lies a little back from the glaring white high road and stands on a lawn fringed with trees. It is thatched and a thatched verandah runs along its front. The thatched roof gives the Rectory house the appearance of a large lofty cottage. As we turned in at the iron gates from the high road and went down the gravel path the Poet was walking in the verandah. He welcomed us cordially and brought us into his drawing room on the right-hand side of the door. He is an old man, over seventy, rather bowed with age, but apparently hale and strong. 'Excuse my study gown,' he said. He wore a dark grey loose gown girt round the waist with a black cord and tassel, black knee breeches, black silk stockings and gold buckled shoes.

I was immediately struck by the beauty and grandeur of his head. It was an Apostolic head, bald and venerable, and the long soft silvery hair flowed on his shoulders and a long white beard fell upon his breast. His face was handsome and striking, keen yet benevolent, the finely pencilled eyebrows still dark and a beautiful benevolent loving look lighted up his fine dark blue eyes . . .

He is a very remarkable-looking man, half hermit, half enchanter.

The Poet seemed pleased with my visit and gratified that I had come such a long way to see him. I told him I had for many years known him through his writings and had long wished to thank him in person for the many happy hours his poems had given me. He smiled and said he was very glad if he had given me any pleasure. Frequently stroking his face and his venerable white beard the Poet told me he had composed his poems chiefly in the evening as a relaxation from the day's work when he kept a school in Dorchester . . .

In describing a scene he always had an original in his mind, but sometimes he enlarged and improved upon the original. 'For instance,' he explained, 'sometimes I wanted a bit of water or wood or a hill, and then I put these in.' 'Pentridge by the river,' he said, was a real place, and so were some others. The river was the Stour.

24 and 25. William Barnes, *Poems of Rural Life in the Dorset Dialect* (1844)

Pentridge by the River

Pentridge! – oh! my heart's a-zwellen
Vull o'jaÿ wi' vo'k a-tellen
 Any news o' thik wold pleäce,
An' the boughy hedges round it,
An' the river that do bound it
 Wi' his dark but glis'nen feäce.
Vor there's noo land, on either hand,
To me lik' Pentridge by the river.

Be there any leaves to quiver
On the aspen by the river?
 Doo he sheäde the water still,
Where the rushes be a-growen,
Where the sullen Stour's a-flowen
 Drough the meäds vrom mill to mill?
Vor if a tree wer dear to me,
Oh! 'twer thik aspen by the river.

There, in eegrass new a-shooten,
I did run on even vooten,
 Happy, over new-mow'd land;
Or did zing wi' zingen drushes
While I plaïted, out o' rushes,
 Little baskets vor my hand;
Bezide the clote that there did float,
Wi' yollow blossoms, on the river.

When the western zun's a-vallèn,
What sh'ill vaïce is now a-callen
 Hwome the deäiry to the païls;
Who do dreve em on, a-flingen

53

Wide-bow'd horns, or slowly zwingen
  Right an' left their tufty taïls?
As they do goo a-huddled drough
The geäte a-leäden up vrom river.

Bleäded grass is now a-shooten
Where the vloor wer woonce our vooten,
  While the hall wer still in pleäce.
Stwones be looser in the wallen;
Hollow trees be nearer vallèn;
  Ev'ry thing ha' chang'd its feäce.
But still the neäme do bide the seäme –
'Tis Pentridge – Pentridge by the river.

The Water-spring in the Leane
Oh! aye! the spring 'ithin the leäne,
A-leäden down to Lyddan Brook;
An' still a-nesslen in his nook,
As weeks do pass, an' moons do weäne.
  Nwone the drier,
  Nwone the higher,
Nwone the nigher to the door
Where we did live so long avore.

An' oh! what vo'k his mossy brim
Ha' gathered in the run o' time!
The wife a-blushen in her prime;
The widow wi' her eyezight dim;
  Maïdens dippen,
  Childern sippen,
Water drippen, at the cool
Dark wallen ov the little pool.

Behind the spring do lie the lands
My father till'd, vrom Spring to Spring,
A-waïten on vor time to bring
The crops to paÿ his weary hands.
  Wheat a-growen,
  Beäns a-blowen,
Grass vor mowen, where the bridge
Do leäd to Ryall's on the ridge.

But who do know when liv'd an' died
The squier o' the mwoldren hall;
That lined en wi' a stwonen wall,
An' steän'd so cleän his wat'ry zide?
  We behind en,
    Now can't vind en,
But do mind en, an' do thank
His meäker vor his little tank.

QUANTOCK HILLS, WEST SOMERSET

26. Richard Jefferies, *Field and Hedgerow* (1889)

From the Devon border I drifted like a leaf detached from a tree, across to a deep coombe in the Quantock Hills. The vast hollow is made for repose and lotus-eating; its very shape, like a hammock, indicates idleness. There the days go over noiselessly and without effort, like white summer clouds. Ridges each side rise high and heroically steep – it would be proper to set out and climb them, but not today, not now: some time presently. To the left massive Will's Neck stands out in black shadow defined and distinct, like a fragment of night in the bright light of the day. The wild red deer lie there, but the mountain is afar; a sigh is all I can give to it for the Somerset sun is warm and the lotus sweet. Yonder, if the misty heat moves on, the dim line of Dunkery winds along the sky, not unlike the curved back of a crouching hare. The weight of the mountains is too great – what is the use of attempting to move? It is enough to look at them. The day goes over like a white cloud; as the sun declines it is pleasant to go into the orchard – the vineyard of Somerset, and then perhaps westward may be seen a light in the sky by the horizon as if thrown up from an immense mirror under. The mirror is the Severn sea, itself invisible at this depth, but casting a white glow up against the vapour in the air. By it you may recognize the nearness of the sea. The thumb-nail ridges of the Quantocks begin to grow harder, they carry the eye along on soft curves like those of the South Downs in Sussex, but suddenly end in a flourish and point as if cut out with the thumb-nail. Draw your thumb-nail firmly along soft wood, and it will, by its natural slip, form such a curve. Blackbird and thrush commence to sing as the heavy heat decreases; the bloom on the apple trees is loose now, and the blackbird as he springs from the bough shakes down flakes of blossom.

SOMERSET LEVELS

27. Adam Nicolson (with Patrick Sutherland),
   Wetland – Life in the Somerset Levels (1986)

Water is a curse turned gift. In the summer, between May and September, when the cows can get out on to the moorland fields, the rhynes and ditches which are used to evacuate the winter rains have water penned up in them to provide wet fences between the fields and ready drinking water for the animals. These summer rhynes, hidden at first as you stare out across the endless and apparently undivided grass, with only odd, arbitrary gates sticking up in the flatness, is where the wetness of the moors concentrates. It is as though the grass were no more than skin, a tightened membrane over the body of water, and these rhynes, incised in that skin with all the precision of improving surgery, had cut through to the substance of the place itself. Each shelters a particular world of butterbur or kingcup, of water mint or a great wedding-show of irises. There is a must in the air above the peaty waters. On either side, there is the dazed flitting of the Minton blue damselflies and the haze of the meadow grasses, both part of the one summer thickness, folding into each other, making an insect haze and a grass hum.

If you sit on the banks of one of these rhynes, the high water in the field soaks up into the cloth of your trousers, so that the only thing to do is swim and move over from the watery peat to the peaty water, a half-noticed change from one half-element to another.

There is no need to step into the rhyne. Simply stand in the shallow margin of the water, next to the winter-mint and the sweet violet, and let your feet slide down over the warm skin of the peat below you. Slowly the body lowers into the cider-soup, crusty with frog-bit and duckweed, with seeds and reed-shells. The points of the arrowhead quiver in your slight wash and, away down the rhyne, the slimed light bodies of the secret eels release a bubble each as they shift away from the strange disturbance. The breadth of the rhyne grows as you come near the surface to a generous, private, pacific width, lobed into by the irises and reeds. The peat must is heady from the broken water and a swan claps in another field. The meadow is riffled in the wind. Heat and vapour wobble in the air above it. The still water is slick on the skin. Nothing is dissolved in it. Everything hangs there in suspension. Time stops. Your body is a golden unnatural brown seen through the whisky water. You hang embedded in the place as though in a tomb, with some strange osmosis of the water sliding into the heart through the skin. It is a soggy, ambivalent fringe world, a world hinged to *both* and *and*. A thousand million years ago, all life was water-life and to float in the semi-substance of a summer rhyne is to return to that antiquity.

But do not be discovered or admit to this odd behaviour. Floating in the rhynes is not what the moor-men do themselves and they will lecture you on the dangers of fluke and other diseases. If you live in a place, some distance must be preserved.

WINSCOMBE, MENDIP HILLS, SOMERSET

28. Theodore Compton, *A Mendip Valley* (1867)

Hardly less important than the postman is the village carrier. Fortunately for us, the railway has made business for itself without running the errand-cart off the road. On the contrary, it now plies twice a week, instead of once. Calling for orders and delivering goods at the different houses here, as well as at villages off the line of rails, the carrier renders services which the railway people do not. He fulfils the useful service of the German and Swiss postman, who brings the goods ordered through the post, and takes the cost and postage. Our carrier executes all kinds of commissions in Bristol for his country customers. He takes our watches to be cleaned, our knives and razors to be set, our furniture to be repaired, and brings back all parcelable things. 'It is always a pleasure to see his honest, country face,' said a lady at Clifton; and it was a true saying.

His dwelling is as rural as himself and his calling. On a bank by the road-side stands his ancient ivy-clad cot, dated 1628. It is one of the few remaining thatched roofs, with thick over-hanging curved eaves, and a rustic porch which shelters the door and the wicker cage of a blackbird. The little garden is gay with flowers, especially when tulips are in season, and in autumn the roof is aglow with the scarlet Virginia creeper.

Before the abolition of toll-bars, our carrier used to start late in the evening, so as to arrive at the first gate after mid-night, and return within the same day. He is now emancipated from that bondage, but still makes his outward-bound or up journey at night, returning the following afternoon. In warm summer weather, the trip must be pleasant enough, along a good road, and through fine hilly country; now along shady lanes by gentlemen's seats, and farms, and villages, and now over high open ground, with views extending far and wide, from the Mendip hills to the distant Welsh mountains. On a moonlight night, though the views are limited, the scenery is still beautiful; indeed, a midsummer night, from sunset to sunrise is one of the most enjoyable parts of the day. But our carrier is familiar with the road, and, happily for his customers, thinks more of his errands than of Midsummer Night's Dreams.

CAMERTON

29. John Skinner, *Diary* (1824)

Saturday, 18 September

I walked up to the Glebe and saw the stadling prepared for the barley, and the two cart loads they had taken yesterday evening placed in a heap near it . . . I then walked into 'Stanley's' field where the barley was cut, and saw there was none set up in cock for tithing. I then said I should not consent to take the tithe unless the cocks were entirely separate and distinct from each other, for if my men only took it up with a pitch and no rake I must be a considerable loser . . .

On Day's coming into the field he walked up to the wagon near which I was standing, and said to the carter, 'What is all this about? Why do you not go on hauling?' The carter replied, 'Mr Skinner objected to the tithing of the barley.' Day then said, 'You go and tithe it, never mind what that fellow says!' The carter accordingly got some boughs and began tithing the wake. I said I never would abide by such tithing, as the cocks were not separate from each other. Day said, 'Never mind him, go on.' He then called a little boy in his service and said, 'You go and walk round each cock, that will be sufficient.' The boy then scuffed away some of the barley with his feet, Day doing some of the others himself of the first line where the boughs had been already placed. I told him that would never do, as the cocks were still not divided and some of the barley still touched. He said it was false, that they did not. I immediately went up to him and asked him what he meant? that anyone might see they still touched. The air of the man was in the extreme menacing; he put his face quite up to mine, shaking his head. I again asked what he meant by saying it was false; that it was he who spoke false in saying so, and it was easy to prove the lie. He said he was not so much a liar as myself. I was scarcely able to restrain myself from striking him . . . I desired my servants to leave the field with the cart, saying that I should not take up the tithe under such circumstances. When Day heard this he called out to one of the women (Garrett's widow) and said, 'You go and see whether his name is on the cart, perhaps he will hereafter deny it was his cart.' The expression of his countenance at this time was more aggravating than the words he spoke, and he walked up to me shaking his head, and, as I looked angrily at him, he called out, 'You need not make those ugly faces, they do not become you' endeavouring by words and actions to irritate me to the utmost of his power, I then walked up to him and said, 'What do you mean by saying I should deny my own name?' 'Only because you have done it before and have a short memory, that is all.' I asked what he meant. He said, 'Ah! I need not tell you. Others know as well as I.' I replied if he alluded to what others might have said of me I could not help that, some of the people of Camerton would for a pot of porter not only say what was false but even swear to it. I should insist upon his telling me what he meant by his insinuation face to face. He said he should not. I then said he was a scoundrel to say what he could not prove. He said I was a rascal. I immediately struck him two blows on the face, one with my right hand, the other with my left. He did not return them, but said, 'This is what I have been wishing for.' He then called out to the carter and said, 'he has given me a bloody nose,' and held down his head which was bleeding. I said he richly deserved what he had got, even had it been more, and added: I supposed he meant to take the law, but I should shew I had been provoked beyond bearing. I am convinced the fellow wished to irritate me to strike him in order to have a setoff against the Exchequer Suit he perceives I am determined to commence, and which he knows will go against him. However, I cannot help it. Such to the best of my knowledge and belief are the circumstances which occurred, and I must abide the consequences.

ANSFORD

30. James Woodforde, *Diary* (1768)

OCT. 26. I had a poor little cat, that had one of her ribs broke and that laid across her belly, and we could not tell what it was, and she was in great pain. I therefore with a small pen knife this morning, opened one side of her and took it out, and performed the operation very well, and afterwards sewed it up and put Friars Balsam to it, and she was much better after, the incision was half an inch. It grieved me much to see the poor creature in such pain before, and therefore made me undertake the above, which I hope will preserve the life of the poor creature.

Nov. 5. I read Prayers this morning at Cary being the 5 of Novem. the day on which the Papists had contrived an hellish plot in the reign of King James the first, but by the Divine hand of Providence was fortunately discovered.

I dined supped and spent the evening at Parsonage. The effigy of Justice Creed was had through the streets of C. Cary this evening upon the [Fire] Engine, and then had into the Park and burnt in a bonfire immediately before the Justice's House, for his putting the Church Wardens of Cary into Wells Court, for not presenting James Clarke for making a Riot in the Gallery at Cary Church some few Sundays back. The whole Parish are against the Justice, and they intend to assist the Church Wardens in carrying on the cause at Wells. The Justice is now at Lord Pawletts at Hinton.

Nov. 11. . . . At Whist this evening with James Clarke, Brother John and Brother Heighes, at which we laughed exceedingly, I lost with them in the whole 0. 0. 6 . . .

Nov. 22. I married Tom Burge of Ansford to Charity Andrews of C. Cary by License this morning. The Parish of Cary made him marry her, and he came handbolted to Church for fear of running away, and the Parish of Cary was at all the expense of bringing of them to, I rec^d of Mr Andrew Russ the overseer of the Poor of Cary for it 0. 10. 6 . . .

DEC. 24. . . . It being Christmas Eve we had the New Singers of C. Cary this evening at Parsonage, and they having been at great expenses in learning to sing, my Father and myself gave them double what we used to do, and therefore instead of one shilling we each gave 0. 2. 0.

DEC. 26. I was very bad in my throat all night, but towards the morning was rather better, only extremely hoarse . . . I could not go to read Prayers this morning at Cary though it was St Stephen, which I hope will be forgiven . . . Sister Jane visited me this morning, and she being deaf and I not able to speak, was good company . . .

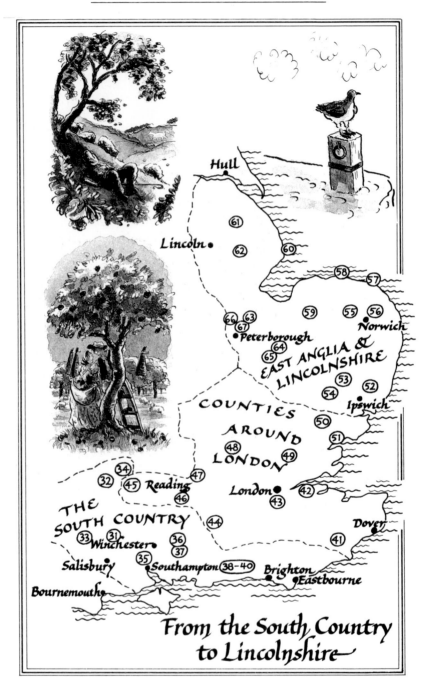

From the South Country
to Lincolnshire

IV

To the South Country

I could have chosen a great old road, the A303, to carry me from Somerset over to Salisbury Plain and the start of a journey along the chalk downs of the South Country. The A303 is a spinal cord to the West Country, a famous holiday road and trade link, streaming with tourist cars all summer and with slowly grinding lorries through the out-of-season winter months. Villages lie a mile or so off the road, connected to their long-distance lifeline by narrow lanes and side roads. Dual carriageway stretches, flyovers and bypasses notwithstanding, the A303 still retains something of the feel of the rough old coaching road it once was. But nowadays it whisks you too fast from place to place. You can leave Parson Woodforde's Ansford at three o'clock, and be walking round Stonehenge before four. To catch the full atmosphere of the slow change from Somerset to Wiltshire, limestone to chalk, closeness of landscape to openness, I found a better route on a far older road.

At Shepton Montague, three miles east of Ansford, is the Montague Arms, an old drovers' inn near the crossroads. These days a quiet village pub, in times past the inn saw trade and profits on a grand scale, for it stands alongside what was a great highway taking pack-horses, drovers and their flocks and herds from Devon to London and back again. This road, named the Harroway ('Hoary Way' or 'Old Road') in Saxon times, can lay claim to be the oldest long-distance road in Britain. Bronze Age traders are known to have used it, bringing Cornish tin from the port of Seaton in Devon up along the backbone of southern England for one hundred and fifty miles to join the ancient North Downs Way in Surrey, then on down to the Channel coast. A high-level Bronze Age trackway, clear across England from west to east – but who knows how long the Harroway had already been used in short, local stretches by Stone Age travellers, keeping high and safe above the swamps, forests and dangers from man and beast in the valley bottoms?

I paused to drink in the drovers' inn and then moved on eastward along the Harroway, hereabouts a dung-spattered lane, between high hedgebanks over which the valley sides rose steeply, past the grandiose turrets of a gatehouse at Redlynch and the quiet dignity of a thatched old manor house at Discove. This is lush green limestone pasture country, in which the Harroway dips into one valley after another, to cross a stream over a tiny bridge and climb under dark oaks to the next ridge. The roadside houses are built of the warm, golden hamstone that lies in a belt across the route. Further east and north the Harroway changes its name to the Hardway. Its character begins to change and harden, too. It straightens and steepens to climb at one in four up Kingsettle Hill, cobbled in the days of the drovers and the packhorse trains to give some purchase in rain, mist and snow. I sweated up, hands on knees and back bent, and was glad to take a breather at a gate halfway up the hill and gaze north over the green miles towards the distant Mendip hills.

There was a much finer view from one hundred and sixty feet in the air at the crest of Kingsettle Hill. On 12 July 1770 Parson Woodforde took an evening walk at Ansford with his brothers and sisters, and 'gave them all a peep through my fine spying glass, to see King Alfred's Tower, now erecting by Mr Hoare on the very highest part of Kingsettle Hill about seven miles off'. Henry Hoare of nearby Stourhead House, 'Henry the Magnificent', built his three-sided brick tower to glorify himself and King Alfred, who had raised his standard against the Danish invaders here in AD 879. I spiralled up the two hundred and six stone steps and stood by the parapet at the top of the tower, half blinded by the wind, a good thousand feet above sea level and master of a panorama of woodland, downland, pasture, cornfields, valleys and hills that stretched fifty miles from Mendip to the Dorset coast.

Looking up and east I could see the Wiltshire Downs waiting for me, their smooth chalk flanks rising in long, rounded snouts from the limestone, white patches showing where scars and scarp edges broke through the turf. And there ran the Harroway, zig-zagging from the trees to the bare top of White Sheet Hill.

From Hardway to Long Lane and back to Harroway the old road switched names as it raised me high to the start of fifty miles of chalk, shaped by man through five millennia on the top of White Sheet Hill into defensive earthworks, burial mounds, ditches, banks, animal pens and water reservoirs. Past the hilltop maze of primitive people's delvings and heapings the Harroway runs straight and deeply hollowed, punctuated by milestones showing in Roman numerals the distance from Salisbury and London. This rutted track was once a great coaching road between London and the West Country, turnpiked in 1750, continuing in use as a fast upland through route until railway competition killed its coach traffic stone dead in the 1840s. Now only the lichened, weather-beaten milestones give a clue of its former import-ance. Over the top of Charnage Down, where larks were singing above every field, I strode along the Harroway with wide downland views all round, to come to a stop where the old road slid under the tarmac of the A303 and roared away east for five traffic-laden miles to Chicklade Bottom. A miserable half mile of buffeting by lorry slipstream was quite enough. I threw in my hand for the day and made off down side roads to the King's Arms at Fonthill Bishop, as quiet and hospitable as ever.

At Chicklade Bottom the Harroway shrugs off its noisy younger brother and rises majestically for a long run on the turf of the downs: fifteen miles of windblown, blissfully lonely walking into the heart of Salisbury Plain. I tramped east and north all the following day, stopping to idle on the outskirts of Groveley Wood where the Harroway briefly joins another ancient trackway and takes on yet another name – the Ox Drove. Before oxen were ever driven along this old track, it was straightened and used by the Romans to transport lead from their Mendip mines; and long before the Romans it carried Mendip coal for British tribespeople. Here, under great beeches with gnarled roots exposed, the two old roads run as one, their banks thick with yellow archangel and garlic-smelling Jack-by-the-hedge, before separating under West Hill. New Age travellers with lumpy dreadlocks swinging to their waists were puzzling over a broken-down car in their trackside encampment of dilapidated buses and vans. One of their children, a fresh-faced little girl picking cow parsley on the Harroway, shyly wished me a good afternoon and called a thin, snarling dog to heel.

The old road runs on high above the villages and woods, up on the roof of the downs where larks rise from chalk clods and fence posts to pour song like a sweet liquid all over the hills and valleys. The Iron Age hill fort at Hanging Langford is a bushy acre or so of shapeless trenches, all but erased by two thousand years of wind, rain and trampling by sheep, cattle and goats. The Harroway dives and climbs through Steeple Langford where the River Wylye spreads itself across the valley floor in pools and side channels; dives and climbs through Berwick St James between two ancient sarsen stones, their backs hollowed by treading – they were once laid flat over the gutter to keep the villagers' feet dry. The Harroway forges ahead, and I forged with it all that afternoon, walking faster and faster, over the crossings of side tracks and tarmac roads, under avenues of lime and coppice edges of beech and oak, mile after mile, until on Normanton Down the familiar, stark, thick shapes of the Stonehenge monoliths pushed up over the swell of the skyline.

Many ancient tracks converge in the Stonehenge area of Salisbury Plain, beaten out by the feet, hooves and wheels of travellers making for that dependable landmark. Stonehenge became the great central exchange of early southern Britain after its completion in about 1400 BC, a natural focus for trade, gossip, ritual, news, magic and politics. Perhaps the only track in the West Country that outdoes Stonehenge in both strategic importance and antiquity is the Harroway, as it runs past the all-attracting stones with its lodestar set ever further to the east.

*

The South Country is all about chalk, a great eastward-running, smooth-backed ridge of it, a hundred miles of chalk from Salisbury Plain to Beachy Head. Here are the famous rolling downs of short turf, wild herbs, and flinty white soil, where tall beech hangers cling to the edge of the escarpments. The downs of the South Country give an irresistible call to the walker. Up on those long, breezy tops there is space, light and springy turf to keep you striding for twenty miles without tiring. Ancient trackways lead off and down to small villages strung out along the roads that parallel the downs in the valleys below; and a rambler can either duck down to their pubs when thirst strikes, or stay high and dry till the end of the day.

The South Country writers included here were most of them great walkers and riders, familiar with other landscapes, but in thrall to the chalk downs. William Cobbett rode the length and breadth of the downs in the 1820s, in the depth of a terrible agricultural depression, gathering impressions, facts and moral indignation for his *Rural Rides*. Richard Jefferies, last met idling on a hot summer's day in the Quantock hills of Somerset, is here on his home ground, confessing a painful nostalgia for boyhood days in his home village of Coate in Wiltshire. A. G. Street writes of Wiltshire shepherds; hearty Tom Hughes of the Vale of the White Horse.

Now we go south through the Hampshire of that quintessential downland writer W. H. Hudson (extolling the contrasting beauties of silence and birdsong) and of Gilbert White and Edward Thomas; then east again into Sussex to hear Richard Jefferies on the virtues of hop-picking. Edward Thomas reappears at the end of the long chalk trail to sum up what it is that makes the South Country downs such a fruitful ground for country writers.

NETHERAVON, WILTSHIRE

31. William Cobbett, *Rural Rides* (1830)

Before you get to Salisbury, you cross the valley that brings down a little river from *Amesbury*. It is a very beautiful valley. There is a chain of farm-houses and little churches all the way up it. The farms consist of the land on the flats on each side of the river, running out to a greater or less extent, at different places, towards the hills and downs. Not far above *Amesbury* is a little village called *Netherhaven*, where I once saw an *acre of hares*. We were coursing at *Everly*, a few miles off; and, one of the party happening to say, that he had seen *an acre of hares* at Mr *Hicks Beech's* at Netherhaven, we, who wanted to see the same, or to detect our informant, sent a messenger to beg a day's coursing, which being granted, we went over the next day. Mr BEECH received us very politely. He took us into a wheat stubble close by his paddock; his son took a gallop round, cracking his whip at the same time; the hares (which were very thickly in sight before) started all over the field, ran into a *flock* like sheep; and we all agreed, that the flock did cover *an acre of ground*. Mr Beech had an old greyhound, that I saw lying down in the shrubbery close by the house, while several hares were sitting and skipping about, with just as much confidence as cats sit by a dog in a kitchen or a parlour. Was this *instinct* in either dog or hares? Then, mind, this same greyhound went amongst the rest to *course* with us out upon the distant hills and lands; and then he ran as eagerly as the rest, and killed the hares with as little remorse. Philosophers will talk a long while before they will make men believe, that this was *instinct alone*.

COATE

32. Richard Jefferies, *Field and Hedgerow* (1889)

I think I have heard that the oaks are down. They may be standing or down, it matters nothing to me; the leaves I last saw upon them are gone for evermore, nor shall I ever see them come there again ruddy in spring. I would not see them again even if I could; they could never look again as they used to do. There are too many memories there. The happiest days become the saddest afterwards; let us never go back, lest we too die. There are no such oaks anywhere else, none so tall and straight, and with such massive heads, on which the sun used to shine as if on the globe of the earth, one side in shadow, the other in bright light. How often I have looked at oaks since, and yet have never been able to get the same effect from them! Like an old author printed in another type, the words are the same, but the sentiment is different. The brooks have ceased to run. There is no music now at the old hatch where we used to sit in danger of our lives, happy as kings, on the narrow bar over the deep water. The barred pike that used to come up in such numbers are no more among the flags. The perch used to drift down the stream, and then bring up again. The sun shone there for a very long time, and the water rippled and sang, and it always seemed to me that I could feel the rippling and the singing and the sparkling back through the centuries. The brook is dead, for when man goes nature ends. I dare say there is water there still, but it is not the brook; the brook is gone like John Brown's soul. There used to be clouds over the fields, white clouds in blue summer skies. I have lived a good deal on clouds; they have been meat to me often; they bring something to the spirit which even the trees do not. I see clouds now sometimes when the iron grip of hell permits for a minute or two; they are very different clouds, and speak differently. I long for some of the old clouds that had no memories. There were nights in those times over those fields, not darkness, but Night, full of glowing suns and glowing richness of life that sprang up to meet them. The nights are there still; they are everywhere, nothing local in the night; but it is not the Night to me seen through the window.

Wiltshire Downs

33. A. G. Street, *Farmer's Glory* (1932)

But sheep are annoying things, and so are a good many shepherds. During a barren late spring, when you were short of grub, most shepherds would delight in seeing how fast they could gallop over it, pitching out larger and larger folds each day, and never grumbling about the extra work. Given a plenteous season, when you wanted the keep cleared faster before it spoiled, the shepherds would feed it in a niggardly fashion. Any suggestion as to speeding up was greeted with the definite remark: 'No, zur, t'wun't do.' From this there was no appeal. The shepherd's word was law. The rest of us just grumbled and carried on.

I don't know whether some shepherds will prosecute me for libel over this, but as a general rule, save for lambing, and other busy times, a shepherd reckoned to finish his actual laborious work by dinner time. After that he studied your sheep. I remember a shopkeeper in a neighbouring town, who retired from business at fifty, and took a farm in this district. Early in his rural career he went out one afternoon, and discovered his shepherd dozing under a bush on the down, with the flock grazing around him. 'What in the world are you doing, shepherd?' asked his employer. 'Lookin' atter your sheep,' replied the shepherd.

'Yes, yes, that's all very well, but you mustn't sit down. I can't pay you to sleep. You must get up and cut thistles, chop down some of these bushes, or do something.'

'Well, I bain't gwaine to. I be studyin' your interests, I tell 'ee, same as I allus have fer any maister.'

The farmer in question told my father about it afterwards. 'When I think of how I used to run up and down behind my counter, it makes my blood boil,' he said.

Both master and man were right in their judgment of the situation, and afterwards had a sound mutual respect for each other. But shepherds were always studying their sheep, and never seemed to tire of it. It always used to amaze me at our harvest suppers, where we could have a choice of beef, mutton, or ham, that our shepherd always chose mutton in large and re-peated helpings. Whether he did so with the idea of supporting his own industry, or in order to get his own back on one of the animals who ruled his whole life, I do not know, but it was always mutton for him.

VALE OF WHITE HORSE, OXFORDSHIRE

34. Thomas Hughes, *Tom Brown's Schooldays* (1867)

But to return to the said Vale of White Horse, the country in which the first scenes of this true and interesting story are laid. As I said, the Great Western now runs right through it, and it is a land of large rich pastures, bounded by ox-fences, and covered with fine hedgerow timber, with here and there a nice little gorse or spinney, where abideth poor Charley, having no other cover to which to betake himself for miles and miles, when pushed out some fine November morning by the Old Berkshire. Those who have been there, and well mounted, only know how he and the staunch little pack, who dash after him – heads high and sterns low, with a breast-high scent – can consume the ground at such times. There being little plough-land, and few woods, the Vale is only an average sporting country, except for hunting. The villages are straggling, queer, old-fashioned places, the houses being dropped down without the least regularity, in nooks and out-of-the-way corners, by the sides of shadowy lanes and foot-paths, each with its patch of garden. They are built

chiefly of good gray stone and thatched; though I see
that within the last year or two the red-brick cottages
are multiplying, for the Vale is beginning to manufacture largely both brick and tiles. There are lots of waste
ground by the side of the roads in every village,
amounting often to village greens, where feed the pigs
and ganders of the people; and these roads are old-
fashioned, homely roads, very dirty and badly made,
and hardly endurable in winter, but still pleasant jog-
trot roads running through the great pasture lands,
dotted here and there with little clumps of thorns,
where the sleek kine are feeding, with no fence on either
side of them, and a gate at the end of each field, which
makes you get out of your gig (if you keep one), and
gives you a chance of looking about you every quarter of
a mile.

One of the moralists whom we sat under in our
youth – was it the great Richard Swiveller, or Mr Stigg-
ins? – says, 'we are born in a vale, and must take the
consequences of being found in such a situation.' These
consequences I for one am ready to encounter. I pity
people who weren't born in a vale. I don't mean a flat
country, but a vale; that is, a flat country bounded by
hills. The having your hill *always* in view if you choose
to turn towards him, that's the essence of a vale. There
he is for ever in the distance, your friend and companion; you never lose him as you do in hilly districts.

And then what a hill is the White Horse Hill! There it
stands right up above all the rest, nine hundred feet
above the sea, and the boldest, bravest shape for a chalk
hill that you ever saw. Let us go up to the top of him, and
see what is to be found there. Ay, you may well wonder,
and think it odd you never heard of this before; but,
wonder or not, as you please, there are hundreds of such
things lying about England, which wiser folk than you
know nothing of, and care nothing for. Yes, it's a
magnificent Roman camp, and no mistake, with gates,
and ditch, and mounds, all as complete as it was twenty
years after the strong old rogues left it. Here, right up on
the highest point, from which they say you can see

eleven counties, they trenched round all the table-land, some twelve or fourteen acres, as was their custom, for they couldn't bear anybody to overlook them, and made their eyrie. The ground falls away rapidly on all sides. Was there ever such turf in the whole world? You sink up to your ankles at every step, and yet the spring of it is delicious. There is always a breeze in the 'camp', as it is called, and here it lies, just as the Romans left it, except that cairn on the east side, left by Her Majesty's corps of Sappers and Miners the other day, when they and the Engineer officer had finished their sojourn there, and their surveys for the Ordnance Map of Berkshire. It is altogether a place that you won't forget – a place to open a man's soul and make him prophesy, as he looks down on that great Vale spread out as the garden of the Lord before him, and wave on wave of the mysterious downs behind; and to the right and left the chalk hills running away into the distance, along which he can trace for miles the old Roman road, the 'Ridgeway' (the 'Rudge', as the country folk call it), keeping straight along the highest back of the hills – such a place as Balak brought Balaam to, and told him to prophesy against the people in the valley beneath. And he could not, neither shall you, for they are a people of the Lord who abide there.

RIVER TEST, HAMPSHIRE

35. Eric Parker, *English Wild Life* (1929)

But the Test water-meadows – they hold other memories besides those of landrail. I think them more beautiful than those of the Itchen, even of the Itchen that travels by St Cross and St Catherine's Hill. They are nearer to the sea; indeed, sea-water comes new and salt to the river of them. And they carry greater fish. Like its neighbour, the Hampshire Avon, the Test has a run of salmon, and when I first fished for them I knew at the end of a happy April day that the Test would always be for me unlike any other river. There are pools between

Nursling Mill and the sea which remind me of the quieter stretches of Tweed running between green banks, but to think of Test side by side with the musical falls and the blue shadows of Deeside under snow, or of the primroses and the deep skies of the Irish Lee, is to realize that with the one is the vigour of the North and with the other the warm winds of the West, but that here is the South, a tranquil stream lucent between beds of cresses, with cowslips and water avens about its banks, and osier thickets chattering with sedge warblers, and swifts and swallows hawking low over the water.

Selborne

36. Gilbert White, *The Natural History of Selborne* (1788)

Selborne, June 8, 1775

Dear Sir,

On September the 21st, 1741, being then on a visit, and intent on field-diversions, I rose before daybreak: when I came into the enclosures, I found the stubbles and clover-grounds matted all over with a thick coat of cobweb, in the meshes of which a copious and heavy dew hung so plentifully that the whole face of the country seemed, as it were, covered with two or three setting-nets drawn one over another. When the dogs attempted to hunt, their eyes were so blinded and hoodwinked that they could not proceed, but were obliged to lie down and scrape the incumbrances from their faces with their fore-feet, so that, finding my sport interrupted, I returned home musing in my mind on the oddness of the occurrence.

As the morning advanced the sun became bright and warm, and the day turned out one of those most lovely ones which no season but the autumn produces: cloudless, calm, serene, and worthy of the south of France itself.

About nine an appearance very unusual began to

demand our attention, a shower of cobwebs falling from very elevated regions, and continuing, without any interruption, till the close of the day. These webs were not single filmy threads, floating in the air in all directions, but perfect flakes or rags; some near an inch broad, and five or six long, which fell with a degree of velocity which showed they were considerably heavier than the atmosphere.

On every side as the observer turned his eyes might he behold a continual succession of fresh flakes falling into his sight, and twinkling like stars as they turned their sides towards the sun.

How far this wonderful shower extended would be difficult to say; but we know that it reached Bradley, Selborne, and Alresford, three places which lie in a sort of a triangle, the shortest of whose sides is about eight miles in extent.

At the second of those places there was a gentleman (for whose veracity and intelligent turn we have the greatest veneration) who observed it the moment he got abroad; but concluded that, as soon as he came upon the hill above his house, where he took his morning rides, he should be higher than this meteor, which he imagined might have been blown, like thistle-down, from the common above: but, to his great astonishment, when he rode to the most elevated part of the down, three hundred feet above his fields, he found the webs in appearance still as much above him as before; still descending into sight in a constant succession, and twinkling in the sun, so as to draw the attention of the most incurious.

Neither before nor after was any such fall observed; but on this day the flakes hung in the trees and hedges so thick, that a diligent person sent out might have gathered baskets full.

The remark that I shall make on these cobweb-like appearances, called gossamer, is that, strange and superstitious as the notions about them were formerly, nobody in these days doubts but that they are the real production of small spiders, which swarm in the fields in fine weather in autumn, and have a power of shooting out webs from their tails so as to render themselves buoyant, and lighter than air. But why these apterous insects should that day take such a wonderful aerial excursion, and why their webs should at once become so gross and material as to be considerably more weighty than air, and to descend with precipitation, is a matter beyond my skill. If I might be allowed to hazard a supposition, I should imagine that those filmy threads, when first shot, might be entangled in the rising dew, and so drawn up, spiders and all, by a brisk evaporation into the region where clouds are formed: and if the spiders have a power of coiling and thickening their webs in the air, as Dr Lister says they have [see his Letters to Mr Ray], then, when they were become heavier than the air, they must fall.

Every day in fine weather, in autumn chiefly, do I see those spiders shooting out their webs and mounting aloft: they will go off from your finger if you will take them into your hand. Last summer one alighted on my book as I was reading in the parlour; and, running to the top of the page, and shooting out a web, took its departure from thence. But what I most wondered at, was that it went off with considerable velocity in a place where no air was stirring; and I am sure that I did not assist it with my breath. So that these little crawlers seem to have while mounting, some loco-motive power without the use of wings, and to move in the air, faster than the air itself.

PRIOR'S DEAN

37. Edward Thomas (1878–1917)

The Manor Farm
The rock-like mud unfroze a little and rills
Ran and sparkled down each side of the road
Under the catkins wagging in the hedge.
But earth would have her sleep out, spite of the sun;
Nor did I value that thin gilding beam

More than a pretty February thing
Till I came down to the old Manor Farm,
And church and yew-tree opposite, in age
Its equals and in size. Small church, great yew,
And farmhouse slept in a Sunday silentness.
The air raised not a straw. The steep farm roof,
With tiles duskily glowing, entertained
The midday sun; and up and down the roof
White pigeons nestled. There was no sound but one.
Three cart-horses were looking over a gate
Drowsily through their forelocks, swishing their tails
Against a fly, a solitary fly.

The Winter's cheek flushed as if he had drained
Spring, Summer, and Autumn at a draught
And smiled quietly. But 'twas not Winter –
Rather a season of bliss unchangeable
Awakened from farm and church where it had lain
Safe under tile and thatch for ages since
This England, Old already, was called Merry.

SUSSEX DOWNS

38. W. H. Hudson, *Nature in Downland* (1900)

This silence of the hills does not impress one at once if
the mind is occupied with thinking, or the eyes with
seeing. But if one spends many hours each day and
many days in lonely rambles (and who would not prefer
to be alone in such a place?), a consciousness of it grows
upon the mind. The quiet too becomes increasingly
grateful, and the contrast between the hills and the
lowland grows sharper with each day. Coming down to
the village where one sleeps, it seems like a town full of
business and noise, and the sound of a train in the
distance has a strangely disturbing effect. The coarse
and common sounds of the lowlands do not penetrate
into the silent country of the hills. The sounds there are
mostly of birds, and these are comparatively few and
are not the loud-voiced. Furthermore, when they are

the same voices which you are accustomed to hear in hedge and field and orchard, they do not seem quite the same. The familiar note of the homestead has a more delicate, spiritualized sound. The common character-istic songsters of the islands and miniature forests of furze are the linnet, whitethroat, dunnock, meadow pipit, yellowhammer, common bunting, whinchat, and stonechat. They are none of them loud-voiced, and their songs do not drown or kill one another, but are rather in harmony and suited to that bright quiet land. I have said that the song-thrush among other birds of the orchard goes to the downs and sometimes breeds there. Now, although I am as fond of the music of this thrush as any one can be, heard from the treetops in woods and lanes and fields, where it sounds best, it was never a welcome voice on the downs. I seldom heard it in those wilder quiet furze islands among the high hills; and if the loud staccato song burst out in such a place I always had a strong inclination to go out of my way and throw a stone at the singer to silence him. On the other hand, I never tired of listening to even the poorest of the characteristic species; even the common bunting was a constant pleasure. In the wide sunny world I preferred him to his neighbour and relation, the yellowhammer. The sound he emits by way of song is certainly bright, and, like some other bird-voices, it is associated in my mind in hot and brilliant weather with the appearance of water spouting or leaping and sparkling in the sun. Doubtless such expressions as 'needles of sound', 'splin-ters', and 'shafts', and 'jets of sound', &c., to be found in writers on bird-music, are not wholly metaphorical, but actually express the connection existing in the writer's mind between certain sounds and sights. The common bunting's little outburst of confused or splintered notes is when heard (by me) at the same time mentally seen as a handful of clear water thrown up and breaking into sparkling drops in the sunlight.

Of the songsters of the furze on the downs the best to my mind is the stonechat. It is true that the linnet has one exquisite note, the equal of which for purest

81

melody and tender expression is not to be found among our feathered vocalists. Those who are so utterly without imagination as to keep a linnet (for the love of it) in a wire prison, cannot hear this note as I hear it. To sing it properly the little bird must be free of the summer sunshine, the wide blue sky and green expanse of earth, the furze bushes, aflame with their winged blossoms and smelling of spice; for that incomparable note, and the carmine colour which comes not on his feathers in captivity, express his gladness in a free aerial life.

39. Richard Jefferies, *Field and Hedgerow* (1889)

In this district, far from the great historic hop-fields of Kent, the hops are really grown in gardens, little pieces often not more than half an acre or even less in extent. Capricious as a woman, hops will only flourish here and there; they have the strongest likes and dislikes, and experience alone finds out what will suit them. These gardens are always on a slope, if possible in the angle of a field and under shelter of a copse, for the wind is the terror, and a great gale breaks them to pieces; the bines are bruised, bunches torn off, and poles laid prostrate. The gardens being so small, from five to forty acres in a farm, of course but few pickers are required, and the hop-picking becomes a 'close' business, entirely confined to home families, to the cottagers working on the farm and their immediate friends. Instead of a scarcity of labour, it is a matter of privilege to get a bin allotted to you. There are no rough folk down from Bermondsey or Mile End way. All staid, stay-at-home, labouring people – no riots; a little romping no doubt on the sly, else the maids would not enjoy the season so much as they do. But there are none of those wild hordes which collect about the greater fields of Kent. Farmers' wives and daughters and many very respectable girls go out to hopping, not so much for the money as the pleasant out-of-door employment, which has an astonishing effect on the health. Pale cheeks begin to glow again in the hop-fields. Children who have suffered from whooping-cough are often sent out with the hop-pickers; they play about on the bare ground in the most careless manner, and yet recover. Air and hops are wonderful restoratives. After passing an afternoon with the drier in the kiln, seated close to a great heap of hops and inhaling the odour, I was in a condition of agreeable excitement all the evening. My mind was full of fancy, imagination, flowing with ideas; a sense of lightness and joyousness lifted me up. I wanted music, and felt full of laughter. Like the half-fabled haschish, the golden bloom of the hops had entered the nervous system; intoxication without wine, without injurious after-effect, dream intoxication; they were wine for the nerves. If hops only grew in the Far East we should think wonders of so powerful a plant.

40. Edward Thomas, *The South Country* (1909)

The road skirts the marshland, the stream and the town, and goes through a gap in the Downs towards another range and more elms and farms at its feet. Stately walks the carter's boy with his perpendicular brass-bound whip, alongside four wagon-horses, while the carter rides. It is a pleasant thing to see them going to their work in the early gold of the morning, fresh, silent, their horses jingling, down the firm road. If they were leading their team to yoke them to the chariot of the sun they could not be more noble. They are the first men I have seen this morning, and truly they create for a little while the illusion that they are going to guide the world and that all will be well in the golden freshness under the blue.

The road now divides to go round the base of the Downs, but a farm track sets out to climb them. There, at the corner, is a church, on the very edge of the flat vale and its elms and ashes in the midst of meadows; a plain towered church, but with a rough churchyard, half graveyard and half orchard, its grass and parsley and nettle uncut under the knotty apple trees, splashed with silver and dull gold-green, dotted by silver buds among yellow-lichened branches that are matted densely as a magpie's nest. The dust from the high road powders the nettles and perfects the arresting melancholy of the desolation, so quiet, so austere, and withal as airy as a dream remembered. But above are the Downs, green and sweet with uplifting grass, and beyond them the sea, darkly gleaming under lustrous white cliffs and abrupt ledges of turf, in the south; in the south-east a procession of tufted trees going uphill in single file; in the south-west the dazzling slate roofs of a distant town, two straight sea walls and two steamers and their white wakes; northward the most beautiful minor range in all the downland, isolated by a river valley at the edge of which it ends in a gulf of white quarry, while on the other side it heaves and flows down almost to the plain, but rises again into a lesser hill with woods, and then slowly subsides. Within a few square miles it collects every beauty of the chalk hill; its central height is a dome of flawless grass only too tender to be majestic; and that is supported by lesser rounds and wavering lines of approach in concavity and convexity, playgrounds for the godlike shadows and lights, that prolong the descent of the spent wave of earth into the plain.

An uncertain path keeps to the highest ridge. The sides of the Downs are invaded by long stream-like gorse-sided coombes, of which the narrow floor is palest green grass. The highest points command much of earth, all of heaven. They are treeless, but occasionally the turf is over-arched by the hoops of a brier thicket, the new foliage pierced by upright dead grey grass. They are the haunt of the swift, the home of wheatear and lark and of whatsoever in the mind survives or is born in this pure kingdom of grass and sky. Ahead, they dip to a river and rise again, their sweep notched by a white road.

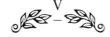

To the Counties Around London

Travelling up from the coast of east Sussex into the wooded Weald of Kent, you make a long and splendid dive from green heights into green depths. The airy, open downland that forms the backbone of Sussex makes its final plunge to ground level just to the west of the genteel holiday town of Eastbourne. From here northwards the landscape tightens and concertinas into valleys, one behind another like rolling waves, becoming ever more fertile and tree-covered the further north they run. Writers on the Wealden countryside tend to foreshorten their viewpoints in tune with the foreshortening landscape, concentrating on the village and parochial scene, in contrast to their South Country counterparts and their celebration of the high and lonely downs.

The northward journey from Eastbourne starts, however, in a landscape far removed in character from either majestic downland or intimate Wealden valleys. To the east of Eastbourne lie the flat marshlands of the Pevensey Levels, smothered on the outskirts of the town under a sprawl of new housing, new industrial estates, new roads and roundabouts among which Eastbourne's retired old folk wait, looking rather bewildered and lost, for their buses to the shopping centres. There's little of marshland feeling about these modern developments, or about the high-banked lane that crosses the Pevensey Levels. Only after a couple of miles do its thick hedges yield gaps wide enough to give long prospects over the marshes. The views, when they do come, are of a flat, dour landscape of dark bushes, ditches full of pondweed and bristling with rushes and reeds, willows unpollarded for generations and wide fields dotted with grazing sheep. The farms of the Pevensey Levels are isolated one from another, battered by the wind, low-lying collections of concrete sheds and rusty Dutch barns with the occasional wall of flint pebbles as a reminder of how they looked in centuries past. Many of their fields are in poor shape, choked with thistles, sedges and docks. The marshland farmers drive their shabby, outmoded cars deliberately, on the crown of the lane at fifteen miles an hour, defying the swervings and honkings of the impatient outsider trapped behind. Sunshine can lighten the whole atmosphere of these marshes, brightening them with gleams on water and wind-blown willow leaves. But their essential sombreness is best shown on a stormy day when the sky blackens and blots out the distant downs beyond Eastbourne, leaving the Levels darkened, swept with rain and sunk in gloom.

Ahead rises the southern edge of the Wealden hills, insignificant compared with the rearing height of the downs, but a pleasure to the eye when set beside the monotony of the marshlands. Oak and ash trees, hedges and verges thick with cow parsley, bracken and foxgloves close in on the lane as if in welcome as it begins its gentle climb up and down these rich slopes. The sand in the soil makes golden gashes in the hedgebanks. At Chapel Row the tiny 'Welcome Stranger' pub carries on its strictly local business in the front room of a cottage by the lane. The red brick cones of oast houses, where hops were dried in pre-mechanization days, begin to appear in back gardens and farm yards, each oast capped with a white wind-hood, many now converted into houses or studios. This easy landscape feels and looks warmer than those bleak Levels, but there's little to be seen of it until the lane climbs to Wood's Corner, one of the highest viewpoints in the Sussex section of the Weald.

From the garden of the Swan inn at Wood's Corner, looking over many miles of densely wooded, dipping country-side, you can appreciate why the Saxons named it 'Andredsweald', the forest where no one lives. The post-Ice

Age meltwaters sculpted the final touches to these clay lands, the exposed heart of the chalk dome whose remaining outer rim now forms the North and South Downs. Thick forest spread to cover the entire expanse of the Weald, from the North Downs to the Pevensey Levels. The Saxons put their pigs into the forest to fatten on acorns and beech mast, and made inroads into the tree cover as they hacked out fields and farmsteads. They gave the Weald many of its placenames, too – the 'steads' (Nettlestead, Brasted), 'hursts' (Salehurst, Goudhurst), 'leys' (Hartley, Wilsley), 'dens' (Hawksden, Horsmonden) – all words signifying Saxon clearings in the great wildwood of Andredsweald. But it was after the Normans arrived – their initial landing was in the Pevensey Levels – that the old forest began to fall in huge swathes, cut down to clear the land for agriculture and for new townships, and to retrieve firewood to power the furnaces smelting the iron ore that lay deep beneath the trees. The Weald became rich, and richer still when Flemish weavers settled here in the reign of Edward III. The view from Wood's Corner shows the landscape that came slowly into being, a patchwork of prosperous villages, small farms and their hedged fields, orchards and hop fields, all set among the still extensive remnants of Andredsweald.

Hereabouts is Squire Jack Fuller's patch. Squire Fuller of Rose Hill was a headstrong individual whose red-blooded approach to life led him into many a tight corner, from which he usually managed to extricate himself with style. After laying a drunken wager that he could see the spire of Dallington Church from his house, he discovered on the morning after that he was mistaken. Nothing daunted, the squire had a replica put up in a position that he *could* overlook – the little cone of stone, known as the Sugarloaf, still stands forlornly in a field just down the road from the Swan inn. There are other Fuller extravaganzas along the lane from Wood's Corner to Goudhurst: a squat, massive observatory to facilitate his love of star-gazing, and the stone needle of an obelisk in a field opposite. Squire Fuller was said to have broadened his horizons with local lovelies, either under the stars in his observatory, or around the Sugarloaf. No wonder he peppered the landscape with phallic symbols.

Two superb country houses lie deep in the valleys here, tucked peacefully away from the world. One is Rudyard Kipling's retreat, Bateman's, all gables and tall chimneys at the turn of a side lane a mile short of Burwash. The other house, Twyssenden Manor, stands off the road to Goudhurst at the end of a bumpy track, a glorious mish-mash of timber framing, golden stone blocks and red pantiles under steep red roofs, mellow to the chimney-tops. This was a stronghold of Catholic sympathizers back in persecution days. At Twyssenden the 'captains' or priests, coming in fear and secrecy up from the coast on their way to London, could rest and recuperate while celebrating the forbidden Mass, sure of a safe retreat in the priest's hole concealed within the manor if the Protestants came to call.

The lanes dip down under the trees, crossing the valley-bottom streams and climbing to the hilltop villages – Burwash, Ticehurst, Goudhurst. All are charming, Goudhurst especially so. Its houses mount the crest of the hill above the River Teise, red roofs and red wall tiles one above another past the duck pond to the top where the stumpy church looks down over the Star and Eagle inn and the steep village street. Shops are dark and old fashioned. People stroll and chat in the middle of the road, staring reproachfully at oncoming cars for which they only reluctantly step aside. No matter that the villagers are mostly commuters to Tunbridge Wells and Maidstone – nowhere in England is village cricket contested, village gossip exchanged or village politics embraced more passionately than in these gorgeous hill villages of the Weald.

The lane narrows as it winds north from Goudhurst towards Curtisden Green past oasts and apple orchards. This is deep countryside with its own flavour, seen at its peak from Curtisden Green's high ground. The converted oast on the village green commands a view that takes some beating, over the cricket nets and through the trees to the weather-boarded houses and winding lanes. But the oast that stands behind the green – a double oast, with twin cones – can better it. Sited on the edge of the ridge, it looks out over valleys rich with hop fields, orchards, vegetable patches, red farms and white oast caps, rising to a long, wooded ridge that frames the whole picture. It was a view much loved by the oast's former owner, Richard Church, a country writer who settled here in 1939. Church had a writing room specially built in the oast tower, but found he didn't care to use it. Isolation, however magnificent, is not what this warm and homely countryside is all about.

Though modern London's influence on its surrounding counties is profound, there's little reference to the Great Wen in these pieces of country writing. We travel in a clockwise direction, encircling the capital from Kent through Surrey, Berkshire and Hertfordshire to Essex, ranging down the years from Izaak Walton's seventeenth-century riverside idyll near Ware to Richard Church's post-war Wealden village. These writers were active before motorways and modern commuting had focused much of the life and industry of these Home Counties on London, and there's a purely parochial feel to many of their descriptions.

Richard Jefferies draws a typically acute contrast between the country labourers at their immemorial work and the pulsating city seen in the distance, but this is London's only influence on scenes within an hour of the city which were for their recorders entirely rural. George Sturt ('George Bourne' to his readers) takes the opposite view to Jefferies, looking up from the streets of his market town of Farnham to delight in the spaciousness of the surrounding green fields and hillsides. Mary Russell Mitford's joyous nutting expedition explores hedgerows now in the grip of a grossly expanded Reading; but most of these places still remain today, outwardly at any rate, much as they were to their writers. The roads of the Lambourne valley in west Berkshire are now tarmacked, no longer 'rough and dusty', but fishermen still sit on the banks of the river among the same wild flowers that 'L.S.' described. Great Bardfield in Essex (C. Henry Warren's 'Larkfield') remains a small, largely agricultural village well out in the sticks. And the passing of a century has not changed one bit the bleakness and mystery of the Essex marshes around Mersea Island.

THE WEALD, KENT

41. Richard Church, *A Window on a Hill* (1951)

What a journey that was through a France paralysed by a general strike! However, I got to England after four days of travel, two of them spent in a Paris of deserted streets, empty restaurants, and snow-filled gutters. And were my forebodings fulfilled? Was I coming back to a Nordic gloom, a Hyperborean complex of cold and darkness?

No, it was not like that. The fog parted as we entered Dover harbour, breaking down over a palette of pastel tints from which the Shakespeare Cliff gleamed like a rampart of pearl. Behind the town the Castle was smudged upon the sky, a building in one of Turner's lightning water-colours. I shut my eyes, and tried to recall the scene from my bedroom window in the villa on the Riviera. But it was already faint, in spite of its hardness: the eastward stretch of coast, broken by two promontories, each with a château to crown it and to throw a sharp reflection upon the calm water; the sun leaping out of that water like an animal, and smacking the hills with flame. No, something was already coming between me and that Homeric scene. The classics were fading out before this insinuation from the North, this drenching atmosphere of home.

After the Customs, and the sound of English voices as subdued as the air that supported them, I left Dover by car, winding out of the town, through Folkestone, then turning inland toward this mid-Kent spot where I sit at this moment in isolation and a quietness the like of which I never found even on the mountain tops down by the Central Sea. As I drove homeward, dusk gathered in the gentle folds of the downs. Nothing stood with distinction. Every colour merged, a smudge of umber or smoky green behind a veil. That veil was the very air itself, visible as the horizontal light was caught and suspended in moisture. Long fins of woodland along the tops of the downs were almost outlined, but not quite. They were just brush-marks on the canvas. A hayrick here and there shone with a self-generated glow, a survival of the summer heat housed there. Some cattle steamed by, followed by a girl on a damp bicycle. All were larger than life, because of the penumbra of shining air around them. The hedgerows between which we hummed along were draped with wet spider-webs, knotted with dewdrops, each knot a point of sulky fire. The cottages and farmhouses, of fire-tinged tiles, burned more boldly on their western walls, harmonizing with the gathering billows of cold smoke that were quenching the sun before he set. He was already withdrawn from fire to orange when we were halfway home, and he went down humbled by the superior glory of his train of vapours.

What had I feared, down there in the hard, Odyssean light? Here was something indeed to return to; a world of beauty such as Homer and Virgil never knew, and no Theocritus could sing; a world of quarter-tones, of infinite gradations, of colour murmuring to itself alone, like the aging Wordsworth with his rapture lost yet remembered. This is what I found coming North.

COOLING MARSHES

42. Charles Dickens, *Great Expectations* (1861)

It was a dark night, though the full moon rose as I left the enclosed lands, and passed out upon the marshes. Beyond their dark line there was a ribbon of clear sky, hardly broad enough to hold the red large moon. In a few minutes she had ascended out of that clear field, in among the piled mountains of cloud.

There was a melancholy wind, and the marshes were very dismal. A stranger would have found them insupportable, and even to me they were so oppressive that I hesitated, half inclined to go back. But I knew them well, and could have found my way on a far darker night, and had no excuse for returning, being there. So, having come there against my inclination, I went on against it.

The direction that I took was not that in which my old home lay, nor that in which we had pursued the convicts. My back was turned towards the distant Hulks as I walked on, and, though I could see the old lights away on the spits of sand, I saw them over my shoulder. I knew the limekiln as well as I knew the old Battery, but they were miles apart; so that if a light had been burning at each point that night, there would have been a long strip of the blank horizon between the two bright specks.

At first, I had to shut some gates after me, and now and then to stand still while the cattle that were lying in the banked-up pathways arose and blundered down among the grass and reeds. But after a little while, I seemed to have the whole flats to myself.

It was another half-hour before I drew near to the kiln. The lime was burning with a sluggish stifling smell, but the fires were made up and left, and no workmen were visible. Hard by, was a small stone-quarry. It lay directly in my way, and had been worked that day, as I saw by the tools and barrows that were lying about.

Coming up again to the marsh level out of this excavation – for the rude path lay through it – I saw a light in the old sluice-house. I quickened my pace, and knocked at the door with my hand. Waiting for some reply, I looked about me, noticing how the sluice was abandoned and broken, and how the house – of wood with a tiled roof – would not be proof against the weather much longer, if it were so even now, and how the mud and ooze were coated with lime, and how the choking vapour of the kiln crept in a ghostly way towards me. Still there was no answer, and I knocked again. No answer still, and I tried the latch.

It rose under my hand, and the door yielded. Looking in, I saw a lighted candle on a table, a bench, and a mattress on a truckle bedstead. As there was a loft above, I called, 'Is there anyone here?' but no voice answered. Then I looked at my watch, and, finding that it was past nine, called again, 'Is there anyone here?'

There being still no answer, I went out at the door, irresolute what to do.

NORTH SURREY

43. Richard Jefferies, *Nature Near London* (1883)

Intent day after day upon the earth beneath his feet or upon the tree in the hedge yonder, by which, as by a lighthouse, he strikes out a straight furrow, his mind absorbs the spirit of the land. When the plough pauses, as he takes out his bread and cheese in the corner of the field for luncheon, he looks over the low cropped hedge and sees far off the glitter of the sunshine on the glass roof of the Crystal Palace. The light plays and dances on it, flickering as on rippling water. But, though hard by, he is not of London. The horses go on again, and his gaze is bent down upon the furrow.

A mile or so up the road there is a place where it widens, and broad strips of sward run parallel on both sides. Beside the path, but just off it, so as to be no obstruction, an aged man stands watching his sheep. He has stood there so long that at last the restless sheep dog has settled down on the grass. He wears a white smock-frock, and leans heavily on his long staff, which he holds with both hands, propping his chest upon it. His face is set in a frame of white – white hair, white whiskers, short white beard. It is much wrinkled with years; but still has a hale and hearty hue.

The sheep are only on their way from one part of the farm to another, perhaps half a mile; but they have already been an hour, and will probably occupy another in getting there. Some are feeding steadily; some are in a gateway, doing nothing, like their pastor; if they were on the loneliest slope of the Downs he and they could not be more unconcerned. Carriages go past, and neither the sheep nor the shepherd turn to look.

Suddenly there comes a hollow booming sound – a roar, mellowed and subdued by distance, with a peculiar beat upon the ear, as if a wave struck the nerve and rebounded and struck again in an infinitesimal fraction of time – such a sound as can only bellow from the mouth of cannon. Another and another. The big guns at Woolwich are at work. The shepherd takes no heed – neither he nor his sheep.

His ears must acknowledge the sound, but his mind pays no attention. He knows of nothing but his sheep. You may brush by him along the footpath and it is doubtful if he sees you. But stay and speak about the sheep, and instantly he looks you in the face and answers with interest.

Round the corner of the straw-rick by the red-roofed barn there comes another man, this time with smoke-blackened face, and bringing with him an odour of cotton waste and oil. He is the driver of a steam ploughing engine, whose broad wheels in summer leave their impression in the deep white dust of the roads, and in moist weather sink into the soil at the gateways and leave their mark as perfect as in wax. But though familiar with valves, and tubes, and gauges, spending his hours polishing brass and steel, and sometimes busy with spanner and hammer, his talk, too, is of the fields.

He looks at the clouds, and hopes it will continue fine enough to work. Like many others of the men who are employed on the farms about town he came originally from a little village a hundred miles away, in the heart of the country. The stamp of the land is on him, too.

FARNHAM, SURREY

44. George Bourne, *Memoirs of a Surrey Labourer* (1907)

Very pleasant it is, as you walk about the old town, to glance through a gap between the houses – down some alley or back-way, or under the entrance to an inn-yard – and catch a glimpse of green hillside a mile away under a great vista of sky telling of far horizons. You look up; as likely as not a rook is sailing overhead. You listen; and if the street chances to be quiet you may hear a lark singing. From a street in my own native town I have watched a hawk poised high in air; one spring day I heard, and looking up caught sight of, a passing cuckoo. Many birds are near at hand. Thrushes and blackbirds are melodious in the back gardens, swallows build under the eaves, now and again a wagtail comes down into the roadway. The summer evenings are vocal with the screaming of swifts; in the summer mornings, if you are up early enough, you may see rooks coolly walking in the streets as though they owned them. Pleasant odours come too. There are hours in June when the town is fragrant with the scent of new hay though you do not see the meadows where it is making. The passing manure-waggon is at worst only half disagreeable, because, after all, it makes you think of farms, and another day the same waggon may bring in for atonement the scent of hops, or of the newly opened heap of mangold. The occasional odour of weeds burning is far from offensive in the street; nor was it at one time offensive, I remember, but rather suggestive of leagues of hot summer weather, when for several days a whole town was perfumed with the penetrating smell of a vast heath-fire six or seven miles away. But, besides these chance reminders of rusticity, there is always the sky, there are always the clouds and the sense of plentiful breathing-room above and around the country town. As you perceive, the shops and dwelling-houses are but a thin screen, a flimsy and often beautiful scene-painting, hiding the open country but not really shutting it out. Rather they frame the sky, and set the imagination dreaming of the fields over which it broods; and while they shut out the eyesores – the neglected farm, the squalid village, or the obtrusively new Cockney villas that too often disfigure the actual country – on the other hand they invite thoughts of the real beauty that lies beyond them. From out there behind the houses and across the valleys comes fancy of coppices full of primroses, hangers fringed with catkins, woodland hollows still open to the April sky, but soon to be curtained in with young leaves. There were never lovelier hedgerows, deeper meadows, more ample downs, or farms more peaceful, than those one is tempted to imagine from the High Street of a country town . . .

LAMBOURNE VALLEY, BERKSHIRE

45. 'L.S.', *Untravelled Berkshire* (1909)

The river Lambourne is almost choked in some places by masses of the yellow monkey flower (*Mimulus Langsdorfer*), an American plant that has now become naturalized; mixed in with it and growing in luxuriance upon the shallow banks is the wild thyme, with its scented mauve flowers. Little wooden bridges span the water all through the villages; here and there a stronger one of red brick or stone. Many and many a happy hour may the fisherman spend upon the banks of the Lambourne. Should he be fortunate enough to find himself in the valley in June, he will probably return home with a heart at peace with the world and a full basket, for trout are numerous in the little river, and leafy June is the best month of all for the sport. A few days' fishing, in the valley during the months of July, August, or September, is an amusement by no means to be despised by those who appreciate the sport.

High up above the villages upon either side lie the Berkshire Downs, sunny and bright and pleasant in summer and autumn; bleak and dreary enough in winter when the wind sweeps over them, and the snow hides all traces of the tracks and footpaths, the only signs of human life.

Now and then a wagon will appear upon the skyline, and move slowly along the ridge, or a group of gleaners working in the harvest-fields. All the women wear the old-fashioned sunbonnets. Now and then, a year or two ago, a smock-frock might actually have been seen, few and far between indeed, perhaps only two or three remaining in the whole of the valley. Even the oldest men have given them up; 'they have grown too proud,' an old woman said to me rather sadly one day. Her husband had given up wearing his before he died, but she 'did like to see him in it when it was washed and clean'. Being of a frugal mind, and apparently not sharing the pride with which she accredited her husband, she had cut it up and made it into a 'wropper' for herself, and 'a beautiful wropper it had made'.

Strange, when one thinks of it, this discontinuance of the smock-frock. Has the need for it departed, with the decrease of human agricultural labour, and the increase of machinery, or is the reason for its disuse to be found simply in a change of fashion? Is it really, as the old woman in the Lambourne valley said, that the men have grown too proud to wear them, or is it not quite possible that the fault lay partly with the women, who no longer possessed the patience required for making them. The beautiful needlework which went to the fashioning of these old country garments needed plenty of that admirable virtue; the smock-frock was not made in a day. Whatever the reason for its departure, it has gone; and when one visits the picturesque villages that now know it no more, one cannot help regretting its absence. For it would still well fit into the picture.

THREE MILE CROSS

46. Mary Russell Mitford, *Our Village* (1819)

The little spring that has been bubbling under the hedge all along the hillside, begins, now that we have mounted the eminence and are imperceptibly descending, to deviate into a capricious variety of clear deep pools and channels, so narrow and so choked with weeds, that a child might overstep them. The hedge has also changed its character. It is no longer the close compact vegetable wall of hawthorn, and maple, and brier-roses, intertwined with bramble and woodbine, and crowned with large elms or thickly set saplings. No!

the pretty meadow which rises high above us, backed and almost surrounded by a tall coppice, needs no defence on our side but its own steep bank, garnished with tufts of broom, with pollard oaks wreathed with ivy, and here and there with long patches of hazel overhanging the water. 'Ah, there are still nuts on that bough!' and in an instant my dear companion, active and eager and delighted as a boy, has hooked down with his walking-stick one of the lissome hazel stalks, and cleared it of its tawny clusters, and in another moment he has mounted the bank, and is in the midst of the nuttery, now transferring the spoil from the lower branches into that vast variety of pockets which gentlemen carry about them, now bending the tall tops into the lane, holding them down by main force, so that I might reach them and enjoy the pleasure of collecting some of the plunder myself. A very great pleasure he knew it would be. I doffed my shawl, tucked up my flounces, turned my straw bonnet into a basket, and began gathering and scrambling – for, manage it how you may, nutting is scrambling work – those boughs, however tightly you may grasp them by the young fragrant twigs and the bright green leaves, will recoil and burst away; but there is a pleasure even in that: so on we go, scrambling and gathering with all our might and all our glee. Oh what an enjoyment! All my life long I have had a passion for that sort of seeking which implies finding (the secret, I believe, of the love of field-sports, which is in man's mind a natural impulse) – therefore I love violeting – therefore, when we had a fine garden, I used to love to gather strawberries, and cut asparagus, and, above all, to collect the filberts from the shrubberies: but this hedgerow nutting beats that sport all to nothing. That was a make-believe thing, compared with this; there was no surprise, no suspense, no unexpectedness – it was as inferior to this wild nutting, as the turning out of a bag-fox is to unearthing the fellow, in the eyes of a staunch fox-hunter.

Oh what enjoyment this nut-gathering is! They are in such abundance, that it seems as if there were not a boy in the parish, nor a young man, nor a young woman – for a basket of nuts is the universal tribute of country gallantry; our pretty damsel Harriet has had at least half a dozen this season; but no one has found out these.

River Thames, Berkshire–Oxfordshire Border

47. Robert Gibbings, *Sweet Thames Run Softly* (1940)

Many of the vistas that one sees between Streatley and Mapledurham might have dropped from gold frames in the Royal Academy. Titles such as 'Where Stately Trees caress the Stream', 'Dappled Meadows', or 'Smooth Hills and Quiet Waters', would be appropriate in their catalogue. Not that I want to disparage the landscape. On the contrary: I have already said that it is among the grandest on the river. It *is* 'lovely' country, the hills *are* 'splendid', the trees *are* 'gorgeous', the houses 'charming', the cottages 'sweet'; but like a Victorian drawing-room it is too rich and comfortable to engender thought.

Pegsdon Barn, Hertfordshire–Bedfordshire Border

48. G. M. Boumphrey, *Along the Roman Roads* (1935)

The Icknield Way led me on down a slope, over a railway and under another, to the little river Hiz, where a ford runs between an elm and a black poplar and by a field of daisies and buttercups – a pleasant spot. And so to the little village of Ickleford where, at the inn, George II puzzled his head as to how on earth the apple got inside the apple dumpling. A little lane between hedges took me one and a half miles to Punch's Cross, and, looking back from here, I had a fine view of fifteen miles and more to Therfield Heath by Royston. Half a mile of metalled road, and then my way swung up a grassy track between high hedges, white with may and guelder rose and full of the song of birds – the chaffinch's sudden fountain of melody and the wistful little tune of the willow-wren. A mile's climbing brought Telegraph Hill, where there was space on the left for a glorious view back the way I had come – Ickleford, Willbury and the downs beyond Baldock – before the hedge shut in again. But only for half a mile. And then the hedge on the right opened and a stile invited me to walk just one hundred yards to the edge of what is said to be the original of John Bunyan's 'Delectable Mountains'. I feel I owe this part of the walk an apology. It was country that I had known only from dashing along the main roads from London in a car. I knew it had a beauty spot or two (and those I generally try to avoid); but London is only thirty miles away and I had always imagined it must be infected with the poison of bad building which reaches so far on every side. It is nothing of the sort. On Pegsdon Barn you are standing on the northern brink of the chalk downs; immediately in front of you the turf sweeps down three hundred feet; and beyond that spread miles and miles of Bedfordshire, Bucks and Cambridgeshire, utterly unspoilt as yet. Just to the left a dry valley runs up into the chalk for two or three hundred yards behind you – and the lines of these chalk valleys are things to be looked at as closely as a piece of sculpture. A mile to the left, trees half hide the entrenchments of Ravensburgh Castle, an old camp, in private grounds. Four miles ahead Wrest Park shows up; and over it unrecognizable miles and miles of country. To the right I could make out, with my glasses, Caesar's Camp at Sandy Gap, ten miles beyond Biggleswade – and *that* is a good ten miles from where I stood. It is a grand spot and one can understand the impression it must have made on John Bunyan.

GREAT AMWELL, HERTFORDSHIRE

49. Izaak Walton, *The Compleat Angler* (1653)

PISC. . . . . And now you shall see me try my skill to catch a trout; and at my next walking, either this evening or to-morrow morning, I will give you direction how you yourself shall fish for him.

VEN. Trust me, master, I see now it is a harder matter to catch a trout than a chub: for I have put on patience, and followed you these two hours, and not seen a fish stir, neither at your minnow nor your worm.

PISC. Well, scholar, you must endure worse luck some time, or you will never make a good angler. But what say you now? There is a trout now, and a good one too, if I can but hold him, and two or three more turns will tire him. Now you see he lies still, and the sleight is to land him. Reach me that landing net; so, sir, now he is mine own, what say you now? Is not this worth all my labour and your patience?

VEN. On my word, master, this is a gallant trout; what shall we do with him?

PISC. Marry, e'en eat him to supper; we'll go to my hostess, from whence we came; she told me, as I was going out of door, that my brother Peter, a good angler and a cheerful companion, had sent word that he would lodge there to-night, and bring a friend with him. My hostess has two beds, and I know you and I may have the best; we'll rejoice with my brother Peter and his friend, tell tales, or sing ballads, or make a catch, or find some harmless sport to content us and pass away a little time, without offence to God or man.

VEN. A match, good master, let's go to that house; for the linen looks white, and smells of lavender, and I love to lie in a pair of sheets that smell so. Let's be going, good master, for I am hungry again with fishing.

PISC. Nay, stay a little, good scholar; I caught my last trout with a worm; now I will put on a minnow, and try a quarter of an hour about yonder trees for another; and so walk towards our lodging. Look you, scholar, thereabout we shall have a bite presently or not

at all. Have with you, sir! o' my word I have hold of him.
Oh! it is a great logger-headed chub; come hang him
upon that willow twig, and let's be going. But turn out
of the way a little, good scholar, towards yonder high
honeysuckle hedge; there we'll sit and sing, whilst this
shower falls so gently upon the teeming earth, and gives
yet a sweeter smell to the lovely flowers that adorn
these verdant meadows.

'LARKFIELD' (GREAT BARDFIELD), ESSEX

50. C. Henry Warren, *England Is a Village* (1940)

The Three Horseshoes is less a house than a honeycomb:
to draw a plan of its oddly shaped cells and passages,
every one on a different level from the other, would be
quite beyond my power. One thing these cells and
passages have in common, however, and that is a
certain severity. There are no rose-satin cushions in the
Three Horseshoes; nothing but good, honest wood. And
there is nothing progressive about Harry. He is only
half, perhaps only a quarter, the landlord of the Three
Horseshoes; the rest of him is a blacksmith. And when,
in his own good time, he comes to bring you your beer,
he brings quite a lot of his forge in with it. The yellow
end of a home-made cigarette (constantly being lit and
as constantly going out again) hangs from his lower lip;
soot colours the rest of his face and his lithe, strong
arms; and instead of a barman's apron he wears a bit of
old leather, cut to ribbons and seared with fire.

In fact, the landlord of the Three Horseshoes has
always been half that and half something else; and one
of Harry's predecessors has left behind him a local
reputation which, however skilled a craftsman he may
be, the very nature of the times will deny to Harry
himself. Many a craftsman, dead and buried these fifty
years or more, still keeps his memory green in the
village by some work of his agile hands – a field-gate
here, good for another quarter of a century, a neat piece
of house-thatching there, or even a scrolled latch in

some out-of-the-way cottage window where mass-production frames have not yet been introduced. And so the memory of Natt Witherby the cooper still lives on, kept green by those oaken harvest-bottles (kegs, as some call them, or costrels) of which he was the master-maker in the locality.

Not that many of Natt's harvest-bottles are still to be seen. Here and there you may find one hanging on a rusty nail in some cottage outhouse, its iron hoops falling away, its paint weathered or gone altogether, and its leather handle and trimly shaped vent-pegs as irretrievably lost as the dark, shining bullock's horn from which its owner drank his beer in the harvest field. But for the most part, Natt's bottles have been broken up and burned, and Natt is remembered less by the sight of them than by the reputation they earned in years gone by.

Harry may have all of Natt's skill in those strong hands of his, but he has to spend it on such severely circumscribed jobs as the mending of stoves and grates, the riveting of cart-wheels, and the patching up of factory products which the craftsman in him abhors. His fate is the fate of most village blacksmiths today, but at least he is more fortunate than most in having his little pub to fall back on. His customers may not be many or very profitable; but they are his friends. All the week they must more or less look after themselves and be content with only an occasional visit from Harry, who stumbles in from the forge for a moment just to see how things are going.

But on Saturday night, washed clean of soot and with a whole cigarette between his lips, he is a host in a hundred. It will be strange if Ned Freeman is not there with his accordion, and many a forgotten country song comes to life over the glasses of beer. And even after closing-time, when his customers should all be gone, Harry sits on in the cloudy tap-room, discussing the mysteries of life with a few chosen cronies.

'No, Jim, you don't want to go home yet awhile. Drat the missus! I should a-thought you had enough of her jaw all the week. Why, I'm only just beginnin' to wake up! Did you see that bit in the paper the other day . . .'

But Jim resists the lure of the landlord's intriguing conversation and goes home. And Harry is left alone, dreaming while the last embers fade.

Old Hall Marshes

51. Sabine Baring-Gould, *Mehalah* (1880)

The rent-paying day was bright and breezy. The tide was up in the morning, and Mehalah and her mother in a boat with sail and jib and spritsail flew before a north-east wind down the Mersea Channel, and doubling Sunken Island, entered the creek which leads to Salcot and Virley, two villages divided only by a tidal stream, and connected by a bridge.

The water danced and sparkled, multitudes of birds were on the wing, now dipping in the wavelets, now rising and shaking off the glittering drops. A high sea wall hid the reclaimed land on their left. Behind it rose the gaunt black structure of a windmill used for pumping the water out of the dykes in the marsh. It was working now, the great black arms revolving in the breeze, and the pump creaking as if the engine groaned remonstrances at being called to toil on such a bright day. A little further appeared a tiled roof above the wall.

'There is Red Hall,' said Mehalah, as she ran the boat ashore and threw out the anchor. 'I have brought the stool, Mother,' she added, and helped the old woman to land dry-footed. The sails were furled, and then Mehalah and her mother climbed the wall and descended into the pastures. These were of considerable extent, reclaimed saltings, but of so old a date that the brine was gone from the soil, and they furnished the best feed for cattle anywhere round. Several stagnant canals or ditches intersected the flat tract and broke it into islands, but they hung together by the thread of sea wall, and the windmill drained the ditches into the sea.

In the midst of the pasture stood a tall red-brick house. There was not a tree near it. It rose from the flat like a tower. The basement consisted of cellars above ground, and there were arched entrances to these from the two ends. They were lighted by two small round windows about four feet from the ground. A flight of brick stairs built over an arch led from a paved platform to the door of the house, which stood some six feet above the level of the marsh. The house had perhaps been thus erected in view of a flood overleaping the walls, and converting the house for a while into an island, or as a preventive to the inhabitants against ague. The sea walls had been so well kept that no tide had poured over them, and the vaults beneath served partly as cellars, and being extensive, were employed with the connivance of the owner as a storeplace for run spirits. The house was indeed very conveniently situated for contraband trade. A 'fleet' or tidal creek on either side of the marsh allowed of approach or escape by the one when the other was watched. Nor was this all. The marsh itself was penetrated by three or four ramifications of the two main channels, to these the sea wall accommodated itself instead of striking across them, and there was water-way across the whole marsh, so that if a boat were lifted over the bank on one side, it could be rowed across, again lifted, and enter the other channel, before a pursuing boat would have time to return to and double the spit of land that divided the fleets. The windmill which stood on this spit was in no favour with the coastguard, for it was thought to act the double purpose of pump and observatory. The channel south of these marshes, called the Tollesbury Fleet, was so full of banks and islets as to be difficult to navigate, and more than once a revenue boat had got entangled and grounded there, when in pursuit of a smuggled cargo, which the officers had every reason to believe was at that time being landed on the Red Hall marshes, and carted into Salcot and Virley with the farmer's horses.

The house was built completely of brick, the windows were of moulded brick, mullions and drip stone, and the roof was of tile. How the name of Red Hall came to be given it, was obvious at a glance.

Round the house was a yard paved with brick, and a moat filled with rushes and weed. There were a few low outhouses, stable, cowsheds, bakehouse, forming a yard at the back, and into that descended the stair from the kitchen door over a flying arch, like that in front.

Perhaps the principal impression produced by the aspect of Red Hall on the visitor was its solitariness. The horizon was bounded by sea wall; only when the door was reached, which was on a level with the top of the mound, were the glittering expanse of sea, the creeks, and the woods on Mersea Island and the mainland visible. Mehalah and her mother had never been at Red Hall before, and though they were pretty familiar with the loneliness of the marshes, the utter isolation of this tall gaunt house impressed them. The thorntrees at the Ray gave their farm an aspect of snugness compared with this. From the Ray, village-church towers and cultivated acres were visible, but so long as they were in the pasture near the Hall, nothing was to be seen save a flat tract of grass land intersected with lines of bulrush, and bounded by a mound.

VI

To East Anglia and Lincolnshire

The best and most characteristic walk from Mersea Island in Essex to the Suffolk farmland north of Ipswich is by way of the upward and outward curve of the coastline. But it's a frustrating business for any walker in a hurry. This is a long hike – some fifty miles in all – and by no means a straightforward one. The miles of easy walking along wide esplanades and concrete sea walls are broken up and interrupted by creeks, stretches of boggy marshland, bridge-less dykes, estuary mouths and a strange, muddy inland sea dotted with tidal islands. The Essex seaside resorts with all their regulated layouts of streets and seafronts are inter-spersed with some of Britain's bleakest and wildest marsh landscapes. You can't follow this coast in one continuous march; water constantly gets in your way, forcing you inland in great sweeping detours to find a bridge or a stretch of firm ground.

This is lonely, wind-whipped walking, too. In summer sunshine, when the saltings smell as fresh and rich as fruit cake and the marshes are speckled purple with sea lavender, the flat views with their glinting pools and creeks have a sombre beauty which, once the eye is schooled to appreciate it, can thrill like no other landscape. Let the sun go in, however, and the temperature drop, and suddenly that brooding Mehalah atmosphere of darkness and desolation sweeps with the cloud shadows across the marshes. All colours except dun brown and steel grey seem to leach out of the landscape. Solitary houses, which in the sunshine of a minute before were standing out cheerfully in their low surroundings, now look stark and in some way menacing. In this mood the Essex marshes turn cold shoulders to the outsider.

The eastern end of Mersea Island trails out in a gravelly spit called the Mersea Stone which faces its counterpart, St Osyth Stone, over the muddy mouth of Brightlingsea Reach. Islands of mud a couple of feet in height lie in the water, as they do across the Reach on the marshy walk down to Colne Point, where the coastline swings from south to east. Jerry buildings and smart seaside second homes rub shoulders at Bel Air and Jaywick. You walk through a wonderful jumble of accommodation, from the flimsiest of wooden huts, converted boats and tin shacks to the grandest of townsmen-by-the-sea bungalow fantasies. All this is by way of introduction to the four-mile sprawl of Clacton-on-Sea and its easterly satellite of Holland-on-Sea. Clacton is a big, blaring exclamation mark to punctuate the walk. Had you come here a little more than a hundred years ago, you would have found nothing but a trio of Martello towers threatening the empty sea from the cliffs. Clacton sprang late into being as a seaside resort, but it sprang with fervour. Its heart beats for those sunny summer days when most of eastern Essex and quite a lot of London come here to bake on the beach and whirl around the fairground attractions on Clacton Pier. A different, more sombre but infinitely more dramatic atmosphere invades Clacton's long sea frontage in winter, when rollers from the North Sea are bursting all over the roads and the gales have torn loose the strings of coloured lights.

Beyond Clacton a path hurdles the wooden groynes along the shore over pebbles and sand patches to enter another four miles of resort frontage. But this is Frinton-on-Sea, gentility and restraint to Clacton's blowsy vigour. On the seaward side of neat greens, and below cliffs blazing with wild flowers, lines of sturdily built wooden beach huts look out on sands where no ice-cream booths or slot arcades are seen. Frinton will not permit them. You have to walk on to the shabbier reaches of Walton-on-the-Naze for a return to resort normality. The landward end of Walton's pier deals in shining rides and slot machines, but out at the far tip it's a fisherman's world. On good days sea anglers find it hard to get space for a decent cast between the almost invisible lines of their neighbours on each side. A world of sandwich-munchers and cigarette-smokers, where damp newspaper packets of ragworms lie at the fishermen's feet on the planking, and half-pound lead weights whistle past the onlooker's ears.

The Naze bulges northwards from Walton, a truncheon-shaped peninsula of low cliffs fast crumbling under the attack of the North Sea waves. To the west of the Naze and sheltering behind it lies Hamford Water, known locally as the Backwaters, an inland sea extending far into the Essex farmlands, whose ten square miles are filled and emptied twice a day by the tides. In the mud of the Backwaters squat low islands – Horsey Island, Skipper's Island, Hedge-end Island, Pewit Island – whose outlines change hourly, shrinking or growing, putting out hundreds of yards of saltings or withdrawing them, drying out or swirling with water as the state of the tide dictates. Some of these islets are con-nected to the shore by slippery, sloppy causeways over the mud, and here in contented isolation live two or three hardy people.

Spending a freezing winter day with the two inhabitants of Horsey Island, and another with the solitary dweller on Skipper's, I marvelled at the richness of the Backwaters' bird life. Peewits, curlews, golden plovers, godwits, redshanks, brent geese, herons, short-eared owls, dunlin – all throng the sodden fields and soft foreshores, where fat seals wallow like great slugs on and off the mud banks. The air rings with bird cries. As the tide rises the islands seem one by one to float free of their underlay of glistening mud, which shrinks, divides and vanishes under the encroaching water. Arthur Ransome set Secret Water (1939) in this remote, watery small world, marooning the Swallows on Horsey Island as he did in real life with his own children. I found the spot where the Swallows set up camp, the farm where the Natives lived and the causeway where Titty, Roger and Bridget almost drowned in the rising tide. Absorbed in the landscape of that childhood story of high adventure, I almost missed my own low-tide crossing of the causeway.

From the Backwaters the coast runs north through creeks and marshes to another blob of civilization at Harwich, the old port tightly packed on to its crooked finger of land where the rivers Stour and Orwell meet to flow into the North Sea. A few miles to the north the River Deben comes down to the sea as well, the three rivers cutting the flat land into peninsulas. Once across Harwich harbour on the ferry there is a long and beautiful walk beside the Deben up to Woodbridge, but to enter Suffolk with due ceremony I'd choose for preference the Orwell and its waterside ramble along the northern shore of the Shotley peninsula. From Shotley Gate, where naval cadets once climbed their training college's tall mast in terror, the path leads west by saltings crammed with wading birds, mile after mile of windy, splendid walking, looking across the half-mile width of the Orwell to the low, wooded Suffolk hinterland. At Pin Mill, halfway between Shotley Gate and Ipswich, walkers with big thirsts and an eye for river scenery might well get no further with their day's journey. The Butt and Oyster, one of the best and most atmospheric pubs in Britain, stands with one foot in the river at high tide, the water's sparkle reflected through the window up on to the ceiling of the dark-panelled, dark-beamed bar. Sitting on the window seat with a pint of Ipswich-brewed Tolly Cobbold bitter and looking out at the old sailing barges moored in the mud banks and the modern-day Swallows splashing around in their tiny dinghies, sniffing in smells of salt water and warm vegetation along with those of the Butt and Oyster's own special fisherman's pie, I have more than once been sorely tempted to abandon an afternoon's walk here.

Above Pin Mill the path runs under the dinosaur legs of a great road bridge and accompanies the river up to the docks at Ipswich. This is a bustling entry into Suffolk's capital town. The untidy sprawl of Ipswich peters away northwards into a gently rolling landscape of copses, large meadows and the fringes of the vast East Anglian corn country.

*

As with many other parts of Britain carrying an overall name that encompasses individual areas – the West Country, for example, or the Scottish Lowlands – East Anglia has no precise boundaries. A general characteristic of the region is flatness, along with a dominant influence of water and sky. Suffolk and Norfolk belong to East Anglia without question, and so do the fenlands of Bedfordshire and Cambridgeshire. For our purposes, East Anglia takes in all these counties, and makes a long northerly leg up into Lincolnshire to the high spine of wolds that overlook the great flat apron of coastline.

We start in two Suffolk villages whose agricultural life has been documented in wonderful detail – Ronald Blythe's 'Akenfield' (Charsfield, ten miles north of Ipswich), and Adrian Bell's 'Benfield St George' (Stradishall, ten miles south-west of Bury St Edmunds). The chapter continues in a northward sweep through Norfolk – the Broads; Weston Longville near Norwich, where Parson Woodforde moved to in 1776 from Ansford in Somerset, to continue chronicling the minutiae of his and his neighbours' everyday lives; Cromer on the north-east coast of the county; the ancient green roads of the River Nar country, explored through the inimitable style and spelling of the King of the Norfolk Poachers, Frederick Rolfe. Rolfe's book *I Walked By Night*, 'born of an old man's loneliness', was licked into shape for publication by Lilias Rider Haggard from the old poacher's pencil scribblings in exercise books and on scraps of paper. From King's Lynn it's north to find Alfred, Lord Tennyson on the Skegness coast and John Hillaby (in the course of a different trek from *Journey Through Britain*) on the Lincoln-shire Wolds. Then south again into the watery world of the fen country: nearly drowning in a dyke with intrepid Celia Fiennes, shooting near Ely with J. Wentworth Day's old-fashioned sporting squire, and finally cruising into the company of a remarkable fenman at Peterborough.

'Akenfield' (Charsfield), Suffolk

52. Ronald Blythe, *Akenfield* (1969)

Brian Newton, aged 19, farm-worker

The older farm-workers aren't all that keen on boys like me. They don't appreciate your running about. There are three men who have been on the farm all their lives and I know they resent me. Two of them have never learned to drive and have nothing to do with the machinery at all, and each year there are more and more jobs they can't do. It is embarrassing for them, I suppose. They'll talk all day about what they did years ago. You'll occasionally meet men who'll say, 'Thank God – those days have gone!' but you'll still meet quite a few who, if they had their way, would be back with the horses tomorrow. They'll fiddle about with some ditch or other miles away, making such a rare fuss of it. It is all quite unnecessary but nobody dare say so, of course. They are so slow. They have to touch everything with their hands – they dislike the idea of not touching things. They must handle, touch . . . They would do the sugar-beeting perfectly – the worst damn job on the farm – even if their fingers were half-dropping off with the cold. If they saw one on the heap with a bit of green left on they'd be scrambling up to get it. All unnecessary. These men are in their early fifties and they hold the idea that theirs is the right way and that we shall have to come round to it. There is another 'stranger' on the farm – a boy from the south. Our ideas are different, we speak different and we even look different – to these village men who have never left their village, unless perhaps for the war. The worst thing about these older workers is that they really do believe that we shall have to come round to their way of thinking. They have some sort of fear of the boss. The boss used to expect them to be hard at it all day, although I don't know that he can expect it these days. What they can't understand is that work is just work – something to be done and paid for. Of course we know that the old men had art – because they had damn-all else! It kept them from despairing. And we young men have efficiency, and I'm not saying that efficiency is enough either. This tractor is efficient. A man is more than a tractor, isn't he?

Jubal Merton, aged 60, wheelwright and blacksmith
Things got worse after the war, yet the land didn't suffer. It went on looking pretty good. The houses came to pieces and the people were hungry and keeping themselves warm with bits of old army clobber, but the fields stayed absolutely perfect. The men forgot that they were the farmer's fields when they were ploughing and planting them, and decked and tended them most perfectly. They were art itself. The farmers like to think that the men did this fine work for them, but they did it for themselves. The farmers had got the upper hand now and wherever he could he made his worker a slave. That was what it was coming to. Have no doubt about it. No man dare open his mouth, or out he went! A man had to be silent to stay in the village. The farmers had become too powerful – and mean! It wasn't their talk which separated them from the gentry, it was their meanness. I'll tell a tale about this.

There was a farmer in the village who gave his men a £5 bonus each for getting the harvest in, and which was money the men counted on for buying the winter boots for their big families. These men, they worked for as long as they could see, day and night, for the first week of the harvest. They were mowing barley mostly and they'd be at it from four in the morning until ten at night. Time made no difference so long as they could see. Well, on the Saturday night they'd had enough so they had a wash and went to the Crown for a drink, which they well deserved. And on the Monday the farmer got them all together and said, 'So you all went home early on Saturday, did you, and left the barley. Well, since you seem to like going home early you can bugger off home now – and stop there!' The men were all still and silent. Nobody dared open his mouth, not because he was afraid for himself but because of his tied-house and his family. Nobody moved. The farmer kept them standing dumb like this well-nigh half an hour and then he said, 'Get to work . . .' The men didn't hurry their harvest; they made a masterpiece of it. It was their defiance. The farmer didn't understand this and Tom Makin heard him boasting in the Great White Horse at Ipswich to some other farmers about how he had made his men 'hustle up'.

OLD NEWTON

53. Arthur Chaplin, quoted by George Ewart Evans, *The Horse in the Furrow* (1960)

'My father tied with another man at an Old Newton furrow-drawing match: both had a quarter-inch *deviation* – it must have been about sixty years ago. Now he had one peculiarity when he was a-ploughin': he had to have his pipe going before he could start. So this particular day at Old Newton, just before he started, he stopped to do the usual: get a good light on his owd pipe. One of the stewards saw him a-doin' this and he say:

'"Hurry up there! We're waiting for you to start. You can't smoke and draw a furrow at the same time."

'"Dew you be quiet. I know what I'm a-dewin' on."

'So he lit up his owd bit of clay pipe, put his hands to the plough and went after his horses. When he had drawn a furrow that everybody could see was one of the best – even before the *stickers* put the sticks on it – they say:

'"See! It's child's play for him. He smokes at it as if he's just a-diggin' in his own garden!"

'They didn't know that he couldn't have drawn a proper furrow let alone a real good 'un if he hadn't got his owd pipe a-drawin' in his mouth! It just shows you: what you're used to, you must do – even if it's in a competition.'

'Benfield St George' (Stradishall)

54. Adrian Bell, *Corduroy* (1930)

All day the loaded wagons come rumbling into the barn. Again and again they are unloaded, and the sheaves stacked in the bays mount gradually higher, till the men can rest, between loads, against the cobwebbed crossbeams. All morning they talk and laugh. They become expansive and reminiscent at harvest-time. The older men speak of harvests that have been, of men they have worked with that are dead, of times and places – of particular crops in particular fields. It is always, 'Do you remember that time when . . . ?' or 'Do you know what became of So-and-so?' As they rise higher, and the country seen through the open doors is spread at their feet, old horizons give place to new, more distant ones, where buildings show faintly, churches or farms, and discussion turns to them, whose or of what village they may be.

Towards evening talk languishes; the intervals between question and answer lengthen. Laughter is peremptory, short-breathed. A grimness then steals over the scene – arms and bodies swaying, forks sweeping to and fro, eyes cast down and little said. Only the rustle of sheaves is heard in the settling gloom. I take my turns at unloading with the rest. At first it is distress, for one must unbuild a load as a stack, taking always the top sheaf, and always that seems the one I am standing on. There is no room to move about on the load of sheaves; they are uneven, slippery. My feet fall into crevices, and I stumble. Uncertain foothold makes double labour of it. Yet the men, unwieldy-figured, balance easily, and bend and thrust up rhythmically. I watch them to learn their ease; the motion that saves the most energy is also the most graceful.

I stand on the stack catching the sheaves as they swing up from below and passing them across. As my fork comes back empty, I find almost automatically another sheaf on its tines. I can labour thus rhythmically, I feel, for ever, but when the rhythm is lost then labour is despair. Comes one sheaf a second – there is a moment when it has left the unloader's fork and not yet reached mine, and pauses in a last sun-ray that transmutes it to a fiery symbol. The next moment it is on my fork, the rich light past, a sheaf of corn again.

My shirt, open to the waist, reveals to me my body at work, the flesh rippling, tightening, and subsiding. What a rare machine this is, able to balance on two feet on a shifting surface and wield weights.

Outside, the moon is up – the harvest moon over harvest fields. It casts a sheen upon the empty stubbles, the bare rounding slopes, so altered from the close-crowded landscape of standing corn. It has glimmering secrets among the trees, and pierces into every entanglement of foliage, and lays faint shadows across the paths. Each finds a ghost of himself beside him on the ground. An elusive radiance haunts the country; the distances have a sense of shining mist. The men move homeward from the field; the last load creaking up the hill behind them, the hoofs of the horses thudding, their breath sounding short. Peace comes, a vision in the fairy armour of moonlight, the peace of 'man goeth forth unto his work until the evening.'

The last load is drawn into the barn to be unloaded in the morning. The horses stand with foam on their bridles, their flanks heaving after the long pull; struggle is in their attitude. It is quite dark in the barn. There is a rattle of chains as the horses are unhitched and led away, the voices of men helping the load into position, a clatter of wood as a block is kicked under a wheel, the music of steel on steel as forks are laid together.

The men straggle out into the moonlight and pause in a group on the roadway, gazing at the sky, at the moon in her glory. (When the men pause in their work they always look at the sky.)

'Don't look much like wet,' says one. 'Don't want neither till the barley's out of the way.'

'Looks like the colour of money to me,' says another.

Bob comes down from the stable. 'Ho, she's regular showing off tonight,' is his tribute. 'Well, I'm goin to see about some supper,' he says. There is a murmur of considered assent, as though there were something original in the idea. With gruff 'Good nights' the group disperses, some going up the road, some down, and some across the fields.

Weston Longville, Norfolk

55. James Woodforde, *Diary* (1776–1790)

June 4 1776 I breakfasted, dined, supped and slept again at Weston. My tooth pained me all night, got up a little after 5 this morning, & sent for one Reeves a man who draws teeth in this parish, and about 7 he came and drew my tooth, but shockingly bad indeed, he broke away a great piece of my gum and broke one of the fangs of the tooth, it gave me exquisite pain all the day after, and my Face was swelled prodigiously in the evening and much pain. Very bad and in much pain the whole day long. Gave the old man that drew it however 0. 2. 6. He is too old, I think, to draw teeth, can't see very well.

June 5 1776 I breakfasted, dined, supped and slept again at Weston. Very much disturbed in the night by our dog which was kept within doors tonight, was obliged to get out of bed naked twice or thrice to make him quiet, had him into my room, and there he emptied himself all over the room. Was obliged then to order him to be turned out which Bill did. My face much swelled but rather easier than yesterday tho' now very tender and painful, kept in today mostly . . .

April 15 1778 . . . We breakfasted, dined, supped and slept again at home. Brewed a vessell of strong Beer today. My two large Piggs, by drinking some Beer grounds taking out of one of my Barrels today, got so amazingly drunk by it, that they were not able to stand and appeared like dead things almost, and so remained all night from dinner time today. I never saw Piggs so drunk in my life, I slit their ears for them without feeling.

April 16 1778 We breakfasted, dined, supped and slept again at home. My 2 Piggs are still unable to walk yet, but they are better than they were yesterday. They tumble about the yard and can by no means stand at all steady yet. In the afternoon my 2 Piggs were tolerably sober.

December 31 1780 . . . This being the last day of the year we sat up till after 12 o'clock, then drank a Happy New Year to all our Friends and went to bed. We were very merry indeed after Supper till 12. Nancy and Betsie Davie locked me into the great Parlour, and both fell on me and pulled my Wigg almost to Pieces. – I paid them for it however.

Feb 3 1781 . . . Had but an indifferent night of Sleep, Mrs Davie and Nancy made me up an Apple Pye Bed last night . . .

Feb 12 1781 . . . We did not go to bed till after 12 this night, the Wind being still very high. We were as merry as we could be, I took of Mrs Davie's Garter tonight and kept it. I gave her my Pair of Garters and I am to have her other tomorrow . . .

May 16 1781 . . . Between 7 and 8 o'clock this morning went down to the River a fishing with my Nets. Ben, Will, Jack, Harry Dunnell and Willm Legate (Ben's Brother) were my Fishermen. We begun at Lenewade Mill and fished down to Morton. And we had the best day of Fishing we ever had. We caught at one draught only ten full Pails of Fish, Pike, Trout and flat fish. The largest Fish we caught was a Pike, which was a Yard long and weighed upwards of thirteen pound after he was brought home.

May 17 1781 . . . Mr Priest of Norwich came to my house about 1 o'clock and he stayed and dined with us and spent the afternoon and in the evening returned to Norwich. I was very glad to see him, as he and wife behaved very civil to Nancy. Mr and Mrs Howes, Mrs Davie, and Mr du Quesne dined and spent the afternoon with us also. I gave my Company for dinner my great Pike which was rosted and a Pudding in his

Belly, some boiled Trout, Perch, and Tench, Eel and Gudgeon fryed, a Neck of Mutton boiled and a plain Pudding for Mrs Howes. All my Company were quite astonished at the sight of the great Pike on the table. Was obliged to lay him on two of the largest dishes, and was laid on part of the Kitchen Window shutters, covered with a cloth. I never saw a nobler Fish at any table, it was very well cooked, and tho' so large was declared by all the Company to be prodigious fine eating, being so moist.

Jan 26 1784 I rejoiced much this morning on shooting an old Woodpecker, which had teized me a long Time in pulling out the Reed from my House. He had been often shot at by me and others, but never could be a match for him till this Morn'. For this last 3 Years in very cold Weather did he use to come here and destroy my Thatch. Many holes he has made this Year in the Roof, and as many before. To Goody Doughty for seven Lemons pd. 0. 0. 6.

April 12 1785 My Servant Willm Coleman was out all the Evening till just 11 o'clock – came home in Liquor behaved very rudely and most impudently to me indeed, I told him that I was determined never more to bear with such Behaviour, and that he shd certainly go to Morr' . . .

April 13 1785 . . . I got up between 5 and 6 o'clock this morning had Will before me as soon as possible, paid him his Wages and dismissed him before 8 o'clock. For a Q^rs Wages at 5 Guineas p^d him 1. 6. 3.

Sept 24 1790 . . . Nancy was taken very ill this Afternoon with a pain within her, blown up so as if poisoned, attended with a vomiting. I supposed it proceeded in great measure from what she eat at Dinner and after. She eat for Dinner some boiled Beef rather fat and salt, a good deal of a nice rost duck, and a plenty of boiled Damson Pudding. After Dinner by way of Desert, she eat some green-gage Plumbs, some Figgs, and Raspberries and Cream. I desired her to drink a good half pint

Glass of warm Rum and Water which she did and soon
was a little better – for Supper she had Water-gruel with
a Couple of small Table Spoonfuls of Rum in it, and
going to bed I gave her a good dose of Rhubarb and
Ginger. She was much better before she went to bed –
And I hope will be brave to Morrow.

NORFOLK BROADS

56. Eric Parker, *English Wild Life* (1929)

Two hopes were in my mind when I set out on the last
day of May for Norfolk; one, to hear a bittern boom, and
the other to see the nest of a bearded tit. And the next
day, when I arrived among the familiar spaces of reeds
and water, I found the landscape strangely altered. The
landmarks I looked for were gone, there were new
horizons, hedges in leaf hid the windmills. But so too
were my hopes changed or increased. For the first
question put to me on arrival was whether I would care
to spend an hour or two in walking to see the nests of a
marsh harrier and a Montagu's harrier. There were
several Montagu's harriers' nests, and one marsh harrier's.

Two hours? But any number! I should never be able
to find such nests for myself. Only a few men in any year
knew exactly where to look for them, and one of them
was with us – indeed, only with his knowledge might we
set out to see them. So we did set out, along high,
straight paths built of woody wreck from the channels
that cut through meadow and reeds; we crossed deep
ditches by swaying fences; and we turned at right angles
down a tiny lane between reeds and sedge, treading on
adder's-tongue fern and brushed by alders and briers, till
our guide held up his hand and beckoned us one by one
forward by a foot-wide track through the sedge.

The track wound snail-ways, in and in. Our guide
halted and pointed. And half a dozen yards away a great
bird rose silently on dark wings and floated up into the
sunlight. And there you had to take but two steps

forward to look at a nest piled in the sedge; invisible to any eye but yours, with four white eggs in it – the only marsh harrier's nest in the British Isles. For that year there were other marsh harriers on the Broads, as there had been in other years, but only one pair built and bred. There above us in the evening sky was the splendid hawk high and far, and here were we with her four lonely eggs.

We made our way back by adder's-tongue and brier, and set out for the next nest, a Montagu's harrier's. That, too, we found, and a clutch of eight eggs – I believe the only clutch of eight on record – and as before we left the confident, sitting bird to circle down to her nest again. Another pair of Montagu's were beating a field on the horizon, the hen with fluttering pauses in her flight; her mate gliding and sliding on even wings. And we sat down on a bank above the reeds to listen for bittern.

All the sounds of the fenland country were about us – the musical wailing of plover, the cry of red-shank, snipe drumming under cirrhus clouds. And suddenly there came to me, as it must have come to fenmen a hundred years ago, and as it will come every year, I hope, now that bitterns breed in England again, the sound of sounds I had been longing to hear, the boom from the bird's air-filled throat that named it for our forefathers boother-boomp and bull-of-the-mire.

It is a sound unlike any other made by an English bird. It is less like a boom than a great in-breathing and out-breathing – almost a snore. Three or four times the bird repeats it, never, I believe, more. We listened to other boomings from other wildernesses as we were quanted home, and as we stepped out on the lodge lawn in the falling dark of the June evening there came across the water two calls that I had never thought to hear together, a bittern's and a cuckoo's.

CROMER TO SIDESTRAND, NORTH NORFOLK

57. Clement Scott, *Poppyland Papers* (1886)

It was on one of the most beautiful days of the lovely month of August, a summer morning with a cloudless blue sky overhead and a sea without a ripple washing on the yellow sands, that I turned my back on perhaps the prettiest watering-place of the East Coast and walked along the cliffs to get a blow and a look at the harvest that had just begun. It was the old story. At a mile removed from the seaside town I had left I did not find a human being. Below me, as I rested among the fern on the lighthouse cliff, there they all were, digging on the sands, playing lawn tennis, working, reading, flirting, and donkey-riding, in a circle that seemed to me ridiculously small as I looked at it from this height. In that red-roofed village, the centre of all that was fashionable and select, there was not a bed to be had for love or money; all home comforts, all conveniences to which well-bred people were accustomed were deliberately sacrificed for the sake of a lodging amongst a little society that loved its band, its pier, its shingle, and its sea. A mile away there were farmhouses empty, cottages to let, houses to be hired for a song; a mile to the right there were sands with no human being on them, deserted cliffs, empty caves, unfrequented rocks; a mile to the left there was not a footprint on the beach, not a footfall on the grassy cliff. Custom had established a certain fashion at this pretty little watering-place, and it was religiously obeyed; it was the rule to go on the sands in the morning, to walk on one cliff for a mile in the afternoon, to take another mile in the opposite direction at sunset, and to crowd upon the little pier at night. But the limit was a mile either way. No one thought of going beyond the lighthouse; that was the boundary of all investigation. Outside that mark the country, the farms, and the villages were as lonely as in the Highlands.

In aimless fashion I strolled on, and attracted by a ruined church tower, took a cut through the cornfields towards a cluster of farms and a distant village. It is difficult to convey an idea of the silence of the fields through which I passed, or the beauty of the prospect that surrounded me – a blue sky without a cloud across it; a sea sparkling under a haze of heat; wild flowers in profusion around me, poppies predominating everywhere, the hedgerows full of blackberry-blossom and fringed with meadow-sweet; the bees busy at their work, the air filled with insect life, the song-birds startled from the standing corn as I pursued my solitary way. So great was the change from the bustle of fashion to this unbroken quiet that I could scarcely believe that I was only parted by a dip of coastline from music and laughter and seaside merriment, from bands and bathing machines, from crochet and circulating libraries. Walking to the cliff's edge, I found a deserted sand; looking across the fields there was no sound but the regular click of the reaping machine under which the golden grain was falling.

MORSTON

58. Richard Mabey, *A Tide in the Affairs* (1981)

I've never understood those who find marshes desolate places. They can be remorselessly hard, especially in winter, but they are never oppressive. They are too open for that. If you look east or west along these flats you can sometimes see for a dozen miles, up to the edge of the Wash, if you are lucky. The view would swallow you if it were not for the rim of the sea itself. It is a shifting edge, but it puts a comforting limit to things. On the tideline, you know where you are. Stand by it and look due north and there is nothing between you and the Arctic Circle. The North Sea here is as dark as anywhere in Britain, and the locals still often refer to it by its stark ancient name, the German Ocean.

Yet turn round and look inland and you could be in the Chilterns. In the mile or so that lies between the sea and the coast-road the marshes gradually assemble themselves. Nearest you are the bare sands and the plastic, shifting muds; then the pastel wash of the first plants, the silver wormwood and lilac sea-lavenders; then the claimed land locked up behind the sea-walls; and finally, backed up against the low swell of the coastal hills, the little villages with their mighty churches, as compact and bright as if they were tucked in a secure inland valley.

It's hard to feel lonely where there is a tide. Whatever else it may be, it is reliable. A tide will come in, always more or less on time, and always, eventually, recede. The signs the spent water leaves on the sand and mudflats are like vanishing footprints. They are soft-edged, fleeting, curiously tidy. Perhaps it is this hus-banding by the sea that gives marshy landscapes what affinities they have with more slowly moulded sceneries inland. It is as if a whole round of seasons – or a whole generation of farming – were enacted twice a day.

GREEN ROADS OF NORTH NORFOLK

59. Frederick Rolfe, *I Walked By Night* (1935)

There are a great many Green roads in Norfolk, but it is not so often they get used these days, the time for them has gone.

There is one running from Wormagay Bridge straight to Swaffham, it catch Pentney, West Billney, and Marham on the way, and then on to Swaffham heath and Narbrough. Of corse it is hardly discernuble in some places, but it is a Publick foot path all the way.

In diffrent Parishes it has diffrent names. At West Bilney it is called the Warren Path, in Pentney it is called Dales Drove, in Marham the Fen lane, outside Marham but still in Marham bounds the Ramper, till it get to Swaffham heath, it is then called Swaffham Road. Then it go on to Pickenham just touching Beachamwell and then still go on.

No doubt it was one of the Ancient roads as some times it is thirty feet wide, at other places it is mearly a foot path.

There is another Green road running over Grimstone Comon. I do not know were it begin, but I know that it go on to Lynn on one side through Barsey and after leaving Grimstone it run on to Gayton Thorpe and East Walton, and away to Southacre and Westacre and then on the Castle Acre. Like the others it is called by diffrent names but the old People always spoke of it as Pot Row.

Many is the time I have traveled them Green roads. Of corse they have tried to abolish them old roads by Plowing them up wen they run over Private land. Just as this road enter Walton Field there is a verry large mound thirty feet high. The old People used to say a great Battle was fought there, any how the plough was always turning up bones and rusty bits of mettall in my time.

Then there is the Pedders way through Norfolk. I do not know were it begin nor yet were it end, all I know is I have traced it from Fincham by Downham Market to Marham, Shuldam and across Narbrough field. It is called Devells Dyke on Narbrough field and is some four feet in hight there. Then it travel on to the bounds of Narford, but of corse in many places it is almost gone, were the plough have been over it.

It cross Narford Estate a verry wide green lane. The late Algeron Fountain once planted it over with small trees and railed it up and thought I supose to be rid of it, but as other foot paths run into it there was a lot of trubble and he had to pull them all up. That was some forty years ago.

Pedders way then run on to Narford, just catch a bit of Westacre, and then on to Castle Acre and Newton, Merton, and I belive to Thetford passing through many villiges on the way. My old Grandfather have told me that the Smugglers used all these Green roads and by ways to smugle there Contraband goods, and that they had there holes and hiden places all along these routs. Were I was Keeper we had a verry large Warren beside the road running from Wormagay. One day the warriners were digging at the botom of a large hill were Oliver Cromwell was suposed to have planted his guns wen he destroyed Pentney Abby, and they came on a large hole about four yards square, which it was plain to be seen had been all timbered up many years before. A Gentleman came and looked at it and said it was one of the Smuglers hides.

LINCOLNSHIRE COAST

60. Alfred, Lord Tennyson (1809–92), *Ode to Memory*

> . . . Artist-like,
> Ever retiring thou dost gaze
> On the prime labour of thine early days:
> No matter what the sketch might be;
> Whether the high field on the bushless
>   Pike,
> Or even a sand-built ridge
> Of heaped hills that mound the sea,
> Overblown with murmurs harsh,
> Or even a lowly cottage whence we see
> Stretch'd wide and wild the waste enor-
>   mous marsh,
> Where from the frequent bridge,
> Like emblems of infinity,
> The trenched waters run from sky to sky . . .

DONINGTON-ON-BAIN, LINCOLNSHIRE

61. John Hillaby, *Journey Home* (1983)

The Bain is a beautiful valley, made the more mysterious that morning by swirling mists that hid the full extent of the flooded pastures, though the high-water mark of the river showed what havoc had been wrought by the storms. Among a sorry assemblage of bales of straw, tomato boxes, and plastic sacks were the swollen corpses of sheep and poultry. It looked as if the moles had had some premonition of what they were in for and had moved up on to higher ground, where more than a hundred hills could be counted in as many paces.

Moles are downright quarrelsome creatures at any time and normally have a well-defined home range. One could imagine the subterranean fights that went on when the riparian population invaded the territory of their more prudent neighbours. It would be actively resented, for a mole's tunnel system is not only its home, but its food shop, its store cupboard, and its dining room.

In Donington-on-Bain, an out-of-the-way village with no evident signs of prosperity beyond the poshed-up water mill, I came across a most hospitable pub, patronized that morning only by locals who went out of their way to welcome a muddy and inquisitive stranger. It could scarcely be described as an unspoiled place, since there wasn't much to spoil except the goodwill of Mary, the lady of the house, and her regulars.

As she clumped down from some business upstairs, one of them warned me what I was in for. 'She'll say she won't serve hikers,' he said. 'But let her go on a bit, y'know.' And he closed one eye, heavily.

She went on at some length. On the day they opened the Viking Way, twenty of 'em in bloody great boots trampled all over the chrysanthemums. No, she'd done with *that* lot, she had. At this I affected to look downcast and walk out slowly. Mild consternation on her part, and chuckles all round. Good rustic humour.

During the ensuing gossip it came out that Lincolnshire had more prematurely retired people to look after than anywhere else in the country. Jobs were desperately scarce. The old-style farms of two hundred acres had meant work for seven or eight men. Today the same number were employed on farms ten times that size. As one of them put it, there were no ladders, no chances of advancement for their sons and grandchildren. Farming had become a deal in the City. What did the fellers rushing about in their bloody great Mercedeses care for the community? Farms were run by people, and people had to be cared for. They hadn't even got a village bus. They were up to their asses in a system they could do nothing about.

LINCOLNSHIRE COUNTRYSIDE

62. Phoebe Hesketh, *A Song of Sunlight* (1974)

> *From a Train Window in Lincolnshire*
> Green miles of rye and barley,
> Gold, green of mustard, kale
> Flank sun-tanned farms and houses
> By riverside and rail –
> No railings, walls or hedges;
> The train slides through the sun
> Past Stickney, Trumble Woodside
> And Coningsby, to run
> By marsh and mere and willow,
> Across unfeatured fen
> And fields where men are hoeing,
> Where scarecrows jerk, and then
> Stand stiff and still, sleeves flapping,
> Outstaring birds and men.

'CROYLAND' (CROWLAND), LINCOLNSHIRE

63. Mrs Burrows (c. 1890)

On the day that I was eight years of age, I left school, and began to work fourteen hours a day in the fields, with from forty to fifty other children, of whom, even at that early age, I was the eldest. We were followed all day long by an old man carrying a long whip in his hand which he did not forget to use. A great many of the children were only five years of age. You will think that I am exaggerating, but I am *not*; it is as true as the

Gospel. Thirty-five years ago (1850–60) is the time I speak of, and the place, Croyland in Lincolnshire, nine miles from Peterborough. I could even now name several of the children who began at the age of five to work in the gangs, and also the name of the ganger.

We always left the town, summer and winter, the moment the old Abbey clock struck six. We had to walk a very long way to our work, never much less than two miles each way, and very often five miles each way. The large farms all lay a good distance from the town, and it was on those farms that we worked. In the winter, by the time we reached our work, it was light enough to begin, and of course we worked until it was dark and then had our long walk home. I never remember to have reached home sooner than six and more often seven, even in winter. In the summer we did not leave the fields in the evening until the clock had struck six, and then of course we must walk home, and this walk was no easy task for us children who had worked hard all day on the ploughed fields.

In all the four years I worked in the fields, I never worked one hour under cover of a barn, and only once did we have a meal in a house. And I shall never forget that one meal or the woman who gave us it. It was a most terrible day. The cold east wind (I suppose it was an east wind, for surely no wind ever blew colder), the sleet and snow which came every now and then in showers seemed almost to cut us to pieces. We were working upon a large farm that lay half-way between Croyland and Peterborough. Had the snow and sleet come continuously we should have been allowed to come home, but because it only came at intervals, of course we had to stay. I have been out in all sorts of weather but never remember a colder day. Well, the morning passed along somehow. The ganger did his best for us by letting us have a run in our turns, but that did not help us very much because we were too numbed with the cold to be able to run much. Dinnertime came, and we were preparing to sit down under a hedge and eat our cold dinner and drink our cold tea, when we saw the shepherd's wife coming towards us, and she said to our ganger, 'Bring these children into my house and let them eat their dinner there.' We went into that very small two-roomed cottage, and when we got into the largest room there was not standing room for us all, but this woman's heart was large, even if her house was small, and so she put her few chairs and table out into the garden, and then we all sat down in a ring upon the floor. She then placed in our midst a very large saucepan of hot boiled potatoes, and bade us help ourselves. Truly, although I have attended scores of grand parties and banquets since that time, not one of them has seemed half as good to me as that meal did. I well remember that woman. She was one of the plainest women I ever knew; in fact she was what the world would call quite ugly, and yet I can't think of her even now without thinking of that verse in one of our hymns where it says:

'No, Earth has angels though their forms are moulded
But of such clay as fashions all below,
Though harps are wanting, and bright pinions folded,
We know them by the love-light on their brow.'

Had I time I could write how our gang of children, one winter's night, had to wade for nearly half a mile through the flood. These floods occur nearly every winter, when the Wash overflows her banks. In harvest-time we left home at four o'clock in the morning, and stayed in the fields until it was dark, about nine o'clock. As a rule the gangs were disbanded during the harvest, each child going to work with its own friends, and when the corn was cut, the whole families would go gleaning the corn left in the fields, this being, of course, the gleaner's own property. A great many families gleaned sufficient to keep them in bread for the whole of the winter.

For four years, summer and winter, I worked in these gangs – no holidays of any sort, with the exception of very wet days and Sundays – and at the end of that time it felt like Heaven to me when I was taken to the town of

Leeds, and put to work in the factory. Talk about White Slaves, the Fen districts at that time was the place to look for them.

Ely, Cambridgeshire

64. Celia Fiennes, *Journal* (1698)

I went 8 mile to Ely which were as long as the 12 I came from St Edmundsbery, the wayes being very deep its mostly lanes and low moorish ground, for 4 miles together I passed over a low ground on each side deffended by the fendiks which are deep ditches with draines; the Fens are full of water and mudd; these also encompass their grounds, each mans part 10 or a dozen acres a piece or more, so these dicks are the fences, on each side they plant willows so there is two rows of trees runns round the ground which looks very finely to see a flatt of many miles so planted, but it must be ill to live there; all this while Ely Minster is in ones view at a mile distant you would think, but go it is a long 4 miles; a mile distant from the town is a little hamlet from which I descended from a steep hill and so cross a bridge over water which enters into the Isleand of Ely, and so you pass a flatt on a gravel Causey which way the Bishop is at the charge to repaire else there would be no passing in the summer; this is secured by some dikes which surround more grounds as the former, full of rows of trees, willows round them which makes Ely looke finely through those trees, and that stands very high.

In the winter this Caussey is over flowed and they have no way but boates to pass in; they cut peate out of some of these grounds; the raines now had fallen so as in some places near the Citty the Caussey was covered and a remarkable deliverance I had, for my horse earnest to drinke ran to get more depth of water than the Caussey had, was on the brinke of one of these diks but by a speciall providence which I desire never to forget and allwayes to be thankfull for, escaped; that bridge was over the River Linn which comes from Norfolke and

133

does almost encompass the Island of Ely, which is 20 mile in bigness in which are severall little towns as Wisbech and many others.

There is another river that joyns with the Linn which composes this land into an Island; at this bridge is a gate but by reason of the great raines the roads were full of water even quite to the town which you ascend a very steep hill into, but the dirtyest place I ever saw, not a bitt of pitching in the streetes so its a perfect quagmire the whole Citty, only just about the Palace and Churches the streetes are well enough for breadth but for want of pitching it seemes only a harbour to breed and nest vermin in, of which there is plenty enough, so that tho' my chamber was near 20 stepps up I had froggs and slow-worms and snailes in my roome – but suppose it was brought up with the faggotts – but it cannot but be infested with all such things being altogether moorish fenny ground which lyes low; its true were the least care taken to pitch their streetes it would make it looke more properly an habitation for human beings, and not a cage or nest of unclean creatures, it must needs be very unhealthy, tho' the natives say much to the contrary which proceeds from custom and use, otherwise to persons born in up and dry countryes it must destroy them like rotten sheep in consumptions and rhumes.

HIGH FEN

65. J. Wentworth Day, *Sporting Adventure* (1937)

You will not find many pointers on the stubble nowadays. Theirs was the day of buskins and muzzle-loaders, of shot flasks and ramrods, of grandfathers in tall hats, drab breeches, and blue waistcoats – good days when your gunner rose at five of the clock, ate fat pork and drank his own home brew for breakfast, put a sandwich of cold bacon as thick as his hand in his pocket, and started out to shoot his manor with no thought of stopping till the sun should swim down in the west.

You will still find men of that sort, albeit they shoot now with breech-loaders, in the lonely parts. You will still find old stranded farms and manors where these men live with horse and gun and a pointer of the old sort. They are good to meet and shoot with, a healthy breath from simpler days. I think the man in the picture must have been of the sort that I knew at High Fen – neither squire nor yeoman, but a blend of both. A thousand-acre man as long as he lived, bred to the old Tory creed of Church and State, a man of fustian and good blood. Everything about the place spoke of the master; horseflesh, stock, crops, and dogs were sound and good. Pointers I think he liked most because of the grace and strength of them, the straight beauty of those firm legs, the depth of chest, the honest width between the eyes, the strength of jaw and the breadth of muscle that meant the best that breeding and brains can put into the form of a dog.

One day stands out above all. We started at six in the morning, the sun glistening on the higher stubbles, struggling with the mist on the lower cattle fens. The old black mill stood up stark out of the fen fog below the stackyard. A skein of mallard from the fen etched straightly their flight above the poplars by the barn. Partridges were calling in the great sixty-acre field beyond where the mangolds billowed away in a green sea; their broad leaves wetted one's gaiters and left glistening drops on Ponto's flanks. In front of me ranged Shot, second of the brace, working on a hundred-yard front. It was pretty shooting on those wide fen fields. You walked in the freshness of morning, the loose black peat crumbling underfoot like coarse sand, the sun sucking up the mists off the level miles; field on field, dyke on dyke, line on line of slim willows, hazing away into the distance where the great lantern on Ely Cathedral shone silver in the morning sun like a palace set upon a hill; brown, peat-stained water gleamed flatly in the dykes; moorhens scuttered up out of the bordering roots and, getting up speed, topped the willows like black woodcock; on the far river wall, against the sky, stood great fen beeves, limned like figures on a fresco. Peewits cried above them, flashing like snowflakes as they turned.

Then, suddenly – stiffened muscles, statuesque limbs, tail like a poker, the whole a blessing to the eye – barely had one time or wit to take in the picture when the covey burst like a shell, cataclysmic, bewildering, speeding a bare yard above the mangold leaves, going like blazes. You got on to the outside right bird, crumpled him up, and saw the water flash in a shower of sun-caught drops as he fell in the dyke.

They swung left, crossing to the 'Master' in his gaiters and brown cords; there came the glint of sun on gun barrels, a white opening flower of smoke, the heavy bang of black powder, and right and left were dropped with pretty skill – to be gathered from the wet roots, with the blue reek of smoke a yard above the ground, the smell of burnt powder stinging the nostrils.

HELPSTON

66. John Clare (1793–1864)

Recollections After an Evening Walk
Just as the even-bell rang, we set out
To wander the fields and the meadows about;
And the first thing we mark'd that was lovely to view
Was the sun hung on nothing, just bidding adieu:
He seem'd like a ball of pure gold in the west,
In a cloud like a mountain blue, dropping to rest;
The skies all around him were ting'd with his rays,
And the trees at a distance seem'd all on a blaze,
Till, lower and lower, he sank from our sight,
And the blue mist came creeping with silence and
    night.
The woodman then ceas'd with his hatchet to hack,
And bent away home with his kid on his back;
The mower, too, lapt up his scythe from our sight,
And put on his jacket, and bid us good night;

The thresher once lumping, we heard him no more,
He left his barn-dust, and had shut up his door;
The shepherd had told all his sheep in his pen,
And humming his song, sought his cottage agen:
But the sweetest of all seeming music to me
Were the songs of the clumsy brown-beetle and bee;
The one was seen hast'ning away to his hive,
The other was just from his sleeping alive –
'Gainst our hats he kept knocking as if he'd no eyes,
And when batter'd down he was puzzled to rise.
The little gay moth, too, was lovely to view,
A-dancing with lily-white wings in the dew;
He whisk'd o'er the water-pudge flirting and airy,
And perch'd on the down-headed grass like a fairy.
And there came the snail from his shell peeping out,
As fearful and cautious as thieves on the rout;
The sly jumping frog, too, had ventur'd to tramp,
And the glow-worm had just 'gun to light up his lamp;
To sip of the dew the worm peep'd from his den,
But dreading our footsteps soon vanish'd agen:
And numbers of creatures appear'd in our sight,
That live in the silence and sweetness of night,
Climbing up the tall grasses or scaling the bough,
But these were all nameless, unnotic'd till now.
And then we wound round 'neath the brook's willow
    row,
And look'd at the clouds that kept passing below;
The moon's image too, in the brook we could see't,
As if 'twas the other world under our feet;
And we listen'd well pleas'd at the guggles and groans
The water made passing the pebbles and stones.
And then we turn'd up by the rut-rifted lane,
And sought for our cot and the village again;
For night gather'd round, and shut all from the eye,
And a black sultry cloud crept all over the sky;
The dew on the bush, soon as touch'd it would drop,
And the grass 'neath our feet was as wet as a mop:
And, as to the town we approach'd very fast,
The bat even popp'd in our face as he past;
And the crickets sang loud as we went by the house,

And by the barn-side we saw many a mouse
Quirking round for the kernels that, litter'd about,
Were shook from the straw which the thresher hurl'd
    out.
And then we came up to our cottage once more,
And shut out the night-dew, and lock'd up the door;
The dog bark'd a welcome, well-pleas'd at our sight,
And the owl o'er our cot flew, and whoop'd a 'good
    night'.

PETERBOROUGH

67. John Seymour, *Sailing Through England* (1956)

Vic Jackson lives in Stanground Creek, for such is the name of his lair, like a pirate king.

He is a hefty, generous man. Generous in build, in nature, in everything. He, like 'Crab' Everitt and like Mackenzie Thorpe, is a member of a type which seems peculiar to the Fen country. His wife is a tall, dark-haired, aquiline-featured woman who wears large ear-rings and is a very fitting wife for Vic.

If you want Vic Jackson for anything during meal times you go, if that great man is indoors, to his back door. You go in, and find yourself in a large kitchen, in which perhaps a dozen people are having a lavish meal. A rough and ready meal perhaps, but a lavish one. For there are hams and sides of bacon slung up in the Jackson larder, huge roasts of beef in the Jackson oven, cases of whisky in the Jackson cellar. On the floor will be perhaps a dozen cats and kittens, and a few dogs, and a baby or two. The people may be Jackson's sons, men working in the yard, tenants, retainers, friends, and hangers on. People in fact, under this aristocrat's protection . . .

Vic Jackson was one of the best talkers I have ever met in my life. If he saw that you were really interested in what he had to say he would talk for hours, eloquently, poetically, beautifully.

What a life those Fen lightermen led. They roamed

the complex system of waterways, penetrating to the remotest farmsteads and villages, they were a law to themselves, they lived off the country, they drank beer, they sang songs, they told stories, they fought. Although they had much in common with the landbound Fenmen they had more in common with each other, and always felt rather that they were a race apart, and they liked to be so.

Jackson owned a fleet of boats, and was something of a master-man. He described to me how he eventually got a steam-tug. He went to Lynn with a large fleet of lighters towing behind this steam-tug, to load up a cargo.

'When I came to muster,' he said, 'I found all me men was in the pub and full of beer. Now I'd given 'em a time to be aboard, and they wasn't, so I thought I'd learn 'em a lesson. I gets hold of three old boys who were hanging about the dock gates at Lynn and I says, "Come on – you're coming a voyage with me!" That pleases them, they was amused, you see, and aboard they get, but they didn't know a thing about it. Instead of having ten good men I had three dud 'uns. And I had to be me own fireman. Well – you know what the flood's like outside Lynn docks, and it was springs – I thought I'd have a job getting round – I had to leave the wheel and run back along the lighters like a cat letting out and taking up the fest ropes – I thought once or twice I never would do it – but I did, and we run alright up to Denver, and . . .' and he describes how he delivered his cargoes, refused to re-engage his repentant and physically suffering crew when they turned up with their tails between their legs, returned to Lynn with his same three old men, discharged them, and then relented and took on all his own boys again. What I liked about this story was the impression one got that he did the whole thing as a joke. It was a prank to slip off up the river without his crew. He did not do it in the bitter spirit of an industrialist staging a lock-out. He did it for fun, and to add another episode to the legend that grows about the names of such men.

Caernarvon
91-2
Wrexham
93
N. MIDLANDS
Chester
Stoke-on-Trent
98
104 103
Chesterfield
102 101
100 99
Nottingham
Barmouth
90
89
Derby
Shrewsbury
Leicester
Aberystwyth
88
WALES
95
96
94
97
Birmingham
68
Warwick
Stratford-upon-Avon
69
Worcester
72
Northampton
79 Hereford
76
86-7
Brecon
78
73
74
70-1
Carmarthen
80
Gloucester
Oxford
85
Swansea
77
81
82-4
75
S. MIDLANDS
Cardiff Bristol

From the Midlands to Wales

VII

To the South Midlands

If anywhere characterizes the divide between East Anglia and the Midlands, Peterborough marks the spot and the River Nene the link. The sprawling boundaries of the city reach east into flatness, west into a rolling landscape; the broad Nene flows from bare fenland to wooded farmland. As you wander westwards the hedges that have been stripped from the fen countryside suddenly reappear, the woodlands stand taller and thicker, and the rich and creamy oolitic limestone begins to make its mark on the village houses and churches. In the short space of a few miles the landscape shifts its mood from openness to intimacy, with Peterborough the hub of this circle of change.

A sour smell from brickfield chimneys greets you as you come into Peterborough from the Cambridgeshire fens. The long, straight fenland roads run embanked a few feet above the drainage ditches and enormous fields of beet, corn and vegetables. The villages stand along the roads in single lines of dull yellow and red brick houses, square and monotonous. Where the roads bend, it is always at a right angle, marshalled strictly to the sharp edges of the hedgeless, featureless fields. One mile unrolls into the next with no variety as the villages and isolated farmhouses go slowly by. Then tall chimneys begin to poke up over the horizon, trailing smoke and that unmistakable, acidic stink of baked clay. The chimneys stand on the edges of vast holes hundreds of yards across, scooped out of the ground, their sides terraced by generations of clay extraction, the ground around them piled high with rubbly hills of misshapen bricks. Children bike happily along the road, never giving a glance at these tremendous wastelands or seeming to notice their smoke and smell.

Peterborough lies flat across the borders of Fenland, its shape hard to grasp with no upstanding features to get one's bearings by. An old city full of history, sacked by Danes and by Hereward the Wake, it lost its enclosed, provincial character when the railways and brickfields opened in the nineteenth century. These days, greatly expanded by new estates housing London overspill families and new business parks clinging to the outskirts, the city struggles to retain what remains of its former character while catering for its two hundred thousand population with new country parks, water parks, footpaths, leisure centres, showgrounds and golf courses. The boundaries of the city push further and further out, covering the fens and meadows with houses, roads and roundabouts, converting its industrial holes and pits into lakes and leisure parks, trying its best to fulfil the fundamentally irreconcilable aims of conservation and development, destroying and creating with the same impressive energy. The best thing to come out of all this upheaval is the Nene Way, a footpath through meadows and under trees that follows the river from the city centre for the best part of twenty miles as it snakes west and south towards the Northamptonshire hills and valleys.

The first few miles of the Nene Way run through a series of water features created by the city to provide the bird-watching, fishing, sailing, canoeing and walking that its inhabitants want, and for which there are not enough open spaces in the city itself. Too often these man-made 'natural' surroundings fail to look anything other than unnatural, landscaped and prettified into a green neutrality. But here the broad Nene, full almost to the brim, lends dignity to the landscape as it curves majestically out of Peterborough, under motorway bridges and past the lakes of Orton Mere. These were once settling ponds for the sugar of the British Sugar Corporation, devourer of sugar beet from those flat fenlands to the east and north. Anglers fish contentedly under the roar of traffic on the A47, the fuming brickfield chimneys beyond the trees far enough away to disperse that acid stink. Osiers and willows hang over the river, which separates round islets into quiet backwaters. The villages along the river already show the limestone influence – silver, cream or yellow-grey depending on the quality of the sunlight. Near Water Newton the Romans built their town of Durobrivae and used the Nene as a highway for their barges. The village lies along the route of the old Great North Road, divided by a stream of traffic until the A1 bypassed it a few years ago. Today it's a silent little strip of houses, with a golden stone mill standing over a reed-fringed millpond on a backwater of the river. Mills punctuate the walk every couple of miles, all tall and solid, all built of the same rich limestone, most converted – more or less harmoniously – into smart houses.

Taking a great northward bend, the Nene flows under the sixteenth-century bridge at Wansford, where the new A1 dual carriageway rushes by a few yards away from the old, deserted Great North Road. Only a trickle of cars and lorries passes between the houses of Wansford these days, though you can guess its past importance to travellers by the number of inns standing along the wide street. The Haycock inn has a good tale attached to it, the salutary story of Drunken Barnabee. Finding a plague cross on the door of the inn one night, Barnabee staggered off into the meadows beside the Nene and fell asleep on top of a haycock. He had a nasty morning-after shock when he awoke. A flood in the night had washed the haycock into the river, and Barnabee was on his way downstream to lands unknown. Soon he passed a group of farm workers on the bank, who shouted out to ask him where he had come from. 'From Wansford Brigg – in England!' replied the baffled Barnabee.

Now the Nene turns southwards past Yarwell, Nassington, Elton and Eaglethorpe, all charming stone villages flanked by the river. Imperceptibly you have been slipping from East Anglia into the Midlands, and hereabouts the change is completed. Sheep graze in the meadows, the trees form dense woods on low ridges, and the Nene narrows and carves a deeper channel under poplars, ash and oak. At Fotheringhay it bends at the foot of the grassy castle mound where Mary Queen of Scots was imprisoned before her execution in 1587. It's an easy climb to the top of the mound which is covered, appropriately, with thistles. Poor Mary, plotted against and plotting, was too hot a property for Queen Elizabeth I to handle. As a symbol and focus of Catholic discontent she had to be removed in a permanent manner. Pale and controlled, she comforted her weeping companions and pardoned her executioner, before kneeling to offer her neck on the block. Two strokes severed her head, 'leaving a little gristle' in the bald words of the contemporary account of the execution. Her lap-dog, who had been hiding under her skirts, ran to lie down between his mistress's head and body. When the head was held up to be viewed, cap and hair both came away. The hair was a wig, under which Mary had concealed her own close-cropped hair that had been turned grey by suffering. Block and clothing were burned to make sure that Catholic sympathizers had no symbols to rally round, and – a final gruesome touch – Mary's blood was thoroughly scrubbed from her little dog so that he, too, could not be seized as a relic.

Past Perio Mill and Tansor the Nene winds on to Cotterstock – another fine mill and handsome small church on the river bank. Here in summer you find fields not far away blazing with the red, white and purple of flowers that agricultural chemicals have long since exterminated from most farmland. Poppies flood these fields with red, cornflowers dot them with blue, daisy-like scentless mayweed freckles them with white. The verges of the lanes have been enriched in the same way by the drifting seeds. It's a touch of vanished pastoral England, brought about by Dr Miriam Lane (née Rothschild) of nearby Ashton Wold. In 1979 she started a project to restore wild flowers to barren places, harvesting seeds and distributing them. Many a motorway and new town roundabout has been enriched with Ashton wild flowers. Pleasure in their beauty, though, is mixed with pain at the thought of the sterility of so many chemically blasted fields and lanes all over Britain. At Ashton Mill, within sight of the needle spire of Oundle Church, wild flower seeds are on sale. May they sprinkle their way from Northamptonshire to Staffordshire. The country writers of the Midlands would say 'Amen' to that.

*

The southern Midlands are quietly celebrated by their country writers, a contented appreciation of broad acres and lush, rolling views that make a smooth buffer between the hard-edged practicality of fenland and the drama and excitement of Welsh mountains, valleys and torrents. Here we roll along the rich band of oolitic limestone, the creamy stone villages and field walls of upland country from Northamptonshire into Oxfordshire, wandering north to Shakespeare country and south again through the Cotswolds past Bredon Hill in Worcestershire and into the Forest of Dean on the Welsh bank of the River Severn. This is the last of the 'soft south', where pastoral beauty still lies unchallenged by any ruggedness in the landscape.

Two pacey hunting scenes gallop across either end of this section of our journey. In between are Flora Thompson's late-Victorian Oxfordshire hamlet of 'Lark Rise' (Juniper Hill) and its nearby main road, caught in the silence of abandonment between stage-coach and motor-car; and Laurie Lee's Slad in the 1920s, in the final stages of its old, isolated existence. There's a high view over Shakespeare country from Sir Arthur Quiller-Couch – 'Q' – and a low one as John Moore looks up from 'Elmbury' (Evesham) to the dominating hump of 'Brensham Hill' (Bredon Hill).

In the few unemphatic lines of his poem *Adlestrop*, Edward Thomas catches perfectly the pervasive mood of these rural southern Midlands: their feeling of time slowed to lazing pace through a sweep of rich, mild countryside.

River Nene, Northamptonshire

68. H. E. Bates, *Down the River* (1937)

The river there was not wide, thirty or forty feet perhaps. There are countries where it would not be a river at all. But to us it was not only *a* river, but *the* river. For me, as a boy, its fascination lay not so much in its breadth as in its depth, in its profound weed-grown darknesses. It had, here and there, the reputation of being bottomless, and to me, standing above, trying to fathom it with my eyes, it looked it. A great sand-coloured shelf protruded out from the bank and then, immediately, there was a drop that seemed to go down into the heart of the world. Yet the men of grandfather's and even my father's time had skated on it with comfort.

So for me that stream had not only a tranquillizing effect, but a terrifying effect. It was a small terror, spasmodic: a sudden shoot of terror up the spine. But then, hadn't I been brought up in terror of it? Hadn't it been dinned and thundered into me never to go near that stream? If I went too near, did I know it would draw me, like a magnet, and drag me in and drown? Did I want to go into the bury-hole?

Yet it fascinated me, in that subtle, powerful way that water does fascinate. In any landscape with water it is the water that catches the eye and holds it and draws it back with some kind of magnetism again and again. The river held my eyes in the same way. It hypnotized me. If it were not the near water, it was the middle distance, where downstream the river forked for the mill back-water, or the far distance, where a greater and older bridge made a stone skyline and shut out the miles of meadows beyond. I was held by the texture and flow of it, by that oily glassiness that falls on water after a hot day, by its brilliance or its almost golden colour after rain, by the spin and ripple and strength of the current moving like great muscles, by the twist and play of it about a reed-flag, by the rise of a fish breaking the surface with great expanding wheels, by the flick and dance of mayflies making their own miniature pin-wheels, by the flap and plop of the small water-waves against the bank or the bridge stones, by endless swaying and swooning motions of those tresses of water-weed, and finally and most constantly by the perpetual implacability and power of it as it flowed on and on.

This is a sensation that you never get with a brook. It

is peculiar to rivers. With a brook there is no sense of strength, or implacability, or terror. There is a feeling almost of cheekiness, of flippancy. With a river there is a concentration, a maturity. It is a force. It is not merely a volume of water travelling on a set course from one point to another. It has become a living thing, with its own defined and complex character, its own idiosyncrasies and with something very like its own soul.

NORTHAMPTONSHIRE COUNTRYSIDE, NEAR NORTHAMPTON

69. G. Whyte-Melville, *Holmby House* (1860)

Yes, there he was, stealing along, his back up, his fur draggled, tangled, and black with mire; his brush drooping, his tongue out, his long knavish countenance woebegone and indicative of thorough physical exhaustion, his whole instincts so intent on his pursuers that he scarcely turned aside at our salutation – there he was, dead-beat, and running short for his life, not a covert or an earth within two miles of him, and the best pack of hounds in England running frantic for his blood in the next field. See, he has nearly reached the old oak tree! one, two, three white hounds are through the fence, the rest following, like a stream of water set free from a dam. How they strain across the ridge and furrow, their bristles erect, their sterns lowered, their hungry eyes flaring out upon him with instinctive hate! He is creeping quite slowly now; but as Harmony and Fairplay near him he turns and shows a long, ominous, gleaming set of teeth. Over they roll, all three together. Marplot and Marygold are close upon them, hounds tumble over each other in hungry confusion, a crash is heard in the fence, and Charles Payne is off his horse in another moment and amongst them. A faint strident noise, like that of a smothered saw, grates upon the ear above the stifled 'worry', 'worry', of the hounds, and ere Charles, the pink of politeness, has time to touch his cap to ourselves (for he takes us for the parson, and therefore a stanch fox preserver, if not fox pursuer), he holds him high up in air, and with a loud 'Who-whoop' proclaims the conclusion of one of those 'best runs of the season' which occur at least once a fortnight.

Who-whoop! indeed. Three more sportsmen have by this time arrived, one over and the other two *through* the fence, which still hides the rest of the field from our eager gaze. Soon a gate opens, and some half a dozen more, including a couple of black coats, make their appearance. There are a good many still *coming*, and a large proportion of the original field that will never get here at all. No wonder; the pastures of Northampton-shire are full of them: they are scattered all over the country. Those who have arrived look wild and heated, and intensely pleased with themselves as they jump off their exhausted horses, and talk and laugh and gesticu-late; the while Charles Payne throws the fox to the hounds, with another encouraging 'Who-whoop!' and the clamorous baying of expectancy is exchanged for the 'worry, worry, worry', of fruition. 'Had a good thing?' we inquire of the first whip, who is appeasing a difference as to a tid-bit between Countess and Caro-line, '*Carpital* thing, sir,' replies that affable function-ary, whose cap and side are plastered with mud, and who looks as pleased as if some one had given him a hundred pounds. '*Carpital* thing, sir. Brought him from Sulby gorse over the finest part of *our* country; never checked but once, down by Cottesbrooke; never touch-ed a covert the whole blessed while! It's eleven miles if it's a yard, and I make it exactly an hour and fifteen minutes from the time I "holloed" him away till we run into him in this here grass field just atween your reverence's legs. Whoop, my darlings! Worry, worry, worry! tear him an' eat him!' Cigars are lit, congratula-tions are exchanged, the bay horse and the brown horse and the chestnut horse receive their due share of praise, a reflective flattery somewhat in this wise: 'How well he carried you, old fellow; and what a stiff line! *I was close to you the whole time!*' From different versions and many contradictory statements we gather a tolerably correct notion of the run; and as its glories gradually flood our still enthusiastic imagination, it is with a pang of regret that we reflect we shall never see gallops such as these again.

Lark Rise (Juniper Hill), Oxfordshire

70. Flora Thompson, *Lark Rise* (1939)

So, for some time, Oxford remained to them a dim blur of bishops (they had seen a picture of one with big white sleeves, sitting in a high-backed chair) and swings and shows and coconut shies (for they knew what a fair was like) and little girls sucking pink-and-white rock and polishing shoes. To imagine a place without pigsties and vegetable gardens was more difficult. With no bacon or cabbage, what could people have to eat?

But the Oxford road with the milestone they had known as long as they could remember. Round the Rise and up the narrow hamlet road they would go until they came to the turning, their mother pushing the baby carriage ('pram' was a word of the future) with Edmund strapped in the high, slippery seat, or, later, little May, who was born when Edmund was five, and Laura holding on at the side or darting hither and thither to pick flowers . . .

As soon as the turning was passed, the flat, brown fields were left behind and they were in a different world with a different atmosphere and even different flowers. Up and down went the white main road between wide grass margins, thick, berried hedgerows and overhanging trees. After the dark mire of the hamlet ways, even the milky-white road surface pleased them, and they would splash up the thin, pale mud, like uncooked batter, or drag their feet through the smooth white dust until their mother got cross and slapped them.

Although it was a main road, there was scarcely any traffic, for the market town lay in the opposite direction along it, the next village was five miles on, and with Oxford there was no road communication from that distant point in those days of horse-drawn vehicles. Today, past that same spot, a first-class, tar-sprayed road, thronged with motor traffic, runs between low, closely trimmed hedges. Last year a girl of eighteen was knocked down and killed by a passing car at that very turning. At that time it was deserted for hours together. Three miles away trains roared over a viaduct, carrying those who would, had they lived a few years before or later, have used the turnpike. People were saying that far too much money was being spent on keeping such roads in repair, for their day was over; they were only needed now for people going from village to village. Sometimes the children and their mother would meet a tradesman's van, delivering goods from the market town at some country mansion, or the doctor's tall gig, or the smart turn-out of a brewer's traveller; but often they walked their mile along the turnpike and back without seeing anything on wheels.

The white tails of rabbits bobbed in and out of the hedgerows; stoats crossed the road in front of the children's feet – swift, silent, stealthy creatures which made them shudder; there were squirrels in the oak trees, and once they even saw a fox curled up asleep in the ditch beneath thick overhanging ivy. Bands of little blue butterflies flitted here and there or poised themselves with quivering wings on the long grass bents; bees hummed in the white clover blooms, and over all a deep silence brooded. It seemed as though the road had been made ages before, then forgotten.

71. William Shakespeare (1564–1616)

Spring

I

When daisies pied and violets blue
  And lady-smocks all silver-white
And cuckoo-buds of yellow hue
  Do paint the meadows with delight,
The cuckoo then, on every tree,
Mocks married men; for thus sings he,
                Cuckoo;

Cuckoo, cuckoo: O, word of fear,
Unpleasing to a married ear!

II

When shepherds pipe on oaten straws,
    And merry larks are ploughmen's clocks,
When turtles tread, and rooks, and daws,
    And maidens bleach their summer smocks,
The cuckoo then, on every tree,
Mocks married men; for thus sings he,
                        Cuckoo;
Cuckoo, cuckoo: O, word of fear,
Unpleasing to a married ear!

Winter

III

When icicles hang by the wall,
    And Dick the shepherd blows his nail,
And Tom bears logs into the hall,
    And milk comes frozen home in pail,
When blood is nipp'd, and ways be foul,
Then nightly sings the staring owl,
                        Tu-who;
Tu-whit, tu-who – a merry note,
While greasy Joan doth keel the pot.

IV

When all aloud the wind doth blow,
    And coughing drowns the parson's saw,
And birds sit brooding in the snow,
    And Marian's nose looks red and raw,
When roasted crabs hiss in the bowl,
Then nightly sings the staring owl,
                        Tu-who;
Tu-whit, tu-who – a merry note,
While greasy Joan doth keel the pot.

CLEEVE PRIOR, WORCESTERSHIRE

72. Sir Arthur Quiller-Couch, *The Warwickshire Avon*
(1892)

We lingered only to look at the building that in
Shakespeare's time was the old Falcon Inn, and soon
were paddling due south from Bidford Bridge. The Avon
now runs straight through big flat meadows towards a
steep hill-side, with the hamlet of Marcleeve (or
Marlcliff) at its foot. This line of hill borders the river on
the south for some miles, and is the edge of a plateau
which begins the ascent towards the Cotswold hills.
Seen from the river below, this escarpment is full of
varying beauty, here showing a bare scar of green and
red marl, here covered with long gray grass and dotted
with old thorn and crab trees, here clothed with
hanging woods of maple, ash, and other trees, straggled
over and smothered with ivy, wild rose, and clematis.
By Cleeve Mill, where clouds of sweet-smelling flour
issued from the doorway, we disembarked and climbed
up between the thorn-trees until upon the ridge we
could look back upon the green vale of Evesham, and
southward across ploughed fields, and cottages among
orchards and elms, to the gray line of the Cotswolds,
over which a patch of silver hung, as the day fought
hard to regain its morning sunshine. The narrow
footway took us on to Cleeve Priors and through its
street – a village all sober, gray, and beautiful. The
garden walls, coated with lichen and topped with
yellow quinces or a flaming branch of barberry; the tall
church tower; the quaintly elaborate grave-stones
below it, their scrolls and cherubim overgrown with
moss; the clipped yew-trees that abounded in all fantastic shapes; the pigeons wheeling round their dove-cote,
and the tall poplar by the manor farm – all these were
good: but best of all was the manor farm itself, and the
arched yew hedge leading to its Jacobean porch, a
marvel to behold. We hung long about the entrance and
stared at it. But no living man or woman approached us.
The village was given up to peace or sleep or death.

Returning, we paused on the brow of the slope above Avon for a longer look. At our feet was spread the vale of Evesham; the river, bordered with meadows as green and flat as billiard-tables; the stream of Arrow to northward, which rises in the Lickey hills, and comes down through Alcester to join the Avon here; the villages of Salford Priors and Salford Abbots; farther to the west, among its apple-trees, the roofs and gables of Salford Nunnery, the village of Harvington. And all down the stream, and round the meadows, and in and out of these

'low farms,
Poor pelting villages, sheepcotes, and mills,'

are willows innumerable – some polled last year, and looking like green mops, others with long curved branches ready to be lopped and turned into fence poles next winter, until they are lost in the hills round Evesham, where the dim towers stand up and the bold outline of Bredon Hill shuts out the view of the Severn Valley.

ADLESTROP, GLOUCESTERSHIRE

73. Edward Thomas (1878–1917)

Yes. I remember Adlestrop –
The name, because one afternoon
Of heat the express-train drew up there
Unwontedly. It was late June.

The steam hissed. Someone cleared his throat.
No one left and no one came
On the bare platform. What I saw
Was Adlestrop – only the name.

And willows, willow-herb, and grass,
And meadowsweet, and haycocks dry,
No whit less still and lonely fair
Than the high cloudlets in the sky.

And for that minute a blackbird sang
Close by, and round him, mistier,
Farther and farther, all the birds
Of Oxfordshire and Gloucestershire.

KINGHAM JUNCTION, GLOUCESTERSHIRE–OXFORDSHIRE BORDER

74. W. Warde Fowler, *A Year with the Birds* (1889)

Beyond the Yantle we come upon a line of railway, running down from Chipping Norton to join the main line to Worcester. Just as the waters of the Evenlode are reinforced at this point in its course by the two contingent streams I described in the last chapter, so the main railway is here joined by two subsidiary lines, the one coming from Chipping Norton and the other from Cheltenham over the Cotswolds. Paradoxical as it may seem, I do not hesitate to say that this large mileage of railway within a small radius acts beneficially upon our bird-life. Let us see how this is.

In the first place, both cuttings and embankments, as soon as they are well overgrown with grass, afford secure and sunny nesting-places to a number of birds which build their nests on the ground. The Whin-chat for example, an abundant bird here every summer, gives the railway banks its especial patronage. The predatory village-boys cannot prowl about these banks with impunity except on Sundays, and even then are very apt to miss a Whin-chat's nest. You may see the cock-bird sitting on the telegraph wires, singing his peaceful little song, but unless you disturb his wife from her beautiful blue eggs you are very unlikely to find them in the thickening grass of May or June. And even if she is on the nest, she will sit very close; I have seen an express train fly past without disturbing her, when the nest was but six to eight feet from the rails. The young, when reared, will often haunt the railway for the rest of the summer, undismayed by the rattle and vibration which must have shaken them even when they were still within the egg. Occasionally a Wheatear will make its appearance about the railway, but I have no evidence of its breeding there; nor is the Stone-chat often to be seen here, though it is a summer visitor not far off among the hills.

Let me say incidentally that no one who has either good eyes or a good glass ought ever to confound the two Chats together. In the breeding season the fine black head of the cock Stone-chat distinguishes him at once; but even the female should never be the subject of a blunder, if the observer has been at all used to attend to the *attitudes* of birds. The Stone-chat sits upright and almost defiant, and is a shorter and stouter bird than the Whin-chat, which perches in an attitude of greater humility, and always seems to me to deprecate your interference rather than to defy it. And it is quite in keeping with this that the 'chat' of the latter is not so loud and resonant as that of the former, as I have satisfied myself after careful observation of both; the Stone-chat penetrating to my dull ears at a greater distance than his cousin. This really means that the bill of the one, and in fact his whole muscular system, is stronger than the same in the other, and the τὸ Θυμοειδεσ of his constitution is more largely developed . . .

Keeping yet awhile to the railway, let us notice that even the station itself meets with some patronage from the birds. In the stacks of coal which are built up close to the siding, the Pied Wagtails occasionally make their nests, fitting them into some hospitable hole or crevice. These, like all other nests found in or about the station, are carefully protected by the employees of the company. In a deep hole in the masonry of the bridge which crosses the line a few yards below the station, a pair of Great Titmice built their nest two years ago, and successfully brought up their young, regardless of the puffing and rattling of the trains, for the hole was in the *inside* of the bridge, and only some six feet from the rails of the down line. A little coppice, remnant of a larger wood cut down to make room for the railway, still harbours immense numbers of birds; here for example I always hear the ringing note of the Lesser Whitethroat; and here, until a few years ago, a Nightingale rejoiced in the density of the overgrown underwood.

A Ring-ousel, the only specimen, alive or dead, which I have seen or heard of in these parts, was found dead here one morning some years ago, having come into collision with the telegraph wires in the course of its nocturnal migration. It was preserved and stuffed by the stationmaster, who showed it to me as a *piebald Blackbird*.

SLAD, GLOUCESTERSHIRE

75. Laurie Lee, Cider With Rosie (1959)

'Can we go out, Mother?'

'Well, don't catch cold. And remember to get some wood.'

First we found some old cocoa-tins, punched them with holes, then packed them with smouldering rags. If held in the hand and blown on occasionally they would keep hot for several hours. They were warmer than gloves, and smelt better too. In any case, we never wore gloves. So armed with these, and full of hot breakfast, we stepped out into the winter world.

It was a world of glass, sparkling and motionless. Vapours had frozen all over the trees and transformed them into confections of sugar. Everything was rigid, locked-up and sealed, and when we breathed the air it smelt like needles and stabbed our nostrils and made us sneeze.

Having sucked a few icicles, and kicked the water-butt – to hear its solid sound – and breathed through the frost on the window-pane, we ran up into the road. We hung around, waiting for something to happen. A dog trotted past like a ghost in a cloud, panting his aura around him. The distant fields in the low weak sun were crumpled like oyster shells.

Presently some more boys came to join us, wrapped like Russians, with multi-coloured noses. We stood round in a group and just gasped at each other, waiting to get an idea. The thin ones were blue, with hunched up shoulders, hands deep in their pockets, shivering. The fat ones were rosy and blowing like whales; all of us had wet eyes. What should we do? We didn't know. So the fat ones punched the thin ones, who doubled up, saying, 'Sod you.' Then the thin ones punched the fat ones, who half died coughing. Then we all jumped up and down for a bit, flapped our arms, and blew on our cocoa-tins.

'What we goin' to *do*, then, eh?'

We quietened down to think. A shuddering thin boy, with his lips drawn back, was eating the wind with his teeth. 'Giddy up,' he said suddenly, and sprang into the air and began whipping himself, and whinnying. At that we all galloped away down the road, bucking and snorting, tugging invisible reins, and lashing away at our hindquarters.

Now the winter's day was set in motion and we rode through its crystal kingdom. We examined the village for its freaks of frost, for anything we might use. We saw the frozen spring by the side of the road, huge like a swollen flower. Water-wagtails hovered above it, nonplussed at its silent hardness, and again and again they dropped down to drink, only to go sprawling in a tumble of feathers. We saw the stream in the valley, black and halted, a tarred path threading through the willows. We saw trees lopped-off by their burdens of ice, cowtracks like pot-holes in rock, quiet lumps of sheep licking the spiky grass with their black and rotting tongues. The church clock had stopped and the weather-cock was frozen, so that both time and the winds were stilled; and nothing, we thought, could be more exciting than this; interference by a hand unknown, the winter's No to routine and laws – sinister, awesome, welcome.

'Let's go an' 'elp Farmer Wells,' said a fat boy.

'You can – I ain't,' said a thin one.

'If you don't, I'll give thee a clip in the yer'ole.'
'Gurt great bully.'
'I ain't.'
'You be.'

The last days of my childhood were also the last days of
the village. I belonged to that generation which saw, by
chance, the end of a thousand years' life. The change
came late to our Cotswold valley, didn't really show
itself till the late 1920s; I was twelve by then, but during
that handful of years I witnessed the whole thing
happen.

Myself, my family, my generation, were born in a
world of silence; a world of hard work and necessary
patience, of backs bent to the ground, hands massaging
the crops, of waiting on weather and growth; of villages
like ships in the empty landscapes and the long walking
distances between them; of white narrow roads, rutted
by hooves and cartwheels, innocent of oil or petrol,
down which people passed rarely, and almost never for
pleasure, and the horse was the fastest thing moving.
Man and horse were all the power we had – abetted by
levers and pulleys. But the horse was king, and almost
everything grew around him: fodder, smithies, stables,
paddocks, distances, and the rhythm of our days. His
eight miles an hour was the limit of our movements, as
it had been since the days of the Romans. That eight
miles an hour was life and death, the size of our world,
our prison.

This was what we were born to, and all we knew at
first. Then, to the scream of the horse, the change
began. The brass-lamped motor-car came coughing up
the road, followed by the clamorous charabanc; the
solid-tyred bus climbed the dusty hills and more people
came and went. Chickens and dogs were the early
sacrifices, falling demented beneath the wheels. The
old folk, too, had strokes and seizures, faced by speeds
beyond comprehension. Then scarlet motor-bikes, the
size of five-barred gates, began to appear in the village,
on which our youths roared like rockets up the

two-minute hills, then spent weeks making repairs and adjustments.

These appearances did not immediately alter our lives; the cars were freaks and rarely seen, the motor-bikes mostly in pieces, we used the charabancs only once a year, and our buses at first were experiments. Meanwhile Lew Ayres, wearing a bowler-hat, ran his wagonette to Stroud twice a week. The carriage held six, and the fare was twopence, but most people preferred to walk. Mr West, from Sheepscombe, ran a cart every day, and would carry your parcels for a penny. But most of us still did the journey on foot, heads down to the wet Welsh winds, ignoring the carters – whom we thought extortionate – and spending a long hard day at our shopping.

But the car-shying horses with their rolling eyes gave signs of the hysteria to come. Soon the village would break, dissolve, and scatter, become no more than a place for pensioners. It had a few years left, the last of its thousand, and they passed almost without our knowing. They passed quickly, painlessly, in motor-bike jaunts, in the shadows of the new picture-palace, in quick trips to Gloucester (once a foreign city) to gape at the jazzy shops. Yet right to the end, like the false strength that precedes death, the old life seemed as lusty as ever.

'BRENSHAM HILL' (BREDON HILL), WORCESTER-SHIRE

76. John Moore, *Brensham Village* (1946)

Almost every morning of their lives the weather-wise people of Elmbury lift up their eyes to glance at Brensham Hill which rises solitary out of the vale, four miles away as the crow flies. According to its clearness or mistiness they make their prognosis of the day; taking into account, of course, the season of the year, the direction of the wind, and the rheumaticky pains in their backs, their legs or their elbows. It is supposed to be a bad sign – in summer at any rate – to see Brensham Hill very plainly. If you can make out the jigsaw pattern of pasture and ploughing, stone wall and hedgerow, quarry and cart-track, furze-patch and bramble-patch, and identify the stone tower atop which is called Brensham Folly, 'twill rain like as not before evening. If the hill appears as a vague grey-green shape, with the larch-plantations showing as faint shadows like craters on the moon, you can get on with your haymaking, for it's going to be fine. But if you cannot see Brensham Hill at all, if the clouds are right down on its seven-hundred-foot summit, then you recollect the old rhyme:

> 'When Brensham Hill puts on his hat,
> Men of the Vale, beware of that,'

and you know you are in for a sousing.

Brensham, therefore, is as much a part of Elmbury's landscape as the great Norman tower of Elmbury Abbey, as the tall chimneys of the flour mills, as the red sandstone bridge which spans with four lovely arches the meandering river. It rises up in front of you as you walk down the wide main street; it appears behind the bowler's arm when you bat on the cricket-field; it is the first landmark of home when you approach Elmbury by train or car; and if you glance round the corner of any of the alleys which compose Elmbury's frightful slums its greenness against the sky holds out to you a prospect of better things. From Tudor House in Elmbury High Street where I spent my childhood I used to look out across the flat green fields to Brensham Hill and think of it as a mountain, its coppices as jungles, its slopes as unmapped contours awaiting an explorer.

FOREST OF DEAN, GLOUCESTERSHIRE

77. Humphrey Phelps, *The Forest of Dean* (1982)

Bracken grows everywhere, uncurling its delicate green fronds in spring, becoming a darker green in summer and turning to bronze as the year advances. The Forester calls it fern and when a young man started courting he used to be asked if he had 'a fern ticket'. Almost everywhere there is gorse which is in bloom most of the year – 'when the gorse is in bloom, kissing is in fashion.' At Tidenham Chase there is genuine heathland. Copper under heather, silver under gorse, gold under bracken, says the farmer metaphorically, but here it is coal under bracken and coal measures don't make good farming land. Beech trees grow where the limestone comes out, not so much because of the lime but because beech trees like well drained soil. The leaves of the beech are so dense that only the earliest plants such as wood anemones can thrive in the beech woods. Nothing, not even bracken, can thrive under the dense cover of conifers and as the acreage of conifers increases the Forest becomes a duller place. Bluebells are widespread, and so are foxgloves which appear in their thousands when hardwoods are clear felled. The silver birch is tolerant of most conditions and will spring up wherever it gets a chance, a colonizer of waste patches, disguising disused industrial sites and old slag heaps. Rose bay willow herb is another colonizer, adding a splash of colour. The tender green of unfolding leaves in spring time caught in the sunlight shows the Forest to better advantage than the heavier leafage of summer, and so do the turning leaves of autumn. There is colour in the woods in winter after the fall of leaves, much more colour than is at first apparent; one must stand and stare.

The true Forester believes that the Forest is the most beautiful place on earth. So beautiful that he sees no reason to go anywhere else, and if he does it only serves to reinforce his opinion that it is the most beautiful place. The Forest is part of Gloucestershire, but the

Forester always, no matter how far he has strayed, says he is from the Forest of Dean, never Gloucestershire. He is content to remain in the Forest, is loth to live elsewhere, and if circumstances compel is consumed with an overwhelming desire to return. To the exiled Forester the noblest sight is the road which leads to the Forest. Any criticism of it is resented, even the mildest will produce an outburst of anger.

The Forest *is* beautiful – in parts; but even at the risk of incurring the united wrath of its natives, I must say that there are warts as well as beauty spots. The latter are the work of nature with some help from man, but the former are all the work of man. This is a working forest and the site of many industries which have left their scars; some are unavoidable and many have been successfully healed by nature. Nevertheless, cosseting, cherishing and preserving can be carried to extremes, only choking the thing which is loved. There are beautiful Cotswold villages, perfectly kept, all they lack is life; whatever anyone may say about Forest villages, that cannot be said. But there are no attractive towns or villages within the Forest proper, and most of them have an air of neglect. The Forest is a land of contrasts; beauty and squalor, and much of the latter is unnecessary.

The area has experienced hard times, it has not had outside money to keep it beautiful as other places have, but even after these and other factors have been taken into consideration the question still remains: why is there so much squalor, mess and neglect? Is it indifference, a case of love being truly blind, or a manifestation of the Foresters' independence, difference or stubbornness? Whatever it is, it certainly is not indifference; indifference to the warts perhaps, but not indifference in the sense of not caring about the Forest. The Forester *does* care about the Forest, passionately; the pride of the Forester for his native land equals – no excels – all others. It is simply the Forest way; part of the jigsaw that is the Forest of which you accept all or none.

WESTERN MIDLANDS AND WELSH BORDERS

78. John Masefield, *Reynard the Fox* (1919)

They crossed the lane to Tolderton,
The hill-marl died to valley clay,
And there before them ran the grey
Yell Water, swirling as it ran,
The Yell Brook of the hunting man.
The hunters eyed it and were grim.

They saw the water snaking slim
Ahead, like silver; they could see
(Each man) his pollard willow-tree
Firming the bank; they felt their horses
Catch the gleam's hint and gather forces;
They heard the men behind draw near.
Each horse was trembling as a spear
Trembles in hand when tense to hurl.
They saw the brimmed brook's eddies curl;
The willow-roots like water-snakes;
The beaten holes the ratten makes.
They heard the water's rush; they heard
Hugh Colway's mare come like a bird;
A faint cry from the hounds ahead,
Then saddle-strain, the bright hooves' tread,
Quick words, the splash of mud, the launch,
The sick hope that the bank be staunch,
Then Souse, with Souse to left and right.
Maroon across, Sir Peter's white
Down but pulled up, Tom over, Hugh
Mud to the hat but over too,
Well splashed by Squire, who was in.

With draggled pink stuck close to skin
The Squire leaned from bank and hauled
His mired horse's rein; he bawled
For help from each man racing by.
'What, help you pull him out? Not I.
What made you pull him in?' they said.
Nob Manor cleared and turned his head,
And cried, 'Wade up. The ford's upstream.'

Ock Gurney in a cloud of steam
Stood by his dripping cob and wrung
The taste of brook mud from his tongue,
And scraped his poor cob's pasterns clean.
'Lord, what a crowner we've a-been.
This jumping brook's a mucky job.'
He muttered, grinning, 'Lord, poor cob!
Now, sir, let me.' He turned to Squire
And cleared his hunter from the mire
By skill and sense and strength of arm.

Meanwhile the fox passed Nonesuch Farm,
Keeping the spinney on his right.
Hounds raced him here with all their might
Along the short firm grass, like fire.
The cowman viewed him from the byre
Lolloping on, six fields ahead,
Then hounds, still carrying such a head
It made him stare, then Rob on Pip,
Sailing the great grass like a ship,
Then grand Maroon in all his glory,
Sweeping his strides, his great chest hoary
With foam fleck and the pale hill-marl.
They strode the Leet, they flew the Snarl,
They knocked the nuts at Nonesuch Mill,
Raced up the spur of Gallows Hill
And viewed him there. The line he took
Was Tineton and the Pantry Brook,
Going like fun and hounds like mad.
Tom glanced to see what friends he had
Still within sight, before he turned
The ridge's shoulder; he discerned,
One field away, young Cothill sailing
Easily up. Pete Gurney failing,
Hugh Colway quartering on Sir Peter,
Bill waiting on the mare to beat her,
Sal Ridden skirting to the right.
A horse, with stirrups flashing bright
Over his head at every stride,
Looked like the Major's; Tom espied

Far back a scarlet speck of man
Running, and straddling as he ran.
Charles Copse was up, Nob Manor followed,
Then Bennett's big-boned black that wallowed,
Clumsy, but with the strength of ten.
Then black and brown and scarlet men,
Brown horses, white and black and grey.
Scattered a dozen fields away.
The shoulder shut the scene away.

VIII

To Wales

John Masefield's Welsh border country is a red and green
land: red earth on green hillsides, red apples among green
leaves, red bulls in green meadows. The broad and wandering River Wye lends a generous spirit to the landscape, which
flows west through Herefordshire in waves of hill and valley
farmland towards the border. Here the mood changes, right
on the boundary between England and Wales. The rolling
hills rise into what in the north of England would be called
fellsides, with rocky bluffs around their rims, and the valleys
steepen into blue depths. The hilltops shed their fields of
grass and corn and their thick woods, and show bare faces to
the sky. Whitewash begins to disappear from the barns and
houses of the small hillside farms, and unadorned red and
grey stone shows through. It's a transition from a land
bathed in peace and plenty to a land stamped with past
centuries of war and want.

In the red and green countryside beyond Hereford, the
Golden Valley runs north-west along the River Dore that
gave the shallow valley its golden name. A few miles to the
west are the valleys of the Black Mountains cut further and
further down between high, dramatic slopes by their respective waters – Dulas Brook, Escley Brook, River Monnow,
Olchon Brook, Afon Honddu. But the Golden Valley is
altogether different. The long ridges each side roll softly on
low skylines, well wooded and patched with rich pink earth,
and the roads that wind up the valley with the river are lined
with hedges sprouting meadowsweet, bindweed, honeysuckle and dog-rose. Walking these narrow roads and lanes,

shaded by tall sycamores and horse chestnuts, your view ahead is of open sky at one moment; then you turn a corner and the sky is sliced diagonally by a green slope where cows or sheep are grazing. Along the main Golden Valley road the villages are spaced out at comfortable intervals of a couple of miles – Ewyas Harold at the foot of the valley; Abbey Dore with its tall red abbey church, remnant of a medieval monastery; Vowchurch lying along the river. Then comes Peterchurch, where the slender spire of the church marks the turning of a lane leading up and across the hills into a contrasting landscape of stronger flavour.

By Urishay and Llanrosser, tiny farming settlements on the heights, the lane twists and turns for ten miles on its switchback way to Hay-on-Wye. Immediately the land steepens and throws out side valleys, narrower and deeper than the Golden Valley, shadowy clefts far below the lane without houses or even roads. Now it is bracken and purple cranesbill in the hedges, and forward views entirely filled by opposing hillsides. The lane climbs past unsignposted side tracks leading to remote farms, past the solid red stone box of the chapel under the trees at Urishay, and tops out at a memorable view. Wales begins on the skyline, across which the long, smooth back of the Hatterall ridge draws a definitive line. The ridge runs north to end abruptly at the sharp downward sweep of Hay Bluff, from which hang-gliders soar and below which local people have a time-honoured picnic spot. The ridge is a natural barrier as well as a political one, a hard-edged frontier if ever there was one.

Views on the Welsh border are constantly changing from long to short focus, and now the lane dips down again to cross the Escley Brook in a dell of bracken and foxgloves where the prospect narrows down to the next bend in the lane, the next roadside oak. Then it's up again, a six-hundred-foot climb by Llanrosser and Tyuchaf, up over the back of a sedgy, thistly hill to another great sweep of countryside spread below – over the head of the Golden Valley and away north and east for fifteen miles across the broad valleys of Wye and Arrow towards Leominster.

Beyond New House you look west to the twin promontor-ies of Hay Bluff and the Twmpa (I prefer its other name, Lord

Hereford's Knob), pushing their blunt prows out in line abreast like green battleships. Here the footpath drops down the steep side of Cusop Hill among sheep under the thorn bushes to reach Tycoch and the little lane at the top of Cusop Dingle.

This area around Hay-on-Wye has many clefts in the hillsides called 'dingle' – Francis Kilvert, the diarist curate of Clyro, whose home ground this is, had a special favourite on his Welsh side of the Wye. Cusop Dingle bends right and left with the trickle of the Dulas Brook, tall oak and ash trees shutting off far views as you descend into the dingle from Tycoch. The whole place rings with the varied songs of chiff-chaffs, finches, blackbirds and thrushes. Under little bridges the brook sparkles as sunlight filters through the leaves to hit the water. Well spaced along the brook stand trim houses, roses and honeysuckle trailing over and through their garden fences. Outhouse roofs slant down almost to ground level, the pincushion mosses on their tiles and slates re-echoing the red and green Herefordshire theme.

But Herefordshire is almost at an end. The border between England and Wales runs along the top of Cusop Dingle and down to Hay and the River Wye. Following its line, you skirt the bookshops and narrow, climbing streets of charming Hay, and come to the bridge over the Wye in the flat belt of river meadows between Herefordshire and Powys hills. From the bridge there is a good view of the shallow Wye rushing over stones and under trees. From the meadows, walking west, you look ahead into Wales to see Francis Kilvert's Clyro at the foot of wooded slopes. For three years, on foot and on the diary page, the restless curate of Clyro worshipped every inch, English and Welsh, of this lovely border valley.

A great deal of the best country writing about Wales is inaccessible to those who cannot read Welsh. For nearly two thousand years Welsh poets have catalogued the magnificence of their mountains and wild interior highlands, the bravery and grandeur of their people and the bloody story of their countryside, both resistant and submissive to the conqueror from across the border. All stirring stuff, shielded from the outsider by a protective barricade of language – and so much the better, many Welshmen would say. However, modern translations have put some of the older heroic prose and poetry within reach of the rest of the world, and other more recent Welsh writers – or writers with Welsh sympathies – have brought the landscape and country life of Wales memorably alive for the foreigner.

The Welsh leg of our journey through Britain makes a great circle from the Herefordshire border down across the Black Mountains and through the deeply cut valleys of the South Wales coalfield, then south and west to the Pembrokeshire islands. Turning north, we wander through the hills of central Wales and along the cliffs of the coastline around Cardigan Bay, into the highest peaks of Snowdonia and east again across North Wales, back to the border in Shropshire. Two of our writers, four centuries apart in time but as one in their emotions, bemoan man's destruction of the countryside of the valleys. Another celebrates the wildlife of remoter regions. But Wales means walking country above all, and here are superb rambles superbly recounted – Francis Kilvert going visiting on his home ground near Clyro, and braving a storm on Cader Idris; W. H. Davies, the 'Supertramp', on the road out of the valleys; Robert Gibbings going up the Wye to its source on Plynlimon. First among many equals is George Borrow, the East Anglian-born but Celtic-blooded eccentric, scrambling to the wildest places in 'Wild Wales' in the 1850s, vibrant with passion for all things Welsh, with out-of-the-way scholarship full of mistakes and misconceptions, and with glee at his own energy and cleverness.

NEWCHURCH, POWYS

79. Francis Kilvert, *Diary* (1870)

Tuesday, 3 May 1870

Started at noon to walk to Newchurch. Went by Whitty's mill. Stopped on the steep hill above the mill to enjoy the sight of the peaceful little hamlet, and the chink of the forge at Pentwyn sounded sweet, clear and busy across the dingle. I turned up by the old deserted kiln house, empty now, silent, desolate, with its high steep brown tiled roof and white dirty walls. This old field path is quite new to me. I have never travelled it before. Just above the kiln I saw and gathered the first red campion. Luxuriantly large cowslips grew on the bank and marsh buttercups in the ditch. It is a strange country between the kiln and Whitehall. The trees look wild and weird and a yew was stifling an oak. The meadow below Whitehall looked sad and strange and wild, grown with bramble bushes, thorns, fern and gorse. Poor Whitehall, sad, silent and lonely, with its great black yew in the hedge of the tangled waste grass-grown garden and its cold chimney still ivy-clustered. I walked round and looked in at the broken unframed windows and pushed open a door which swung slowly and wearily together again. On another door at the house end were carved two figures of ploughs. A dry old mixen withered before and close to the front entrance. Here were held the Quarterly Dances. What fun. What merry makings, the young people coming in couples and parties from the country round to dance in the long room. What laughing, flirting, joking and kissing behind the door or in the dark garden amongst the young folks, while the elders sat round the room with pipe and mug of beer or cider from the 'Black Ox' of Coldbrook hard by. Now how is all changed, song and dance still, mirth fled away. Only the wind sighing through the broken roof and crazy doors, the quick feet, busy hands, saucy eyes, strong limbs all mouldered into dust, the laughing voices silent. There was a deathlike stillness about the place, except that I fancied once I heard a small voice singing and a bee was humming among the ivy green, the only bit of life about the place. From the old long low brown cottage of Whitehall with its broken roof with a chimney at each gable end I went up the lane to Pant-y-ci speculating upon the probable site of the Coldbrook and the Black Ox which was the house of call on Clyro Hill for the drovers of the great herds of black cattle from Shire Carmarthen and Cardigan on their way down into England. I thought I saw the place where the house probably stood. No one was at home at Pant-y-ci so I stuck a cowslip in the latch hole by way of leaving a card and went on to Crowther's Pool.

By Tyn-y-cwm Meadows to Newchurch village and in turning in at the old Vicarage garden door I heard the hum of the little school. The door under the latticed portch was open and as I went in a pretty dark girl was coming out of an inner door, but seeing me she retreated hastily and I heard an excited buzzing of voices within the schoolroom and eager whispers among the children: 'Here's Mr Kilvert – It's Mr Kilvert.' Not finding the good parson in his study I went into the schoolroom and fluttered the dove cot not a little. The curate and his eldest daughter were away and pretty Emmeline in a russet brown stuff dress and her long fair curls was keeping school bravely with an austere look in her severe beautiful face, and hearing little Polly Greenway read. Janet and Matilda dressed just alike in black silk skirts, scarlet bodices and white pinafores, and with blue ribbons in their glossy bonny dark brown curls, were sitting on a form at a long desk with the other children working at sums. Janet was doing simple division and said she had done five sums, whereupon I kissed her and she was nothing loth. Moreover I offered to give her a kiss for every sum, at which she laughed. As I stood by the window making notes of things in general in my pocket book Janet kept on interrupting her work to glance round at me shyly but saucily with her mischievous beautiful grey eyes. Shall I confess that I travelled ten miles today over the hills for a kiss, to kiss that child's sweet face. Ten miles for a kiss.

I do think the way the Vaughan girls wear their short curling hair is the most natural and prettiest in the world. Oh if fashionable young ladies could but see and perceive and understand and know what utterly ludicrous guys they made of themselves, with the towers and spires and horns and clubs that they build and torture their hair up into! But slaves to fashion must its gods adore.

FROM EBBW VALE TO ABERGAVENNY, GWENT

80. W. H. Davies, *A Poet's Pilgrimage* (1927)

On making inquiries I learned that there were three ways to get to Brynmaur, a town I would have to go through to get to Abergavenny. One way was a path over a steep mountain, which was supposed to get me to Brynmaur in about twenty minutes, but which I suspected would turn out in the end to be the longest way of all. I had not forgotten what I had seen in Ebbw Vale, the extraordinarily steep places on the hillside, where rows of houses were built. Some of the roads to these houses were so very steep that the people who lived in them could almost have gone to bed by walking up the outside walls of their houses without taking the trouble to go indoors to use the stairs. The second road I was told was good, but that there was a bad dip before I reached Brynmaur. I did not like the sound of this, for if an Ebbw Vale man took the trouble to mention a dip at all, and to describe it as bad, it must be bad indeed.

The third road was much longer, but good all the way. So I came to the conclusion that the long road was the shortest after all, judging it by time. After I had been walking about an hour I came to a small town called Beaufort, which was only a short way from Brynmaur. In passing through this little town I was considerably struck by the difference in its looks from the little towns in Glamorganshire. Although the houses and cottages were no larger, yet for all that they looked richer and ever so much more superior. The doors had brass knockers, brass letter boxes and brass numbers, which gave the little houses a refined look. And when I looked at the window curtains and saw how clean they were, I knew that I had at last come among people that took a pride in their homes, however small their houses were. Again, I saw several women polishing the brass on the doors, scrubbing the threshold, or window cleaning, and none of them were gossiping. To my surprise these women did not look at all like household drudges, but were dressed clean and neat enough to welcome any visitor that might come along unexpectedly.

It was not long before I began to realize that I was entering a different kind of country altogether, from bare, rocky hills to leafy ones. In fact, the change was so sudden, all within a couple of miles, that it took me completely unawares. I began to see woody hills that reminded me by their beauty of those that had been so common in the Neath valley. When I came to an inn called the Forge Hammer, I had to force my way past a great fat pig that lay sleeping in the doorway. This proved to me at once that I had left collieries, tin, copper, plate and iron works behind me, and that I was now in an agricultural country. Moreover, I began to see stables at the side of the houses, and all the little cottages had laburnum, laurel and other trees in front of them. Instead of meeting pale, sinewy colliers, I began to see a number of fat, red-faced farmers driving fat horses to and from Abergavenny. I could get clean lodgings at a place called the Hen and Chickens I had been told in Ebbw Vale. So when I got near the town I began to make inquiries, and having found it, paid for my bed and went out to see the main buildings.

Seeing a respectable-looking inn, after I had been walking here and there for nearly an hour, I went into it and remained long enough to drink six glasses of ale. At this house the ale must have been very strong, for, to my surprise, I felt that I had had quite enough for that day. However, I did not show it much, except that I was perhaps a little slower in movements and speech.

Glyn Cynon, Mid-Glamorgan

81. Anon (sixteenth century)

Glyn Cynon Wood
Aberdare, Llanwynno through,
all Merthyr to Llanfabon;
there was never a more disastrous thing
than the cutting of Glyn Cynon.

They cut down many a parlour pure
where youth and manhood meet;
in those days of the regular star
Glyn Cynon's woods were sweet.

If a man in sudden plight
took to flight from foe,
for guest-house to the nightingale
in Cynon Vale he'd go.

Many a birch-tree green of cloak
(I'd like to choke the Saxon!)
is now a flaming heap of fire
where iron-workers blacken.

For cutting the branch and bearing away
the wild birds' habitation
may misfortune quickly reach
Rowenna's treacherous children!

Rather should the English be
strung up beneath the seas,
keeping painful house in hell
than felling Cynon's trees.

Upon my oath, I've heard it said
that a herd of the red deer
for Mawddwy's deep dark woods has left,
bereft of its warmth here.

No more the badger's earth we'll sack
nor start a buck from the glade;
no more deer-stalking in my day,
now they've cut Glyn Cynon's shade.

If ever a stag got into a wood
with huntsmen a stride behind,
never again will he turn in his run
with Cynon Wood in mind.

If the flour-white girl once came
to walk along the brook,
Glyn Cynon's wood was always there
as a fair trysting nook.

If as in times gone by men plan
to span the mountain river;
though wood be found for house and church
Glyn Cynon's no provider.

I'd like to call on them a quest
of every honest bird,
where the owl, worthiest in the wood,
as hangman would be heard.

If there's a question who rehearsed
in verse this cruel tale,
it's one who many a tryst has kept
in the depth of Cynon Vale.

GILFACH GOCH

82. Richard Llewellyn, *How Green Was My Valley* (1939)

The first thing I saw was the slag heap.

Big it had grown, and long, and black, without life or sign, lying along the bottom of the Valley on both sides of the river. The green grass, and the reeds and the flowers, all had gone, crushed beneath it. And every minute the burden grew, as cage after cage screeched along the cables from the pit, bumped to a stop at the tipping pier, and emptied dusty loads on to the ridged, black, dirty back.

On our side of the Valley the heap reached to the front garden walls of the bottom row of houses, and children from them were playing up and down the black slopes, screaming and shouting, laughing in fun. On the other side of the river the chimney-pots of the first row of houses could only just be seen above the sharp curving back of the far heap, and all the time I was watching, the cable screeched and the cages tipped. From the Britannia pit came a call on the hooter as the cages came up, as though to remind the Valley to be ready for more filth as the work went on and on, year in and year out.

'Is the pit allowed to do this to us, Mr Gruffydd?' I asked him.

'Do what, my son?' Mr Gruffydd asked.

'Put slag by here,' I said.

'Nowhere else to put it, my son,' he said. 'Look up by there at the top of the mountain, by the Glas Fryn. There are the daffodils, see.'

And indeed, there they were, with their green leaves a darker sharpness in the grass about them, and the yellow blooms belling in the wind, up by the Glas Fryn and all along the Valley, as far as I could turn my head to see.

Gold may be found again, and men may know its madness again, but no one shall know how I felt to see the goldness of daffodils growing up there that morning. The Glas Fryn was the nearest place to our house where they grew. It was later that I pulled bulbs to grow in our garden, but the garden was so small and the earth so blind with dust from the slag that they gave up trying and died.

But that morning Mr Gruffydd put me down among them all, close to them, where I could take them in my hands to breathe the cool breath of them and give thanks to God.

Below us, the river ran sweet as ever, happy in the sun, but as soon as it met the darkness between the sloping walls of slag it seemed to take fright and go spiritless, smooth, black, without movement. And on the other side it came forth grey, and began to hurry again, as though anxious to get away. But its banks were stained, and the reeds and grasses that dressed it

were hanging, and black, and sickly, ashamed of their
dirtiness, ready to die of shame, they seemed, and of
sorrow for their dear friend, the river.

83 and 84. R. S. Thomas, *Later Poems* (1983)

The Chapel

A little aside from the main road,
becalmed in a last-century greyness,
there is the chapel, ugly, without the appeal
to the tourist to stop his car
and visit it. The traffic goes by,
and the river goes by, and quick shadows
of clouds, too, and the chapel settles
a little deeper into the grass.

But here once on an evening like this,
in the darkness that was about
his hearers, a preacher caught fire
and burned steadily before them
with a strange light, so that they saw
the splendour of the barren mountains
about them and sang their amens
fiercely, narrow but saved
in a way that men are not now.

Good

The old man comes out on the hill
and looks down to recall earlier days
in the valley. He sees the stream shine,
the church stand, hears the litter of
children's voices. A chill in the flesh
tells him that death is not far off
now: it is the shadow under the great boughs
of life. His garden has herbs growing.
The kestrel goes by with fresh prey
in its claws. The wind scatters the scent
of wild beans. The tractor operates
on the earth's body. His grandson is there
ploughing; his young wife fetches him
cakes and tea and a dark smile. It is well.

SKOKHOLM ISLAND, DYFED

85. Ronald Lockley, *Dream Island* (1930)

I walk each day around the island, counting the flock
and tending the ewes with lambs; making sure that they
have sought shelter on windy days, and that all is well. I
confess it is an easy task, and much to my liking, this
long perambulation along the cliffs, counting my precious flock, and welcoming the new-born lambs and
seeing that they are able to stand sturdily on their long
legs and take nourishment . . .

In walking every day around the island upon this
work I am able to satisfy my desire to know how my
little kingdom progresses, what new arrivals are here,
what birds gone: whether the tadpoles are hatched
under the starwort in the main pond, whether the lesser
black-backs have yet occupied the bog, whether the
ravens have brought their young off, whether any more
black redstarts have come, whether the vernal squills,
the campion or the cowslips are flowering, and a
hundred other events of early spring. In summer the
thousand daily events and adventures of the walk are
almost bewildering. On hot days, when the long walk
over rough ground and through bracken and heather –
perhaps for four miles – following the indentations of
the coastline, is likely to exhaust too much energy and
time, the pony is saddled, and the rounding-up is
accomplished at a gallop . . .

When we have examined the sheep, and have had
breakfast, the main work of the day begins. We hurry off
to the day's fishing, eager to see what wondrous things
of the sea we have caught in our basket pots, and all day
long we are in the boat at this pleasant task. Though the
hauling up of the pots is not light work, it is extremely
fascinating to peer into each pot to see what Neptune
has given us. The pots are each baited with three pieces
of gurnet for the snaring of lobsters, crayfish and crabs,
and, although we get our fair share of these, we also

have many unexpected hauls of such fish as conger-eels, cuttle-fish, jelly-fish, star-fish, sea-slugs, prawns, 'spider' and other strange crabs, and many another strange-looking denizen of the deep . . .

From our goats we obtain milk, butter and cheese; from our garden, fruit and the produce of the soil; from the chickens and gulls, eggs; from the island and the sea, rabbits and fish. We have only to grow and grind our own wheat in order to be self-supporting. I have even suggested to Doris that we spin our own wool and weave our own garments! So far, however, we rely on others, and I think for these we shall always do so, not being so entirely self-reliant that we desire to discard the advantages and conveniences of civilization.

From the sea we obtain our firewood. So far the coal from the schooner has lasted us three years, and I think will hold out for another five. If we do not have another wreck by the end of that time we shall dig peat from the 'turbary' on the bog. This 'turbary', an area of a few acres, supplied the fuel of turf or peat which the inhabitants of the island used over a hundred years ago . . .

Happily illnesses are unknown in this healthy, salt air. The coast-dwelling folk of Pembrokeshire have a reputation for longevity, and I like to picture myself an old salt, with a flowing white beard, and at eighty years of age still hauling my pots and driving my sheep. But Doris, as yet, does not approve of a beard.

Thus you will see my one-time dreams have come true, for I dwell on an island, far from the turmoil of a city, and accessible only to the chosen few. I have all the birds I could wish for, and welcome every one. In the summer I can reckon there are over thirty thousand on our island, of which two-thirds comprise puffins and shearwaters. In variety, so far, over a hundred different species are recorded, and there is a peculiar delight in welcoming new species; more particularly in such a well-defined area as an island.

Each summer brings us fresh cruising adventures, and when the North wind is true and steady we shall be sailing once more out to far distant Grassholm to see again the gannets and seals.

And so live happily ever after!

Llandovery to Llangadog

86. George Borrow, *Wild Wales* (1862)

On the tenth I departed from Llandovery, which I have no hesitation in saying is about the pleasantest little town in which I have halted in the course of my wanderings. I intended to sleep at Gutter Vawr, a place some twenty miles distant, just within Glamorgan-shire, to reach which it would be necessary to pass over part of a range of wild hills, generally called the Black Mountains. I started at about ten o'clock; the morning was lowering, and there were occasional showers of rain and hail. I passed by Rees Pritchard's church, holding my hat in my hand as I did so, not out of respect for the building, but from reverence for the memory of the sainted man who of old from its pulpit called sinners to repentance, and whose remains slumber in the churchyard unless washed away by some frantic burst of the neighbouring Towey. Crossing a bridge over the Bran just before it enters the greater stream, I proceeded along a road running nearly south and having a range of fine hills on the east. Presently violent gusts of wind came on, which tore the sear leaves by thousands from the trees of which there were plenty by the roadsides. After a little time, however, this elemental hurly-burly passed away, a rainbow made its appearance and the day became comparatively fine. Turning to the south-east under a hill covered with oaks, I left the vale of the Towey behind me, and soon caught a glimpse of some very lofty hills which I supposed to be the Black Mountains. It was a mere glimpse, for scarcely had I descried them when mist settled down and totally obscured them from my view.

In about an hour I reached Llangadog, a large village. The name signifies the Church of Gadog. Gadog

was a British saint of the fifth century, who after
labouring amongst his own countrymen for their spiritual good for many years, crossed the sea to Brittany,
where he died. Scarcely had I entered Llangadog when a
great shower of rain came down. Seeing an ancient-
looking hostelry I at once made for it. In a large and
comfortable kitchen I found a middle-aged woman
seated by a huge deal table near a blazing fire, with a
couple of large books open before her. Sitting down on a
chair I told her in English to bring me a pint of ale. She
did so and again sat down to her books, which on
inquiry I found to be a Welsh Bible and Concordance.
We soon got into discourse about religion, but did not
exactly agree, for she was a bitter Methodist, as bitter as
her beer, only half of which I could get down.

Leaving Llangadog I pushed forward. The day was
now tolerably fine. In two or three hours I came to a
glen, the sides of which were beautifully wooded. On
my left was a river, which came roaring down from a
range of lofty mountains right before me to the south-
east. The river, as I was told by a lad, was the Sawdde or
Southey, the lofty range the Black Mountains. Passed a
pretty village on my right standing something in the
shape of a semi-circle, and in about half-an-hour came
to a bridge over a river which I supposed to be the
Sawdde which I had already seen, but which I subsequently learned was an altogether different stream. It
was running from the south, a wild fierce flood amidst
rocks and stones, the waves all roaring and foaming.

After some time I reached another bridge near the
foot of a very lofty ascent. On my left to the east upon a
bank was a small house, on one side of which was a
wheel turned round by a flush of water running in a
little artificial canal; close by it were two small
cascades, the waters of which and also those of the
canal passed under the bridge in the direction of the
west. Seeing a decent-looking man engaged in sawing a
piece of wood by the roadside, I asked him in Welsh
whether the house with the wheel was a flour-mill.

'Nage,' said he, 'it is a pandy, fulling mill.'

'Can you tell me the name of a river,' said I, 'which I have left about a mile behind me? Is it the Sawdde?'

'Nage,' said he. 'It is the Lleidach.'

Then looking at me with great curiosity he asked me if I came from the north country.

'Yes,' said I, 'I certainly come from there.'

'I am glad to hear it,' said he, 'for I have long wished to see a man from the north country.'

'Did you never see one before?' said I.

'Never in my life,' he replied: 'men from the north country seldom show themselves in these parts.'

'Well,' said I; 'I am not ashamed to say that I come from the north.'

'Ain't you? Well, I don't know that you have any particular reason to be ashamed, for it is rather your misfortune than your fault; but the idea of any one coming from the north – ho, ho!'

'Perhaps in the north,' said I, 'they laugh at a man from the south.'

'Laugh at a man from the south! No, no; they can't do that.'

'Why not?' said I; 'why shouldn't the north laugh at the south as well as the south at the north?'

'Why shouldn't it? why, you talk like a fool. How could the north laugh at the south as long as the south remains the south and the north the north? Laugh at the south! you talk like a fool, David, and if you go on in that way I shall be angry with you. However, I'll excuse you; you are from the north, and what can one expect from the north but nonsense?'

87. Huw Llwyd (c. 1568–1630)

The Fox's Counsel
Good morning, fox of the cave,
Every tame fowl's arch-foeman,
Your ripple I recognize,
Welcome to fertile country.
Describe, in the fair meadow,

Your life, bold soft-bellied beast.
Fair and clean, you are noted,
And shapely in every part:
You were dyed with dark colour,
Red and gold that will not fade;
Your narrow nose is savage,
Your teeth, they are marvellous,
Strange pincers, swiftly gripping,
And able to crunch through bones;
And your eye's glowering look
You turn like an old traitor.
On your head, fine beast, always,
Is the semblance of stiff stumps;
Your neck beneath was well-dressed,
Shaped like a ridge, you're splendid;
Bulging belly in coarse cloth,
A belly full of malice!
Short leg, bold through thick-branched grove,
Keen trotter towards weak lambkins.
Your tail, the length of mid-day,
Thick coarse cloth, is your pillow;
That tail is a yard-long brush,
A roll extremely swollen.
Kindling on the cairn's summit,
Kindled lad in a stout den,
Well-designed is your dwelling,
A hide-out from terriers.

Sorry scheme, you live yonder,
Paunchy lad, by plundering,
Pilfering, when it's quiet,
And strolling through leaves all day:
Kid's meat, when it's to be had,
Ewes, if they're for the taking;
A fine life, when there are lambs,
Blameless for you to tithe them.
Take hereafter, yours freely,
A goose and hen, unrebuked:
Clever you are, bird-snatching,
Hillside or bog, wild and tame.

All accomplishments your gift,
When closed in, you're a lion.
And if you come with twilight
Is there one so full of sense,
Or any with tricks slicker
Than yours, savage-snarling fox?

PLYNLIMON, POWYS–DYFED BORDER

88. Robert Gibbings, *Coming Down the Wye* (1942)

It was mid-winter when I first tried to reach the source
of the Wye, on Plynlimon. In the morning, when I left
Llangurig, the sun had risen in a clear sky, and was
throwing its radiance over the snow-covered hills. To
the west the sky was green as olives and the ice-fringed
river, reflecting that colour, showed all the lights of an
aquamarine. Higher in the hills the water in the
tributaries flowed through crystal gorges. It was as if
some giant crucibles of molten glass had been spilled
along either bank. In sheltered pools, where the water
was deep and calm, delicate fern-like plates of ice
stretched out to meet each other over mid-stream, but
on windier stretches the frozen surface was rippled and
polished, and dark as the water flowing beneath. Where
there had been a waterfall there were now caverns of
ice, festooned with stalactites, the rock faces on either
side shining like chandeliers with frozen spray.

Although there wasn't a cloud to be seen small
snow-flakes began to fall, each one dazzling bright in
the sunlight, and the higher I climbed the larger these
flakes became. But they soon lost their brilliance. By
midday the horizons were blotted out, and the tussocks
of grass at my feet were crested with fresh snow. The
ice-flecked stream had become the colour of pewter.
The snow fell thicker and thicker, and a cold wind
swept down the valley. Soon I became enveloped in this
mild blizzard. My only guide was the Wye itself, beside
me, now no wider than an old man's jump. Then I found
a dead sheep, stretched out stiff and cold under a slab of

rock. If that could happen to an animal that's covered all over with a thick fleece what chance would I have, I thought, with no more than a few hairs on my chin. I decided to retrace my steps.

Three months later I was more successful in my attempt to reach the top. The day was diamond clear, with tufts of high white cloud throwing purple shadows over spur and combe, as they sped away to the south. In all directions there was a tumult of hills: on all sides there were glimpses of distant lakes. From the sheltered slope on which I sat I could watch the silver line of the Wye winding towards the old lead mine above Pant Mawr. A mile to the west the Severn started on its course. Behind me the Rheidol had its source in the flanks of the same great hill.

Plynlimon is not a single peak, but a marriage of many, two of its highest points being three miles apart. These and the surrounding country are some of the oldest hills in the world, older by far than the Alps, the Andes, or the Himalayas, yet it is possible almost anywhere on their surface to pick up slabs of shaly rock which show not only the tide ripples of a time when they were submerged beneath the sea, but also the clearly marked tracks of worms who moved and had their being in those seas some five hundred million years ago.

I was at the source of the Wye. After a gentle murmuring underground the water welled up, brushing aside the young spring grass, to form a pool no bigger than a bowler hat. Then gently it glided between rich tussocks of moss and rushes still bent from their load of winter snow, until it tumbled like a shower of sequins over the black velvet of a peat face. The pool below this was wider and deeper, and with every yard of its flow the strength of the rivulet increased. Small streams from successive dells and dingles joined in, and so, between thick felts of sphagnum moss starred with cotton grass, and over rocks long since worn smooth, it frisked and dived towards its first main tributary a thousand feet below.

CADER IDRIS, GWYNEDD

89. Francis Kilvert, *Diary* (1871)

Tuesday, 13 June 1871

About this time the wind changed and flew suddenly round into the S. The head of Idris, which had been cowled in cloud, had cleared for a while, but now an impenetrable dark cloud settled down upon it and the mist came creeping down the mountain. The sky looked black and threatened rain. Now there lay before us vast tracts and belts of large stones lying so close together that no turf could be seen and no grass could grow between them. It was broken basalt, and huge lengths of basalt, angled, and some hexagonal, lay about or jutted from the mountain side like enormous balks of timber and with an unknown length buried in the mountain. We passed quarries where some of the great columns had been dug out to be drawn down the mountain on sledges. Cader Idris is the stoniest, dreariest, most desolate mountain I was ever on. We came now to the edge of a vast gulf or chasm or bason almost entirely surrounded by black precipices rising from the waters of a small black tarn which lay in the bottom of the bason. Here the guide showed me the place at the foot of an opposite precipice where Mr Smith's body had been found. Then we stumbled and struggled on again over rough tracts and wildernesses of slate and basalt. The sun was shining on the hills below, but the mist crawled down and wrapped us as if in a shroud blotting out everything. The mists and clouds began to sweep by us in white thin ghostly sheets as if some great dread Presences and Powers were going past and we could only see the skirts of their white garments. The air grew damp and chill, the cloud broke on the mountain top and it began to rain. Now and then we could discern the black sharp peak which forms the summit looming large and dark through the cloud and rain and white wild driving mist, and it was hidden again. It is an awful place in a storm. I thought of Moses on Sinai.

The rain grew heavier. The old guide could not get on very fast and told me to go on alone to the top and shelter in the hut as I could not miss the path. So I went on up the last sharp peak looming black through the dark mist and cloud, by a winding path among the great rocks and wildernesses of loose stone. For a few minutes I was alone on the top of the mountain. The thought struck me, suppose the old man should be seized with cramp in the stomach here, how in the world should I get him down or get down myself in the blinding mist? The cloud and mist and rain swept by and drove eddying round the peak. I could hear the old man chinking his iron-shod staff among the rocks and stones, as he came up the path, nearer and nearer, but till he got close to me I could not discern his white figure through the dense mist. 'This is the highest point of *Cader Idris*,' he said, laying his hand upon a peak of wet living rock, 'not *that*,' looking with contempt at the great conical pile of stones built upon the peak by the sappers and miners during the Ordnance Survey. He said, 'The Captain of the surveying company had his tent pitched on the top of Cader Idris for 3 summer months and never left the place. He had 18 men to wait upon him. And how many clear views do you think he got in that time?' 'Twelve,' I hazarded. 'Nine,' he said.

He took me down to a rude 2-roomed hut built of huge stones by his father just under the shelter of the peak, and produced for my benefit a hard-boiled egg and some slices of bread and butter. Also he gave me a woollen comforter to wrap round my neck. Then he vanished. The mist drove in white sheets and shapes past the doorless doorway and past the windows from which the window frames had been removed and the wind whistled through the chinks in the rude walls of huge stones. A large flat block of stone in the middle of the room on which I sat formed the table. It is said that if any one spends a night alone on the top of Cader Idris he will be found in the morning either dead or a madman or a poet gifted with the highest degree of inspiration. Hence Mrs Hemans' fine song 'A night upon Cader Idris'. The same thing is said of the top of Snowdon and of a great stone at the foot of Snowdon. Old Pugh says the fairies used to dance near the top of the mountain and he knows people who have seen them.

Presently I heard the old man clinking his stick among the rocks and coming round the hut. He came in and lighted his pipe and we prepared to go down by the 'Foxes' Path'. And indeed it was a path fit only for foxes. After leading me a few steps he began to go over what seemed to me to be the edge of a precipice, depth unknown and hidden in the mist. The side of the mountain was frightfully steep here and required great care in going down. Suddenly the old man stopped at a beautiful little spring in the almost perpendicular bank, pulled out his tumbler and gave me a draught of the clear sparkling water, much colder than the water from the spring of Dysyni. About the spring the grass grew brilliant green and there was a long winding riband of bright green where the waters overflowing from the spring trickled down through the grass stems to feed the lake at which the foxes drink just below. Next we came to a broad belt of loose rocks lying close together which the guide cautioned me to beware of and not without reason saying they were as slippery as glass and that a sprained ankle was an awkward thing on the mountain. Down, down and out of the cloud into sunshine, all the hills below and the valleys were bathed in glorious sunshine – a wonderful and dazzling sight. Above and hanging overhead the vast black precipices towered and loomed through the clouds, and fast as we went down the mist followed faster and presently all the lovely sunny landscape was shrouded in a white winding sheet of rain. The path was all loose shale and stone and so steep that planting our alpenstocks from behind and leaning back upon them Alpine fashion we glissaded with a general landslip, rush and rattle of shale and shingle down to the shore of the Foxes' Lake. The parsley fern grew in sheets of brilliant green among the grey shale and in the descent we passed the largest basaltic columns of all protruding from the mountain side. In the clefts and angles of the huge grey tower columns grew beautiful tufts and bunches of parsley fern. We passed another lake and after some rough scrambling walking over broken ground at the mountain foot we came back into the turnpike road at the lake that we had passed in the morning. As we entered Dolgelly the old man said, 'You're a splendid walker, sir', a compliment which procured him a glass of brandy and water.

Barmouth, Gwynedd

90. Siôn Phylip (d. 1620)

The Seagull
Fair gull on the water's bank,
Bright-plumed breast, well-provided,
Hawk does not seize or pursue,
Water drown, nor man own you.
Nun feasting on the ocean,
Green sea's corners' coarse-voiced girl,
Thrusting wide through the lake's neck;
And then shaking a herring,
Salt water's clear white sunlight,
You're the banner of the shore.
The blessed godchild are you,
Below the bank, of Neptune:
A sorrow for you, the change
Of your life, cold your christening,
Brave white bird in rough waters,
Once a girl in a man's arms.

Halcyon, fair slim-browed maiden,
You were called in your kind land,
And after your man, good cause,
To the waves then you ventured,
And to the wild strait's seagull
You were changed, weak-footed bird.
You live, quick fish-feeding girl,

Below the slope and billows,
And the same cry for your mate
You screech loudly till doomsday.

Was there ever on the sea
A more submissive swimmer?
Hear my cry, wise and white-cloaked,
The hurt of the bare sea's bard:
My breast is pained with passion,
Pining for love of a girl.
I have begged from my boyhood
That she'd make one tryst with me,
And the tryst was for today:
Great was grief, it was wasted.
Swim, forget not my complaint,
To the dear maiden's region;
Fly to the shore, brave brightness,
And say where I was held fast
By the mouth, no gentle wave,
Of rough Bermo, cold foaming,
In all moods a sorry spot,
A cold black sea for sailing.

I rose, I travelled as day was
Breaking towards that dear bright face.
Dawn came on a thorny seastrand,
A cold day from the south-east.
A foul wind winnowed gravel,
Stripping stones, the whirlwind's nest.
The signs grew darker with dawn,
Twrch Trwydd drenching the beaches.
Inky was the wind's gullet
Where the western wind draws breath.

Harsh is the shore in conflict
If the western inlet's rough:
The sea spews, turning rocks green,
From the east spews fresh water.
Deep heaves from the ocean-bed,
In pain the pale moon's swooning.
The green pond is heaved abroad,
A snake's heave, sick from surfeit.

Sad heave where I saw tide ebb,
Rain's drivel that came pouring,
Cold black bed between two slopes,
Salt-filled briny sea-water.
Furnace dregs, draff of hell-spit,
Mouth sucking drops from the stars,
A winter night's greedy mouth,
Greed on the face of night-time,
Crock-shaped wet-edged enclosure,
A ban between bard and girl,
Foul hollow gap, raging pit,
Foggy land's filthy cranny,
Cromlech of every sickness,
Narrow pit of the world's plagues.
The pit was the sea-pool's haunt,
High it leaped, pool of prickles.
As high as the shelf it climbs,
Spew of the storm-path's anguish.
It never ebbs, will not turn:
I could not cross the current.

Three waters could flow eastwards,
Three oceans, these are the ones:
The Euxin, where rain wets us,
The Adriatic, black look,
The flood that runs to Rhuddallt,
Ancient Noah's flood turned salt.
The water-gate at Bermo,
Tide and shelf, may it turn land!

SNOWDONIA

91. Roger A. Redfern, *Rambles in North Wales* (1968)

A lovely sunny morning in June among the high hills.
All about were innumerable alpines in full bloom and
ground beetles were everywhere. It was a shame to go
on. One hour later the steep, broken slopes falling to the
Afon Nant Peris and Gwastadnant had been negotiated,
the Titanian woods of oak and leaning hazel above

Nant Peris had been trodden under and the cuckoo's call came across the even grass slopes of Elidir Fawr. The south-east face of this giant hill-mass is one of my favourites, long and almost unbroken and spacious to every vapour and often dotted with Welsh Mountain ewes and lambs. There can be no bigger mountainside south of the Highlands, two thousand feet from base to summit ridge and catching all the morning's bright sunlight. I was thankful for the bottle of lemonade placed a few days before beneath a broken wall where rushes grew luxuriantly.

From the sweeping, shattered ridge Elidir Fach (2,964 feet) rolled away a quarter of a mile to the north and that was my next summit. The wind was very strong on the crossing from this lesser peak to its greater neighbour but by eleven o'clock the cache upon the 3,029-foot summit of Elidir Fawr was reached. It was later than I had anticipated when still in the valley, though even then it was my belief that by 2.30 p.m. I could be ascending the first slopes of the Carneddau.

Dark-shadowed clouds crowded low over the Carneddau summits and from this Elidir perch the very air seemed lonely. The strong wind blew, the clouds cast black gloom north-eastwards and I hadn't seen one soul that day. Now, however, it was time to climb on, down the terraces of scree with wide views over into the northern cwm which contains Llyn Marchlyn Mawr, memories of a bathe there long ago, on a day of alto-cumulus clouds and thunderstorms. High up on the north-eastern slope of Elidir Fawr peers Craig Cwrwgl. This is the most isolated peak in Snowdonia, a great wedge of cliff that claims to possess a summit attainable only after many feet of rock climbing.

On over the grassy, sheep-dense top of Mynydd Perfedd and so by a rocky way to the lovely Foel Goch and giant Y Garn, the armchair mountain at the head of the Nant Ffrancon which cradles a favourite pool of earlier days, Llyn Clyd. I gained the top of Y Garn half an hour after noon, just eight hours after leaving Pen-y-Pass; with the sun still shining here I could look

to the eastern mountains carrying wisps of grey mist
around their heads.

92. Hywel ab Owain Gwynedd (d. 1170)

Exultation

A foaming white wave washes over a grave,
the tomb of Rhufawn Pebyr, regal chieftain.
I love today what the English hate, the open land of the
   North,
and the varied growth that borders the Lliw.
I love those who gave me my fill of mead
where the seas reach in long contention.
I love its household and its strong buildings
and at its lord's wish to go to war.
I love its strand and its mountains,
its castle near the woods and its fine lands,
its water meadows and its valleys,
its white gulls and its lovely women.
I love its soldiers, its trained stallions,
its woods, its brave men and its homes.
I love its fields under the little clover,
where honour was granted a secure joy.
I love its regions, to which valour entitles,
its wide waste lands and its wealth.
O, Son of God, how great a wonder,
how splendid the stags, great their possessions!
With the thrust of a spear I did splendid work
between the host of Powys and lovely Gwynedd.
On a pale white horse, a rash adventure,
may I now win freedom from my exile.
I'll never hold out till my people come;
a dream says so and God wills so.
A foaming white wave washes over a grave.

A white wave, near the homesteads, foams over,
coloured like hoar-frost in the hour of its advance.
I love the sea-coast of Meirionnydd,
where a white arm was my pillow.
I love the nightingale in the wild wood,
where two waters meet in that sweet valley.

195

Lord of heaven and earth, ruler of Gwynedd,
how far Kerry is from Caer Lliwelydd!
In Maelienydd I mounted on a bay
and rode night and day to Rheged.
May I have, before my grave, a new conquest,
the land of Tegeingl, fairest in the world.
Though I be a lover of Ovid's way,
may God be mindful of me at my end.
A white wave, near the homesteads, foams over.

PISTYLL RHAEADR, CLWYD

93. George Borrow, *Wild Wales* (1862)

There are many remarkable cataracts in Britain and the neighbouring isles, even the little Celtic Isle of Man has its remarkable waterfall; but this Rhyadr, the grand cataract of North Wales, far exceeds them all in altitude and beauty, though it is inferior to several of them in the volume of its flood. I never saw water falling so gracefully, so much like thin beautiful threads as here. Yet even this cataract has its blemish. What beautiful object has not something which more or less mars its loveliness? There is an ugly black bridge or semicircle of rock, about two feet in diameter and about twenty feet high, which rises some little way below it, and under which the water, after reaching the bottom, passes, which intercepts the sight, and prevents it from taking in the whole fall at once. This unsightly object has stood where it now stands since the day of creation, and will probably remain there to the day of judgment. It would be a desecration of nature to remove it by art, but no one could regret if nature in one of her floods were to sweep it away.

As I was standing on the planks a woman plainly but neatly dressed came from the house. She addressed me in very imperfect English, saying that she was the mistress of the house and should be happy to show me about. I thanked her for her offer and told her that she might speak Welsh, whereupon she looked glad and said in that tongue that she could speak Welsh much better than Saesneg. She took me by a winding path up a steep bank on the southern side of the fall to a small plateau, and told me that was the best place to see the Pistyll from. I did not think so, for we were now so near that we were almost blinded by the spray, though, it is true, the semicircle of rock no longer impeded the sight; this object we now saw nearly laterally rising up like a spectral arch, spray and foam above it, and water rushing below. 'That is a bridge rather for ysprydoedd [spirits] to pass over than men,' said I.

'It is,' said the woman; 'but I once saw a man pass over it.'

'How did he get up?' said I. 'The sides are quite steep and slippery.'

'He wriggled up the side like a llysowen [eel], till he got to the top, when he stood upright for a minute, and then slid down on the other side.'

'Was he any one from these parts?' said I.

'He was not. He was a dyn dieithr, a Russian; one of those with whom we are now at war.'

'Was there as much water tumbling then as now?'

'More, for there had fallen more rain.'

'I suppose the torrent is sometimes very dreadful?' said I.

'It is indeed, especially in winter; for it is then like a sea, and roars like thunder or a mad bull.'

After I had seen all I wished of the cataract, the woman asked me to come to the house and take some refreshment. I followed her to a neat little room where she made me sit down and handed me a bowl of buttermilk. On the table was a book in which she told me it was customary for individuals who visited the cataract to insert their names. I took up the book which contained a number of names mingled here and there with pieces of poetry. Amongst these compositions was a Welsh englyn on the Rhyadr, which though incorrect in its prosody I thought stirring and grand. I copied it, and subjoin it with a translation which I made on the spot.

'Crychiawg, ewynawg anian – yw y Rhyadr
Yn rhuo mal taran;
Colofn o dwr, gloyw-dwr glan,
Gorwyllt, un lliw ag arian.'

'Foaming and frothing from mountainous height,
    Roaring like thunder the Rhyadr falls;
Though its silvery splendour the eye may delight,
    Its fury the heart of the bravest appals.'

IX

To the North Midlands

The three rivers that flow within a few miles of each other out of the hills of north-east Wales towards the Shropshire border seem to presage in their abrupt names – Teme, Clun and Lugg – the blunt practicality that characterizes so many of the North Midlands working towns. But there's nothing blunt or downbeat about the landscape of their origins, a tremendous series of rolling hill ranges that are the last eastward heaves of the great mountain masses of North Wales. The up-and-down landscape continues well into the English side of the border, too, in the humped shapes of the Long Mynd and Wenlock Edge, and further south the exciting hill country around Ludlow and Leominster.

Though this is essentially a landscape running east and west, there is one feature – a man-made one – that knits the country of Teme, Clun and Lugg together from north to south, itself a small portion of an ancient barrier between Welsh and English that runs the entire length of the border between the two countries, far straighter and more directly than today's political boundary. Offa's Dyke is a symbol of division and mistrust, rather than of a meeting of the hearts and minds of the two nations between which it runs in intermittent stages for eighty miles. A low bank of earth and stones, five or six feet high, is all you are likely to see of the Dyke on the ground, broken in places by field paths and

199

tractor ways, overgrown with brambles or sprouting a line of ragged thorns, running from a hill crest down into the valley and up the other side in a more or less dead straight line. Seen from the air, or from a hilltop with a clear view, the Dyke can be made out winding round bluffs, clinging to the edges of escarpments and diverging to cross rivers at suitable points – almost always with a clear view into the country lying to the west. There was a good reason for this westward aspect. The Dyke was built in about AD 790 on the orders of Offa, King of Mercia, to mark the boundary between his then relatively peaceful kingdom and his long-term Welsh adversaries. It provided not only a tangible, undeniable frontier and statement of separateness of the two countries and their cultures, but also an excellent grandstand from which Offa's people could observe and report back to their king what the unruly neighbours were up to. An extraordinary amount of organization must have been needed in planning the Dyke, surveying it and gathering the labourers to build it to its original height of twelve feet or more. Twelve hundred years later it still stands along the border to perpetuate the name of King Offa and the memory of his domination of southern England.

From the small border town of Montgomery, I followed Offa's Dyke on a hot summer day from Wales into England – and back into Wales, and then into England again as the earthwork slices decisively across the wavering curves of the political border. A mile out of town I found the Dyke running on the same line as the border over three miles of flattish fields, a bank low enough to jump over, with bare earth patches in its sides where sheep had hollowed out snoozing dens. They lay flicking their ears at the flies, too hot to move as I brushed past them. Oak trees growing in the top of the Dyke gave some shade, their roots clamped in the crumbling structure. The Dyke looked in poor shape, and soon vanished altogether under the scrapings and ploughings of local farmers. There was compensation for dykelessness in the view – a large shallow valley rimmed with low hills to the north, but beginning to rise into the steep humps and hillsides of Clun Forest to the south. The tall, jagged ruins of Montgomery Castle, overlooking the valley from their mound, were soon left behind as I crossed the River Caebitra from England back into Wales and began the climb into the hills at Cwm.

As soon as it starts to snake up and down the hills and valleys, the Dyke changes character. No longer a faint scar in a low landscape, it charges the hill slopes like a roller-coaster; not much higher than in the fields near Montgomery, but much more visible, a straight green channel that attracts the eye immediately from each new hill crest. Ramshackle black-and-white farmhouses, powdered pale pink near ground level by rain-blown earth, stand in the valley bottoms by streams thick with rosebay willowherb and kingcups, isolated from their nearest neighbours by slopes hundreds of feet high that press in claustrophobically. This is closed-in countryside, all level ground farmed, the slopes too steep for farming set with tiny conifer plantations. Yet in spite of its agricultural nature, there is an atmosphere of wildness and remoteness that makes the solitary rambler glad to have the Dyke as a companion.

There are steep and sweaty hills to climb, beyond Cwm and at Edenhope just after the final crossing into England, short but muscle-cracking ascents on which the Dyke gives no quarter. Straight up – a bend at the top – straight down. At Churchtown, in the middle of this wilderness of hills, a couple of cottages and a plain little church stand beside the Dyke, which vanishes into a plantation. But there it was when I had struggled up the slope, plunging on and on round the side of Hergan Hill to a tiny cluster of houses at Mardu. One more climb and fall beside the Dyke, suddenly grown into a tall and impressive bank, and I staggered with twanging calf muscles down to Newcastle in the valley of the River Clun; narrow enough, but a broad plain after the tight little valleys of Clun Forest. The Dyke disappears again here as it crosses the river, but soon it reappears on the southern side to hurdle its remorseless way southward towards Knighton and another incursion into Welsh territory. I was more than happy to laze on the bridge at Newcastle after ten miles that had tired me as twenty in more kindly terrain would not have done. The relentless directness and purposefulness of the Dyke had been both inspiring and exhausting,

201

but now I could sit and stare idly down the Clun valley into the country of the 'Shropshire Lad'.

From the most greenly rural of Shropshire scenery to the blackness of Staffordshire's industrial landscape; back out and across to green rurality and black industry side by side in Nottinghamshire; up again through the high and remote Peak of Derbyshire to the tiny moorland village that marks the start of the Pennine Way – and an end in the murky, fiery, industrial cityscape of Sheffield. Our route through the northern Midlands brings together, as many of the region's writers themselves do, landscapes as pastorally peaceful and as thoroughly industrialized as any in Britain.

For A. E. Housman, the 'Shropshire Lad', for Mary Webb at Hope, near Shrewsbury, and for Alison Uttley up in the Peak at Cromford, the beauty of their own beloved regions is felt with an intensity more like pain than pleasure. D. H. Lawrence, in one of his earliest pieces of writing, sees a mood-plunge from elation to despair echoed by the birds of his native countryside. And the same contrast of highs and lows, subtle beauty and stark ugliness, is the theme that runs through the writing of Elihu Burritt and Arnold Bennett on the nineteenth-century Black Country and Potteries land-scapes, and through J. B. Priestley's *English Journey* of the 1930s through the man-made mountains and smog-thick-ened air of the ravaged countryside where Derbyshire meets the South Riding of Yorkshire and the outskirts of the industrial north.

Shropshire–Worcestershire Border

94. A. E. Housman, *A Shropshire Lad* (1896)

> As through the wild green hills of Wyre
> The train ran, changing sky and shire,
> And far behind, a fading crest,
> Low in the forsaken west
> Sank the high-reared head of Clee,

My hand lay empty on my knee.
Aching on my knee it lay:
That morning half a shire away
So many an honest fellow's fist
Had well-nigh wrung it from the wrist.
Hand, said I, since now we part
From fields and men we know by heart,
For strangers' faces, strangers' lands, —
Hand, you have held true fellows' hands.
Be clean then; rot before you do
A thing they'd not believe of you.
You and I must keep from shame
In London streets the Shropshire name;
On banks of Thames they must not say
Severn breeds worse men than they;
And friends abroad must bear in mind
Friends at home they leave behind.
Oh, I shall be stiff and cold
When I forget you, hearts of gold;
The land where I shall mind you not
Is the land where all's forgot.
And if my foot returns no more
To Teme nor Corve nor Severn shore,
Luck, my lads, be with you still
By falling stream and standing hill,
By climbing tower and whispering tree,
Men that made a man of me.
About your work in town and farm
Still you'll keep my head from harm,
Still you'll help me, hands that gave
A grasp to friend me to the grave.

HOPE, SHROPSHIRE

95. Mary Webb, *Gone to Earth* (1917)

Hazel, in the fields and woods, enjoyed it all so much
that she walked in a mystical exaltation.

Reddin in the fields and woods enjoyed himself only.
For he took his own atmosphere with him wherever he

went, and before his footsteps weakness fled and beauty
folded.

The sky blossomed in parterres of roses, frailer and
brighter than the rose of the briar, and melted beneath
them into lagoons greener and paler than the veins of a
young beech-leaf. The fairy hedges were so high, so
flushed with beauty, the green airy waters ran so far
back into mystery, that it seemed as if any moment God
might walk there as in a garden, delicate as a moth.
Down by the stream Hazel found tall water-plantains,
triune of cup, standing each above the ooze like
candelabras, and small rough-leaved forget-me-nots
eyeing their liquid reflections with complaisance. She
watched the birds bathe – bull-finches, smooth-coated
and well-found; slim willow-wrens; thrushes,
ermine-breasted; lusty blackbirds with beaks of crude
yellow. They made neat little tracks over the soft mud,
drank, bathed, preened, and made other neat little
tracks. Then they 'took off', as Hazel put it, from the top
of the bank, and flew low across the painted meadow or
high into the enamelled tree, and piped and fluted till
the air was full of silver.

Hazel stood as Eve might have stood, hands clasped,
eyes full of ecstasy, utterly self-forgetful, enchanted
with these living toys.

'Eh, yon's a proper bird!' she exclaimed, as a big
silken cuckoo alighted on the mud with a gobble, drank
with dignity, and took its vacillating flight to a far ash-
tree. 'Foxy ought to see that,' she added.

Silver-crested peewits circled and cried with their
melancholy cadences, and a tawny pheasant led out her
young. Now that the dew was gone, and cobwebs no
longer canopied the field with silver, it was blue with
germander speedwell – each flower painted with
deepening colour, eyed with startling white, and carry
ing on slender stamens the round white pollen-balls –
worlds of silent, lovely activity. Every flower-spike had
its family of buds, blue jewels splashed with white, each
close-folded on her mystery. To see the whole field not
only bright with them, but brimming over, was like

watching ten thousand saints rapt in ecstasy, ten thousand children dancing. Hazel knew nothing of saints. She had no words for the wonder in which she walked. But she felt it, she enjoyed it with a passion no words could express.

Mrs Marston had said several times, 'I'm almost afraid Hazel is a great one for wasting her time.' But what is waste of time? Eating and sleeping; hearing grave, sedulous men read out of grave, sedulous books what we have heard a hundred times; besieging God (whom we end by imagining as a great ear) for material benefits; amassing property – these, the world says, are not waste of time. But to drink at the stoup of beauty; to lift the leafy coverlet of earth and seek the cradled God (since here, if anywhere, He dwells), this in the world's eye is waste of time. Oh, filthy, heavy-handed, blear-eyed world, when will you wash and be clean?

Hazel came to a place where the white water crossed the road in a glittering shallow ford. Here she stayed, leaning on the wooden bridge, hearing small pebbles grinding on one another; seeing jewel-flashes of ruby, sapphire and emerald struck from them by the low sunlight; smelling the scent that is better than all (except the scent of air on a barren mountain, or of snow) – the scent of running water. She watched the grey wagtails, neat and prim in person, but wild in bearing, racing across the wet gravel like intoxicated Sunday-school teachers. Then, in a huge silver willow that brooded, dove-like, over the ford, a blackcap began to sing. The trills and gushes of perfect melody, the golden repetitions, the heart-lifting ascents and wistful falls drooping softly as a flower, seemed wonderful to her as an angel's song. She and the bird, sheltered under the grey-silver feathers of the tree, lived their great moments of creation and receptivity until suddenly there was a sharp noise of hoofs, the song snapped, the willow was untenanted, and Reddin's horse splashed through the ford.

'Oh!' cried Hazel, 'what for did you break the song? A sacred bird, it was. And now it's fled!'

IRONBRIDGE

96. H. J. Massingham, *The Wisdom of the Fields* (1945)

Harry's very workshop is as close to the river as human house can get, being a long weather-boarded hut built on piles, like a Lake Village, on the lowest terrace of the south bank a few steps below the girders of the Iron Bridge. He keeps his coracle under it and the workshop itself, with its chains, ropes, nets, corks, flotsam, paddles, timber and coracle-laths, might be a beached barge. His profession, if Harry can be said to have a definite profession, is rabbiting and coracle-making. He is also a mole-catcher, making his own wooden mole-traps and salting the skins. This is another indication which pushes him back into the Iron Age. He has actually figured in a coracle race as an ancient Briton. I found nothing peculiar in the thought of this timeless picaresque 'coracle mon of Siv'n' paying a call on the Goidelic or Brythonic coracle men who dared the tricky waters of his river in a craft you carry on your back and yet have your arms free.

For making coracles he uses axed ash-laths for the frame which is now covered with tarred calico for the ancient hide which perhaps conditioned its size and cupped shape. The split shaft of the paddle is also ash, but the long rectangular blade has to be of seasoned oak. Harry gets his from the timbers of demolished old cottages but also from floating timber which his maternal Severn yields up to him. He lives by Severn in other ways than floating on it in a craft much frailer, lighter and more sensitive to current and ripple than an empty brandy-cask. The flowing surface of the broad stream brings him part of his living, for any floating junk is grist to Harry's mill, and he puts it to a variety of surprising usages. Thus, he lives for the river, from the river, by the river and on the river, a life as semi-aquatic as the bank-vole's, as buoyant on the water as the tufted duck's and up and down the river, though further than, the kingfisher's.

After a lengthy sitting with him, I was so fortunate as to witness a moment of one of his river-lives – that of on the river. Entirely on his own initiative, he fished out his coracle from under the floor of the workshop and gave an exhibition – Harry is the born showman – of what he could do with it on Severn's bosom. When you consider that to scratch or look over the edge of the craft or stretch out a leg, almost to cough and certainly to sneeze, is enough to upset it, his performance may be regarded as one of the few marvels left in a now wonderless world. He got this thistledown affair into mid-stream (you work the paddle in front, if a craft nearly as round as half an orange can be said to have a front) and proceeded to whirl it round and round, as though it were a kind of water-top. Then he lunged to and fro, sporting with the flimsy thing as though he were riding one of Neptune's nags. After that, without the slightest warning, he tumbled off the plank-seat across the middle and with knees drawn up and head tucked in like a Neolithic burial pretended to go to sleep. Up and with a breath-catching gesture he flung the paddle twenty yards away into the current, stretched himself at full length across the plank and like an inverted turtle swam with his hands after the paddle which he easily recovered. But this circus-prowess was as nothing to what a friend saw him do one day. His coracle was towing a landing-stage and a tree-trunk behind it under Buildwas Bridge and all through the Gorge, with the river in semi-flood and flowing like a mill-race between the cliffs. How old Drayton's Naiads of Sabrina would have clapped their hands to see a sight like this!

Black Country, West Midlands

97. Elihu Burritt, *Walks in the Black Country and its Green Border-Land* (1868)

For an unpoetical man like myself, it is difficult to get hold of similes which would enable the reader to picture

the scene in his mind. A writer of a military turn of
fancy might say that it was the sublimest battle-scene
ever enacted on earth; that ten thousand Titans were
essaying to breach heaven with a thousand mortars,
each charged with a small red-hot hill. It might look
like that not only to General Grant or Sherman, but
even to men who never wore a sword. There was an
embattled amphitheatre of twenty miles span ridged to
the purple clouds. Planted at artillery intervals on this
encircling ridge, and at musket-shot spaces in the dark
valley between, a thousand batteries, mounted with
huge ordnance, white at the mouth with the fury of the
bombardment, were pouring their cross-fires of shot and
shell into the cloud-works of the lower heavens.
Wolverhampton, on the extreme left, stood by her black
mortars which shot their red volleys into the night.
Coseley and Bilston and Wednesbury replied bomb for
bomb, and set the clouds on fire above with their lighted
matches. Dudley, Oldbury, Albion, and Smethwick, on
the right, plied their heavy breachers at the iron-works
on the other side; while West Bromwich and distant
Walsall showed that their men were standing as bravely
to their guns, and that their guns were charged to the
muzzle with the grape and canister of the mine. The
canals twisting and crossing through the field of battle,
showed by patches in the light like bleeding veins.
There were no clouds except of smoke over the scene;
but there were large strips of darkness floating with
crimson fringes into the red sea, on which the white
moon rode like an ermined angel of peace.

For all that glowing empire was peace. Peace has her
battle-fields as well as war, and this was her Waterloo.
Here she had mustered fifty regiments of her swart
veterans, armed with all the weapons of her exhaustless
arsenal – with Minié picks and Schneider hammers, and
file-edged swords that cut at their sides. Those great-
mouthed mortars, belching forth globes of fire, were her
huge muzzle-loaders. And all this was the thick of one
of her great battles by night – only one of the three
hundred a year she fights in that dark valley with the

elements. What are all the mines and counter-mines of war compared with the hundreds her sappers have dug fifty fathoms below the visible surface of this battle scene! Where or when did war ever dig such deep trenches or fill them with such battalions, or bring its land and sea forces into action with such united and concentrated power! Here were 10,000 pickmen sending up from holds, 500 feet deep, cartridges for loading the cupola cannon that were reddening the night with their blaze. Here were the deck or surface brigades standing to their batteries, and making each other look like the old picture of *The Defence of Gibraltar*. There were the Brades Works at the right centre of the line, discharging a thousand spades, hoes, trowels, and pruning-hooks an hour. Further down toward Birmingham there was a well-manned battery that poured forth a shower of bolts and nuts; and Chance's great fortress was all ablaze, with its hot fountains sending out acres of glass to be parcelled into panes of every size. To the right of us, to the left and front of us, the whole amphitheatre was in close action, working out for the world the thousand small arms of peace – cotton hoes for Brazil and harpoons for Behring's Straits, and, for all the countries between, every tool used in honest labour.

The moon rode up with its bland face a little flushed over the scene, and the whole heavens were suffused with the red illumination, as if in honour of human industry. Then at that moment all the church bells of Dudley sent forth a shower of mirthful music, which pattered like silver rain against the purple garments of the night; and the widest streets and the market place of the town were doubly lighted, while the home-stars of all the houses up to the dark hilltops, looked like so many constellations, grouped like those we everywhere see by night. It was a scene worthy of a great poet's inspiration, and I hope his pen will some day do better justice to it than mine has done . . .

Having surveyed the Black Country from Dudley Castle, the tourist or visitor of the district should go immediately to another view-tower but a few miles distant, which commands a scenery of remarkable contrast with the iron region of fire and smoke. This is the Clent hills, in or rather over Hagley. It is doubtful if such a contrast can be found elsewhere in any country. It is a contrast which affects equally all the senses and faculties of enjoyment, and therefore all the more difficult to describe. From the Castle Hill of Dudley Nature has the under-hand, and from the crown of her head to the sole of her foot she is scourged with cat-o'-nine-tails of red-hot wire, and marred and scarred and fretted, and smoked half to death day and night, year and year, even on Sundays. Almost every square inch of her form is reddened, blackened, and distorted by the terrible tractoration of a hot blister. But all this cutaneous eruption is nothing compared with the internal violence and agonies she has to endure. Never was animal being subjected to such merciless and ceaseless vivisection. The very sky and clouds above are moved to sympathy with her sufferings and shed black tears in token of their emotion. When you have sated the eye with this scene, even without being affected with these sentimental fancies, just go over to Hagley and ascend the citadel hill of the Clent range, and you will see what Nature is where she has the upper hand, and breathes free from the asthma and rheumatism of the other condition. You see her in all the various dresses she has worn from her birth. On this furzy-breathing hill you see the simple and homely dress she wore when man first found her here two thousand years ago or more; and it is all redolent with the thymy odour that perfumed it then. But from this hilltop see what manner of robes she wears all along down into the deep, quiet valley and up its gentle, undulating slopes that meander to the distant horizon. The fingers of the Creator made the first garment for man, but He left to human hands the clothing of naked Nature; and these are the beautiful garments they have worked for her – dresses how varied of green and gold and of every tint the rainbow's pallet can blend and bring to the adornment! Here she reigns in all her peaceful and summer glory over a vast rural domain – a great picture of living and breathing beauty in an encircling frame of emerald, gilded by undulating lines of golden sky.

Stoke-on-Trent, Staffordshire

98. Arnold Bennett, *The Old Wives' Tale* (1908)

Those two girls, Constance and Sophia Baines, paid no heed to the manifold interest of their situation, of which, indeed, they had never been conscious. They were, for example, established almost precisely on the fifty-third parallel of latitude. A little way to the north of them, in the creases of a hill famous for its religious orgies, rose the river Trent, the calm and characteristic stream of middle England. Somewhat farther northwards, in the near neighbourhood of the highest public house in the realm, rose two lesser rivers, the Dane and the Dove, which, quarrelling in early infancy, turned their backs on each other, and, the one by favour of the Weaver and the other by favour of the Trent, watered between them the whole width of England, and poured themselves respectively into the Irish Sea and the German Ocean. What a county of modest, unnoticed rivers! What a natural, simple county, content to fix its boundaries by these tortuous island brooks, with their comfortable names – Trent, Mease, Dove, Tern, Dane, Mees, Stour, Tame, and even hasty Severn! Not that the Severn is suitable to the county! In the county excess is deprecated. The county is happy in not exciting remark. It is content that Shropshire should possess that swollen bump, the Wrekin, and that the exaggerated wildness of the Peak should lie over its border. It does not desire to be a pancake, like Cheshire. It has everything that England has, including thirty miles of Watling Street; and England can show nothing more beautiful and nothing uglier than the works of nature and the works of man to be seen within the limits of the county. It is England in little, lost in the midst of England, unsung by searchers after the extreme; perhaps occasionally somewhat sore at this neglect, but how proud in the instinctive cognizance of its representative features and traits!

Constance and Sophia, busy with the intense pre-occupations of youth, recked not of such matters. They were surrounded by the county. On every side the fields and moors of Staffordshire, intersected by roads and lanes, railways, watercourses and telegraph lines, patterned by hedges, ornamented and made respectable by halls and genteel parks, enlivened by villages at the intersections, and warmly surveyed by the sun, spread out undulating. And trains were rushing round curves in deep cuttings, and carts and waggons trotting and jingling on the yellow roads, and long, narrow boats passing in a leisure majestic and infinite over the surface of the stolid canals; the rivers had only themselves to support, for Staffordshire rivers have remained virgin of keels to this day. One could imagine the messages concerning prices, sudden death, and horses, in their flight through the wires under the feet of birds. In the inns Utopians were shouting the universe into order over beer, and in the halls and parks the dignity of England was being preserved in a fitting manner. The villages were full of women who did nothing but fight against dirt and hunger, and repair the effects of friction on clothes. Thousands of labourers were in the fields, but the fields were so broad and numerous that this scattered multitude was totally lost therein. The cuckoo was much more perceptible than man, dominating whole square miles with his resounding call. And on the airy moors heath-larks played in the ineffaceable mule tracks that had served centuries before even the Romans thought of Watling Street. In short, the usual daily life of the county was proceeding with all its immense variety and importance; but though Constance and Sophia were in it they were not of it.

The fact is, that while in the county they were also in the district; and no person who lives in the district, even if he should be old and have nothing to do but reflect upon things in general, ever thinks about the county. So far as the county goes, the district might almost as well be in the middle of the Sahara. It ignores the county, save that it uses it nonchalantly sometimes as leg-stretcher on holiday afternoons, as a man may use his back garden. It has nothing in common with the county; it is richly sufficient to itself. Nevertheless, its self-sufficiency and the true salt savour of its life can only be appreciated by picturing it hemmed in by county. It lies on the face of the county like an insignificant stain, like a dark Pleiades in a green and empty sky . . . You cannot eat a meal in decency without the aid of the Five Towns. For this the architecture of the Five Towns is an architecture of ovens and chimneys; for this its atmosphere is as black as its mud; for this it burns and smokes all night, so that Longshaw has been compared to hell; for this it is unlearned in the ways of agriculture, never having seen corn except as packing straw and in quartern loaves; for this, on the other hand, it comprehends the mysterious habits of fire and pure, sterile earth; for this it lives crammed together in slippery streets where the house-wife must change white window-curtains at least once a fortnight if she wishes to remain respectable; for this it gets up in the mass at six a.m., winter and summer, and goes to bed when the public houses close; for this it exists – that you may drink tea out of a teacup and toy with a chop on a plate. All the everyday crockery used in the kingdom is made in the Five Towns – all, and much besides. A district capable of such gigantic manufacture, of such a perfect monopoly – and which finds energy also to produce coal and iron and great men – may be an insignificant stain on a county, considered geographically, but it is surely well justified in treating the county as its back garden once a week, and in blindly ignoring it the rest of the time.

EASTWOOD, NOTTINGHAMSHIRE

99. D. H. Lawrence, *The White Peacock* (1911)

They decided to bury him in our churchyard at Grey-mede under the beeches; the widow would have it so, and nothing might be denied her in her state.

It was a magnificent morning in early spring when I watched among the trees to see the procession come down the hillside. The upper air was woven with the music of the larks, and my whole world thrilled with the conception of summer. The young pale wind-flowers had arisen by the wood-gale, and under the hazels, when perchance the hot sun pushed his way, new little suns dawned, and blazed with real light. There was a certain thrill and quickening everywhere, as a woman must feel when she has conceived. A sallow tree in a favoured spot looked like a pale gold cloud of summer dawn; nearer it had poised a golden, fairy busby on every twig, and was voiced with a hum of bees, like any sacred golden bush, uttering its gladness in the thrilling murmur of bees, and in warm scent. Birds called and flashed on every hand; they made off exultant with streaming strands of grass, or wisps of fleece, plunging into the dark spaces of the wood, and out again into the blue.

A lad moved across the field from the farm below with a dog trotting behind him – a dog, no, a fussy, black-legged lamb trotting along on its toes, with its tail swinging behind. They were going to the mothers on the common, who moved like little grey clouds among the dark gorse.

I cannot help forgetting, and sharing the spink's triumph, when he flashes past with a fleece from a bramble bush. It will cover the bedded moss, it will weave among the soft red cow-hair beautifully. It is a prize, it is an ecstasy to have captured it at the right moment, and the nest is nearly ready.

Ah, but the thrush is scornful, ringing out his voice from the hedge! He sets his breast against the mud, and models it warm for the turquoise eggs – blue, blue,

bluest of eggs, which cluster so close and round against
the breast, which round up beneath the breast, nestling
content. You should see the bright ecstasy in the eyes of
a nesting thrush, because of the rounded caress of the
eggs against her breast!

What a hurry the jenny wren makes – hoping I shall
not see her dart into the low bush. I have a delight in
watching them against their shy little wills. But they
have all risen with a rush of wings, and are gone, the
birds. The air is brushed with agitation. There is no lark
in the sky, not one; the heaven is clear of wings or
twinkling dot—.

Till the heralds come – till the heralds wave like
shadows in the bright air, crying, lamenting, fretting for
ever. Rising and falling and circling round and round,
the slow-waving peewits cry and complain, and lift
their broad wings in sorrow. They stoop suddenly to the
ground, the lapwings, then in another throb of anguish
and protest, they swing up again, offering a glistening
white breast to the sunlight, to deny it in black shadow,
then a glisten of green, and all the time crying and
crying in despair.

The pheasants are frightened into cover, they run
and dart through the hedge. The cold cock must fly in
his haste, spread himself on his streaming plumes, and
sail into the wood's security.

There is a cry in answer to the peewits, echoing
louder and stronger the lamentation of the lapwings, a
wail which hushes the birds. The men come over the
brow of the hill, slowly, with the old squire walking tall
and straight in front; six bowed men bearing the coffin
on their shoulders, treading heavily and cautiously,
under the great weight of the glistening white coffin; six
men following behind, ill at ease, waiting their turn for
the burden.

100. Alan Sillitoe, *Nottinghamshire* (1987)

A double row of houses down the hill known as 'The
Breach', where Lawrence spent most of his young life,
are more substantial than those of the street on which

he was born. I set off along the lane towards Coney Green Farm, and then on to Willey Wood Farm about a mile away, a gentle climb of two hundred feet. When I turn to look, Eastwood sprawls up the opposite hill, but in front there is green countryside, flesh that is sweetest when close to the bone, bucolic pockets described in precise and loving detail by Lawrence.

Going down the hill to Moorgreen Reservoir, the thousand yards by a main road is far enough in traffic to make me glad when I get to the bottom and turn again on to a footpath. In *Women in Love* the Criches at the nearby house give a party, and the lake is called Willey Water which was 'blue and fair, the meadows sloped down in sunshine on one side, the thick dark woods dropped steeply on the other'. During the festivities the daughter of the house, Diana, is drowned and when the water is drained she's found with 'her arms tight round the neck of the young man, choking him' – Dr Brindell who had tried to rescue her.

The woods look somewhat scruffy, the water metallic and half dead, and I only want to get into High Park Wood that packs the darkened east side. Silence is a luxury, to be sought for and, if necessary, endured like a refugee. The spirit bruises itself against noise. The multiple dinning machines of modern life box in any thought, however trivial. There is no way beyond the surrounding perimeter of engines. They roar overhead, blotting out the sky.

But not in this damp wood, not yet, only the crunch of a few dead twigs blown by the wind. The feet alone can get you to silence. Lodge gates channel me into damper air, and to a part of Nottinghamshire, on the eastern side of the Erewash Valley, that has its own special character. The emphasis of Lawrence has made it slightly unreal, and I find it necessary to put his works out of mind for a while, which is not more difficult than forgetting Hardy's novels while in Dorset.

I see the land freshly because it is finally more powerful than those who write about it. The land is there for people to walk over, and for writers to use like farmers, to harvest it into their books for the benefit of consuming readers, who reap its food for the soul as surely as a farmer produces earthly bread. But you don't know the land until you feel the texture under your boots, view the shades of green, notice the dullness, smell the bark and loam. Only then does it come to life.

Each generation of writers describes the countryside afresh so as to keep the appreciation of it alive. The people are related to the landscape, and change little, in spite of technology and the meretricious overlay of flash advertising. A writer relates people to their landscape, which thereby deepens the portrait of both. When this relationship vanishes from writing, art loses its centre.

Rainworth

101. J. Whitaker, *Scribblings of a Hedgerow Naturalist* (1904)

There is no inland county in England which offers more attractions to wildfowl than Nottinghamshire, and no place in this county more tempting to them than the Rainworth Valley with its numerous lakelets, secluded and sheltered, here they can enjoy quiet and food, without which no great quantity will remain. Dotted about in north Notts., and also in the forest district, are beautiful sheets of water, many of very considerable extent; some of them lie in great parks, and are rarely or ever disturbed; on these, large flocks of wildfowl congregate, and from them scatter over the ponds, and streams, of this favoured district, and sea-loving ducks are often tempted away from their haunts by the river Trent, which runs through the county from south-west to north-east, and forms a crystal highway from the silver sea. Ducks of all kinds love to follow the course of a big river, and thus are brought into places without which inducement they would never frequent. Once there, and finding food, and quiet, they attract others, till large companies collect, and form a delightful picture with their various colours, and curious call notes; but it matters not how quiet the retreat is, ducks always leave it at flight time to seek other quarters where to feed during the night, and return to the lake to rest in the day. It is during this flight and feeding time that they run the risk of being shot, and many a one returns no more. Rainworth being in a line of flight for the Rufford and Thoresby ducks, which come to these ponds and also pass over to Newstead and Annesley, gives one an opportunity, now and again, of shooting a couple or so, but the greater part fly well out of gunshot. One very clear night, some winters back, my son counted the ducks passing over, and on adding up, after the flight, we found two hundred and fifty had flown up the Valley, but not one within shot. There is no doubt there are not the quantity of ducks we had in the old days, but where one person shot then, now there are half a dozen; still, after a sharp frost, when the ice is melted, a lot of wildfowl arrive, and good sport is had. Three of us, on such a day, got forty-eight ducks on Rainworth Water. There is no greater satisfaction than in circumventing a duck, and no bird keeps its eyes and ears open wider than Anas Boscas, but when you do get him there is no bird on the list which is better eating. I well remember my father saying, 'I have lived seventy years, and I don't know now which is the better bird – a red grouse or a wild duck?' There is no regular decoy in Notts., but there are duck traps at Annesley, and Park Hall, in both of which many birds are taken during the season. It is quite wonderful the difference between a shot duck and a decoyed one: the juices run out through the shot holes, but are retained in the hand-killed bird, and when cooked it is as good again.

CROMFORD, DERBYSHIRE

102. Alison Uttley, *Country World* (1984)

I dipped my little china mug into the bucket as the girl hauled it out on to the flags, and I drank the sweet water.

The memory comes back to me, and I taste the exquisite coldness of that pure water as I sipped it with tiny eager shivers of delight, long ago. The home of my childhood, eternal and green, appears before my inward eye, and I live again in the brightly coloured circle of hills where I was born. No matter where I am, I seek unconsciously for resemblances to that beloved spot. A draught of spring water, an uncut hedgerow, a broken wall, these bring back visions so real that I cannot tell in which life I am living, the present, or the crystal-clear past, when as a child I ran with arms outstretched to catch the wind down the well-known grassy hillsides.

In that green country with its cool deep valleys and fantastic rocks, the narrow paths wind over the hills, linking village to hamlet; they cross streams and wander through woods with ancient names, a thousand intersecting paths, which have been used by the countryman from Saxon times. From the highest parts one can trace the grass-covered roads, along which no cart travels. There are curling hedges which hold protecting arms round odd little fields, and dark lichened stone walls cutting and dividing the green, and everywhere there are woods, beech woods, a flaming fire in the back end of the year, soft as clouds in Spring, oak woods, rough and sturdy, plantations of dark fir and tender larch, and mixed woods of many colours and sounds, sheltering fox and badger, woods full of enchantment.

A portion of that land I know so well that I can see the contours of the hills, the patterns of the fields, the irregularities of the diverse landscape as plainly as if they were painted before me. I know every flower-filled ditch, leafy hedge-bottom, and daisied bank, better than I know the lines of my own hand, for during all my earliest years my senses had no distractions from the daily scenes of wood and field and hillside. They became part of me, like the cold air I breathed, and I had no conception of other lands beyond our own farm and its neighbourhood, the countryside which filled the crumpled circle of England displayed before my infant eyes.

The Pennine Way

103. A. Wainwright, *Pennine Way Companion* (1968)

But yes, it is interesting: the variety and gradual changes of scenery make it so. Black moors alternate with green valleys. There are desolate hilltops but pleasant rivers too. The barren uplands give place to woodlands and forests, the moss and bog and heather of the heights to flowery meadows. One walks at first, starting from Edale, on a lofty causeway of gritstone between industrial towns, and it is an odd experience here, crossing the rough desolate moors, to meet the many trans-Pennine roads, busy with traffic: strips of tarmac, pulsating with noise and movement, thrown across the lifeless deserts of peat. Then follows a region of rolling foothills, still bare but less wild, to the pastoral peace of Airedale. There is a too-brief encounter with the fascinating limestone country of Craven, and moors again to the lovely reaches of upper Teesdale. Cross Fell, the summit of the Pennine Way, next dominates the route before being succeeded by further valley-walking. The Roman Wall is reached and inspires the imagination for a few miles before the spruce forests of the Border are entered. A long high traverse of the Cheviot hills completes the journey. On the way, one sees ancient castles and earthworks, many evidences of former mining activity, now derelict, and places with literary or historical associations. Interesting too are the changes in local dialects as you pass from one district to another, the way the brooks become becks and then burns, the different breeds of sheep from Peak to Border . . . Yes, it is all interesting, but weeping skies deaden enthusiasm, and fine weather is needed for a full appreciation of the Pennine Way. In any conditions, however, it will always be an invigorating exercise for the limbs, a complete change of environment, the perfect tonic for a jaded mind and a cure for urban depression. If you want to 'get away from it all', here, ideally, is the escape. You can't get further from the familiar than on the Pennine Way. You live for a time in a new world, and you forget the other.

CHESTERFIELD (DERBYSHIRE) TO SHEFFIELD (SOUTH YORKSHIRE)

104. J. B. Priestley, *English Journey* (1934)

Between Chesterfield and Sheffield, where the fields are preserved in the place-names and hardly anywhere else, the countryside looked very queer. Industrial man and Nature sing a rum sort of duet in those parts. I saw a row of sharply conical little hills that looked like a topographical freak until I came close to them and then realized that they were old slag heaps now almost entirely covered with grass. Further on we passed a hill that might have been brought from some other planet. It was black where the low rays of the sun were not faintly gilding it, and was everywhere deeply scarred and seamed. Not even passing through mountainous Nevada, where the landscape is only so much geology, have I seen so strange and desolate a hill as this; only of course Nature had not been at work here, for this was really a colossal slag heap, the biggest I have ever seen. We were now drawing near to Sheffield. There was some fine high country on the left, good Pennine stuff. The sun was low but still shining strongly and, with the increasing smokiness of the air, it made a strange chiaroscuro, as northern as high tea and the proper short 'a' sound. For one minute Sheffield, far below, looked like the interior of an active volcano. The road ran along a ridge. Down below, on the left, were rows and rows of little houses, acres of slanting and gleaming slates. We ran under the murky canopy and were in Sheffield.

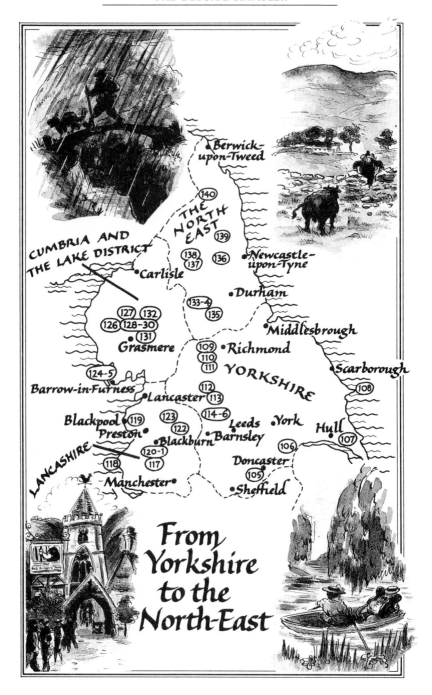

Berwick-
upon-Tweed

THE
NORTH
EAST

140

139

CUMBRIA AND
THE LAKE DISTRICT

138
137

136

Newcastle-
upon-Tyne

Carlisle

Durham

133-4

135

127 132

Middlesbrough

126 128-30

131

Grasmere

109

110

111

Richmond

YORKSHIRE

Scarborough

124-5

112

108

Barrow-in-Furness

Lancaster

113

114-6

Leeds

York

Hull

Blackpool 119

123

122

Barnsley

Preston

120-1

Blackburn

106

107

LANCASHIRE

118

117

Doncaster

Manchester

105

Sheffield

From
Yorkshire
to the
North-East

To Yorkshire

The savour of the south Yorkshire countryside is at its sweetest after a strong, bitter draught of south Yorkshire industry. Only when you have seen the hand of industrial man laid crushingly on the landscape, digging, twisting and bending it to his will, can you appreciate the resurgence of nature in the countryside beyond, moulded and made green by no influence more aggressive than the gently meandering River Don. There is no sudden transition from the grey to the green, the foul to the fair, as you leave the mighty manufacturing city of Sheffield on the railway line towards Doncaster. This is a landscape of heavy industry, coal and iron, that has spread and sprawled over seven or eight centuries, linking up the villages and towns into a vast mass of steelworks, coal mines, waste heaps, scrap yards and terrace after terrace of uniform brick housing. Even now, with heavy industry tramping its final retreat into history, it's a devastating and awe-inspiring sight.

The train leaves Sheffield station between black walls of stone under a succession of high black bridges. Black streets and black canals lie below the line as it emerges from the cuttings and tunnels to a wide view over the city. Functional industrial workshops still in use are soon left behind, and the great bowl of low-lying land is filled with acre upon acre of abandoned buildings and derelict ground. Outmoded steelworks buildings, some as tall and impressive as many a stately home, stand with shattered windows and walls broken into jagged gaps above scrap yards piled with unrecognizable heaps of metal. This central part of Sheffield was still open common land until the early nineteenth century, but after being enclosed it soon vanished under the shoulder-to-shoulder cutlery manufactories and steelworks. From the hillsides around the rim of the bowl the ranks of Victorian terraces look down on this jumble of grey, red and black. Newer houses have climbed almost to the top of Wincobank Hill, where Iron Age men built the strongest fort in south Yorkshire to defend the crossing of the River Don against attack from the south. These earthworks, visible from the train as green ledges in what remains of the open hillside, were strong enough to halt the advance of Roman soldiers trying to break through towards the northern hills. Now they jut from their vanishing hilltop, all but obliterated.

The train runs through a great blackened steelworks, brick sheds on one side and scrapheaps on the others, to come to Brightside station – an ironic name, enclosed as it is by tall black walls. Ironworking has been the lifeblood of Brightside for eight hundred years, its coal and minerals irresistible to industrial man. His latest achievement stands beyond, a great curving motorway bridge spanning river, roads and railway line. Two cooling towers make graceful shapes against the harsh angularity of steelworks sheds, their sides converging to slender waists and widening out again towards their crowns, welcome curves in a landscape of right angles and sharp corners. Storage cylinders, silos and tanks go by – a square mile of low modern sheds in green, red and brown – a green flash of municipal grass – a plunge again into a coaly, metallic no man's land of industrial waste. No plants can get a roothold or an ounce of nourishment from these sterile leavings that form miniature ridges, hills and mountain ranges beside the railway. 'C. F. Booth Ltd, Buyer of all Grades of Scrap Metals' says the sign on the scrapyard, where a skeleton of girders frames an enormous magnetic crane. Five thousand battered car bodies lie roughly piled in stacks of ten at a time, fodder for Mr Booth or his descendants.

These eastern outskirts of Sheffield have crushed their underlying landscape between industry and waste, and as Sheffield blurs seamlessly into Rotherham the grip grows ever tighter. Rotherham's blackened church spire marks the start of three miles of industrial dominance and decay, centred around the vast steelworks at Rawmarsh. A bleak name for a bleak and desolate place. The train rattles past broken segments of wall sprayed with graffiti – cheerful in silver and orange aerosol paints against the red, black and grey – to thread its way, one of a tangled web of lines, through the Rawmarsh complex. Grey sheds with peaked roofs and forbidding lines of brick office buildings on this side of the line; on the other, spotlights high against the sky on skeleton legs, rusty railway waggons on sidings, cranes, chimneys of metal with spiral twists in them, chimneys of brick two hundred feet tall, more enormous sheds, miles of bright yellow pipework, water towers up on stilts above the roofs of the works. And a great desert of slag from the furnaces, dull red and lifeless, the unwanted excretions of the industry, incapable of being used even by the ingenious creators of this steelworking megalopolis.

Then it's all over. The train leaves Rawmarsh behind, and the hills close gradually in. The blackened earth is clothed in green grass, woods appear on the hillsides, and the Don comes close in to the railway. The river has been crawling unnoticed nearby all the way from the centre of Sheffield, but out here in the green it reclaims its place at the heart of the landscape. Poplars grow tall and dark on the banks and along the sides of streams coming down the hill slopes to join the river. Swinton with its estates of semi-detached brick houses, Mexborough on its rise of ground and the rapidly greening colliery site at Conisbrough are still there to break up the rural landscape, but the staggering, unsettling industrialism of Rotherham and Sheffield is only faintly echoed here. At Conisbrough the tall castle keep stands dramatically up from the trees, reflected in a wide bend of the Don. Disembarking here one can walk the riverside footpath for miles, through orchid woods and round the edge of ponds teeming with ducks, songbirds and butterflies, undarkened by the least shadow of the enormities left behind.

As England's largest county, and one that experienced more widely than any other the apocalyptic changes brought about by the Industrial Revolution, Yorkshire contains within its borders vast tracts of countryside entirely overwhelmed by industry. These have given rise to their own literature, rooted in those abruptly created and all-consuming towns and cities: writing which falls outside the scope of this book. The country writers of Yorkshire have had equally striking and completely separate materials to work with – the county's great range of landscapes of moorland, coastline, hill and dale, where the influence of industry lies only lightly or not at all. The following chapter takes an anticlockwise swing east and north, then west and south, picking a few choice fruits from Yorkshire's laden tree of country writing.

One or two southerners are allowed their say – J. Wentworth Day with a funny story from the country of the inland River Humber, H. V. Morton another on the cliffs at Flamborough Head. But it is Yorkshire men and women, by birth or by adoption, who dominate these selections, as every self-respecting Yorkshire man and woman would agree is only right and proper. Through the succession of glorious limestone dales they take us, and down into the gritty moorland corridor between West Yorkshire and Lancashire: loose-living Charles Fothergill in Wensleydale in 1805, on his way to dally with his lady friend; James Herriot blundering in a cowshed somewhere between Wensleydale and Coverdale; J. B. Priestley and David Pownall recording these uplands in their grimmest aspects; John Hillaby spurning the grit in favour of the lime. And to bring the perambulation of Yorkshire to a close, Emily Brontë in the country of *Wuthering Heights*, all but swept away by the naked emotion with which those sombre moors flooded her.

River Don, South Yorkshire

105. John Tomlinson, *Rambles Twenty Miles Round
Doncaster* (19th century)

Those who love to glide through the water in a light
trim boat (and who does not?) would greatly enjoy the
excursion from Sprotborough to Conisborough. Having
secured the attendance of two amateur oarsmen, who
made up by earnestness what they lacked in skill, and,
taking myself an easy position at the helm, we started
one bright morning in June from the Copley Arms. As
we pushed off into the middle of the stream a hundred
little songsters from Engine Wood and Sprotborough
plantings hailed us with musical honours, while on the
green bank two or three kine and a young colt cocked
their tails and ran as if determined to herald our
progress. If you wish for rosy health and a light heart,
get up in the morning early, and pay your respects to
Nature. The fresh young breeze kisses your cheek softly;
the half awakened shrubs and flowers as they nod in
recognition, shake from their crest a glittering dew-
drop, while old King Sol, beholding the joy of his realm,
beams smiles all around. (Here the reader must utter a
great sigh and think of dyspeptics and the nightmare.)
Our little boat appeared like the nautilus on the stream
in comparison with surrounding objects. On the left,
rising almost perpendicularly from the river to the
height of eighty feet, was Levitt Hag, studded here and
there with large conical lime-kilns, and small but clean
cottages; to the right is a pleasing diversity of forest and
meadow, with the Pot-ridings and Ward Wood skirting
the bank for a considerable distance. After many a long
and strong pull we came within a short distance of
Conisborough. That first view of the castle from the
river will not easily pass away from the memory. Your
attention is riveted to the magnificent old round keep,
looking as if it had grown out of that huge earthwork
which slopes somewhat abruptly down nearly to the
river. Having parted with the boatmen and crossed a
garden to the ancient ferry, a boy, by the aid of a rope

thrown across the weir, landed me in his boat on the opposite side, and from thence I climbed the hill to the castle grounds. A beautiful green carpet covers the entire court-yard, where for centuries tramped the feet of armed men, while moss and ivy flourish luxuriantly on the fragments of huge walls. I sat down by the old grey keep, and, amid the stillness and desolation, thought on the strange vicissitudes with which it is associated.

RAWCLIFFE

106. J. Wentworth Day, *Sporting Adventure* (1937)

Picture a fiery-faced gentleman, in a cutaway, green, brass-buttoned shooting coat; curly brimmed, bell-topped hat; thigh gaiters buttoned with innumerable buttons armed with a gun five feet long, astride a bull on a Yorkshire grouse moor. Ahead of this terrific Nimrod stalks a large black sow. Suddenly the sow stiffens in the heather. Its snout and head straighten out like a poker. The pig stands rigid. The bull and its rider draw nearer.

On the instant, from the heather bursts a covey of grouse like a bomb-shell. The sportsman raises his ferocious piece, an instant's deliberate aim, and the gun vomits a yard of flame and a bellying cloud of smoke. A grouse drops to the shot.

This is no Bertram Mills nightmare. It is a fact. It happened, to be accurate, about a hundred and twelve years ago. The rider of the bull was the eccentric Mr James Hirst, of Rawcliffe. He had trained the pig to point grouse as accurately as any dog. And he went hunting on the bull. The habit arose from his strenuous objection to paying taxes. Horses and dogs in those days were heavily taxed. Bulls and pigs were not. Hence the odd, but frequent, sight of a gentleman in ratcatcher attending meets of the Badsworth Hounds on a bull and shooting grouse over a pig.

RIVER HUMBER, EAST YORKSHIRE

107. Winifred Holtby, *South Riding* (1936)

Lydia hauled up the basket, then scrambled herself to the top of the bank and looked.

She stood, shading her eyes, the wind whipping her bare legs, her arms, her hair, and she looked across the salt-marsh and the Leame to Lincolnshire.

It was here at last, the river that she knew so well from a distance, and yet had never till now approached.

A fleeting gleam of silver, the lights on a ship, a word from an old gossip – she knew the Leame all right.

But here it was at last, spread wide before her.

Immediately below the bank stretched the grey-green carpet of salt-marsh. Sea-samphire and sea-aster grew there, and the coarse puffing sea-meadow grass; here and there lay pools blinking up into the vivid blue of the sky; an overflow stream rounded into a pond, and beyond the pond lay more marsh, and beyond the marsh another, lower bank, the last rampart of the county, and beyond the bank the bold silver sweep of the Leame itself.

It was high tide. From Lincolnshire to Yorkshire the Leame filled its banks. Its waters, five miles wide, lapped against the little rivulets and indentations, sucking and gurgling. A tramp-steamer went chugging out to sea, sending ripples to beat against the mud. A motor yacht, light as a bird, swished down the smooth wide water.

'Oh!' cried Lydia, and though she had always known the sea, grew aware of a new and strange exhilaration, as though she had been released from a captivity.

FLAMBOROUGH HEAD

108. H. V. Morton, *The Call of England* (1928)

An idiot desire to collect a guillemot's egg with my own hands possessed me, so that in a rash moment I asked to be allowed to go over the top. To my surprise and horror, he agreed. I could not draw back.

He took off his gear and they strapped me into it, placed the tin hat on my head, and the bags over my shoulders. They tied the rope to the waist-ring, put the guide-rope in my hand, and told me to 'let myself go' over the edge of the cliff.

I found myself on an almost perpendicular ledge of rock. I braced myself against it with my feet as I hung passionately with both hands to the rope, so that I was at right angles to the rock. I felt like a fly on a ceiling. Above me was the rough grass edge of the cliff against the sky and the voices of the egg-gatherers shouting to me: 'Let yourself go!'

My problem, which was one of gravity plus pure funk, was solved for me when something gave way, leaving me swinging at the end of the rope, kicking the cliff for a foothold. Voices from the sweet world above said that I was 'getting on fine!'

All might have been well had I not struck a piece of chalk with my foot, which broke away when I was in a position to follow its descent. I watched it fall, down down, down, through a flight of gulls, through a cloud of kittiwakes, down, down into the distant steaming sea. That second's glimpse collected all my nerves in the pit of my stomach. Death did not seem so awful as the possibility of swinging or spinning or turning turtle. A few gulls, attracted by my plight, screamed round me in the most insulting way. The rope seemed a live and evil thing, ready to give to me the instant I had the pluck to take a downward step. That moment never came!

Why do some people rush into rash situations? I felt angry with myself. Why did I want to rob the gentle guillemot? The view downward between my feet was simply appalling: a wall of chalk falling sheer beneath me for three hundred feet, and then the steel-grey sea hissing over spikes and needles of rocks. I gave a frantic pull-up signal and felt the rope tighten as they hauled. Four amused faces greeted my eggless return.

'Well,' said the chief hauler-up, 'you're not the first that's turned back by a long way!'

'Thanks,' I said bitterly, as I unbuckled myself in an agony of self-contempt.

Then Sam Leng took the harness and slipped over the cliff nimbly, nervelessly, returning in fifteen minutes with a sack full of the loveliest blue-green and black eggs you have ever seen. At that moment I would rather have done that than have received a chestful of decorations.

SWALEDALE, NORTH YORKSHIRE

109. J. S. Fletcher, *The Enchanting North* (1908)

Beyond Reeth, Swaledale becomes a country to be explored with some determination and courage. There is little to see at Reeth itself except its fine and capacious green, but it boasts a good inn, with excellent accommodation, and is a good centre for exploring the surrounding district. Here one is really out of the world. Railways seem to be a thousand miles away, and one is apt to forget that the telegraph wire has found its way into these solitudes – lingering here, indeed, one has no wish to know that the *way* has been found. It is true that, after all, one is not so far from the swift means of returning to any point of the compass – it is only five miles over the hills to Redmire in Wensleydale, and only ten back to Richmond. But looking about one at the hillsides, pitted with the scars from whence human hands have dug forth lead for at least two thousand years, and at the valleys, fading away amongst the mountains, and apparently devoid of all but the scantiest evidences of human life, one can easily, with the aid of a little imagination, believe that one has come into a solitude which nothing ever has disturbed and nothing can ever transform.

Yet there is life in these desolate regions, and life which is clean, and sweet, and health-giving and honest. The people of the dales, far removed as they are from towns and cities, are of a sturdy mind, a solid independence, and they possess an intelligence and a sharpness of wit and perception which will often put the mere townsman to shame. Only they themselves know what it is to live in these regions, where amidst wide solitudes a village or a hamlet is found –

> Each with its little span of sky
> And little lot of stars—

but their surroundings breed in them a loftiness of character which soon becomes apparent to the stranger who goes amongst them. Beyond Reeth, in the far reaches of Upper Swaledale, beyond even Muker and Keld, far away in the most desolate reaches of wild scenery, where one hears nothing but the voice of a shepherd, the bleating of sheep, the distant barking of a dog or the cry of a bird, one comes across men who, dwelling far away from where men are crowded together, are yet sharp of wit, clear of mind, sure of speech. And for that reason, if for no other, any man who wishes to know the *spirit* of the Dales should think not only of the easily accessible and historic parts of them, but should penetrate to their very deepest recesses.

WENSLEYDALE

110. Charles Fothergill, *Diary* (1805)

111th Day: SEP. 6 1805

This day I wished to go to Richmond on several accounts: I wished to see Fryer and J . . . and I fell short of large drawing paper and pencils and some other articles. It rained however so hard in the morning that I could not go 'till after dinner. It was fine when I sat out, but by the time I reached Askrigg it came on the most tremendous thunder storm I was ever out in: the thunder crackled about my ears and echoed in the mountains with the most tremendous and awful sounds, and the lightning played about my head and ran along the road before me in a terrible manner. I never was so immediately *in* a storm of this terrific kind; for two miles I was in minutely expectation of being struck; birds were knocked down, cattle affrighted almost to death and the people who were riding Askrigg boundarys galloping for their lives. I thought myself as safe walking along as under shelter, I therefore took little notice of what a woman told me who stood at the door of a house as I passed: 'You'l surely be lost if you go along' cried she. 'I hope not' thought I and went forward. Soon after I passed Nappa I had the pleasure to find I had left it all behind me. I felt thankful for my preservation and walked cheerily along.

I passed through Carperby: it appears to have been a market town; there is a market cross in the middle of its single long street that appears ancient; there is yet an annual fair held here: nearly all the market places in this contry have crosses. A little beyond, fine view of Bolton Castle: appearance of entrenchments by the road; Redmire, a pint of ale at the public house, a pretty girl, knitters. Scarth nick; the exquisite view from the top; 'tis surely unequalled for grandeur as well as beauty: in this view there is all that can be wished in a landscape; wild moors only partly enclosed to the halfpenny house; felt a pleasure in drinking a pint of ale here because my grandfather so much frequented it: wild and quick walk of five miles in the dusk of the evening over high moors to Richmond: heard the Golden Plover pipe frequently as I passed: vast deal of wet, dirty and uncomfortable. On my arrival at Richmond do not like the appearance of the quarters recommended to me by my deary: seek out Fryers and lodge there.

Swaledale/Coverdale

111. James Herriot, *It Shouldn't Happen to a Vet* (1972)

My last call was just outside Darrowby and I could hear the church clock striking a quarter past seven as I got stiffly out of the car. After my easy day in the service of the government I felt broken in mind and body; I had to suppress a scream when I saw yet another long line of cows' backsides awaiting me. The sun was low, and dark thunder clouds piling up in the west had thrown the countryside into an eerie darkness; and in the old-fashioned, slit-windowed byre the animals looked shapeless and ill-defined in the gloom.

Right, no messing about. I was going to make a quick job of this and get off home; home to some food and an armchair. I had no further ambitions. So left hand on the root of the tail, right hand between the hind legs, a quick feel around and on to the next one. Eyes half closed, my mind numb, I moved from cow to cow going through the motions like a robot with the far end of the byre seeming like the promised land.

And finally here it was, the very last one up against the wall. Left hand on tail, right hand between legs . . . At first my tired brain didn't take in the fact that there was something different here, but there was . . . something vastly different. A lot of space and instead of the udder a deeply cleft, pendulous something with no teats anywhere.

I came awake suddenly and looked along the animal's side. A huge woolly head was turned towards me and two wide-set eyes regarded me inquiringly. In the dull light I could just see the gleam of the copper ring in the nose.

The farmer who had watched me in silence, spoke up.

'You're wasting your time there, young man. There's nowt wrong wi' HIS bag.'

MALHAM TARN

112. David Pownall, *Between Ribble and Lune* (1980)

Malham Tarn has many faces – from my own, peering over the side and looking back up at me – to the brawling, foam-flecked waves which are flogged up by the north-west and north-east winds. From a day spent in limpid sunshine when the surface is as still as a mirror to the grey saw-blades of storm-water, is a transformation seldom seen in the course of one day, but the impression of altering moods moved by a random force is a strong one, strong enough to give the lake a human feel.

Observing the cycles of high spirits, melancholy, dullness and inspiration in oneself – suffering the perpetual struggle to diagnose and understand the reasons for them is enough to make a bond between that changing face of hydrogen and oxygen, remorselessly dead up there in the hills, and life. If Wordsworth was trying to say anything other than that God is Nature, then this, I think, was his thesis. We are conscious of eternal parallels between our spiritual states and the physical expressions of the world's motion, chemistry and constitution. Malham Tarn is not an eye, a soul, a woman. But it is *me* and that metaphor is true, not a device of literature. We influence each other beyond the dispute between the animate and inanimate. Nature is an individual to each.

I took my agent up to the lake with my son on a day when I should have known better than even to attempt to fish. After an hour of skulking round the shores to avoid the wind which was howling over a saddle of ground to the north-east, I decided that we should cross the lake. When we got to the opposite shore, the waves were starting to come aboard and I headed for the boat-house, having agreed that we must give up. I could not get the boat back, but remained stuck off one promontory, heaving away until my arms were cracking. My son took an oar and we tried together but got nowhere.

It was the only time that I have noticed even a
scrap of fear in myself up there. It was not fear of
drowning, or even of wrecking the boat, it was fear of
resistance. All those immovable, ageing, circling
nightmares in my own psyche – death, desertion, despair – were pouring into the boat, racing over the
tormented scene, blocking us off. It was that bond
between what was in me and what was out there
which made the oars sink deeper into the waves and
bend my back to break the wind's deadlock on that
corner. When we got to the boat-house I looked back
out at the grey storm and hated it.

WHARFEDALE

113. J. B. Priestley, *English Journey* (1934)

In the afternoon we returned down Upper Wharfedale,
but then cut east and climbed up to Blubberhouses. The
sun had disappeared; the day was cloudy and sagging,
with imminent signs of rain. Now we got that other and
familiar aspect of these moorlands, seeing them as a
high, grey desolation, with the winds shooting over
them, threatening to shatter the heavy clouds. The long
stone walls and the few stone buildings did not suggest
man's handiwork or his presence, but seemed to be
natural outcroppings of the grey rock. Not a soul was
about. A few birds went beating up against the wind
and crying desolately, that was all. The country was
Thibetan in its height and emptiness. It was impossible
to believe that in half an hour we might have dropped
into Harrogate and taken the waters. I tried to remember exactly where it was that, years before in this
region, I had stumbled upon a genuine deserted village.
There it was, on the moors, with two small factories and
several rows of cottages, and completely uninhabited.
(Something, I believe, went wrong with the water
supply.) I remember eating my sandwiches inside one of
the cottages, from which most of the roof was gone. I
stared at the gaping doorways and the grass-grown

street; and not even a mouse stirred. No village I saw in the war area, I think, gave me the same complete picture of desolation as that empty shell of a moorland village did. And it was somewhere in these parts, though behind what misty ridge I could not remember. The sagging clouds broke, and it rained good and hard, as it always does up there.

BRONTË MOORS, WEST YORKSHIRE

114. John Hillaby, *Journey Through Britain* (1968)

Fortunately for poets and those who like to walk about in the open air, the beauty of landscape is not something that can be reduced easily to basic geology or a few ready-wrapped phrases about what places are used for. Preference and prejudice creep in. Mine are apparent in a love of limestone and a dislike of grit, two geological bed-fellows as unlike as chalk and cheese. You get the feel of both from the Wolf Stones on the edge of the Brontë moors.

Stand on that gritstone and look north and you are looking into limestone country. It looks far brighter than the moors to the south. The acid squelch is replaced by wholesome springy turf, the cotton-grass by fescues that sheep enjoy. Flowers abound in the hedgerows: water-avens, wild garlic, Solomon's seal, and lilies-of-the-valley; the bird song is clamorous and the local inhabitants talk about something more interesting than the probability of rain.

As if to impress you with the sparkle and variety of their native stone, the dalesmen patch their pale walls with black splintery chert, full of the remains of ancient sponges; the shepherds push in bits of quartz-like grit and grey-brown slabs of Uredale sandstone a-glitter with mica and you feel there is something more than utility in those bright mosaics.

'Wuthering Heights' (Top Withens)

115. Emily Brontë, *Wuthering Heights* (1847)

Wuthering Heights is the name of Mr Heathcliff's dwelling. 'Wuthering' being a significant provincial adjective, descriptive of the atmospheric tumult to which its station is exposed in stormy weather. Pure, bracing ventilation they must have up there at all times, indeed: one may guess the power of the north wind, blowing over the edge, by the excessive slant of a few stunted firs at the end of the house; and by a range of gaunt thorns all stretching their limbs one way, as if craving alms of the sun. Happily, the architect had foresight to build it strong: the narrow windows are deeply set in the wall, and the corners defended with large jutting stones.

116. Emily Brontë (1818–48)

High waving heather, 'neath stormy blasts bending,
Midnight and moonlight and bright shining stars;
Darkness and glory rejoicingly blending,
Earth rising to heaven and heaven descending,
Man's spirit away from its drear dongeon sending,
Bursting the fetters and breaking the bars.

All down the mountain sides, wild forests lending
One mighty voice to the life-giving wind;
Rivers their banks in the jubilee rending,
Fast through the valleys a reckless course wending,
Wider and deeper their waters extending,
Leaving a desolate desert behind.

Shining and lowering and swelling and dying,
Changing for ever from midnight to noon;
Roaring like thunder, like soft music sighing,
Shadows on shadows advancing and flying,
Lightning-bright flashes the deep gloom defying,
Coming as swiftly and fading as soon.

To Lancashire

The Pennine Way long-distance footpath is the grand high road from the West Yorkshire moors to the moors of east Lancashire. The Way is essentially a moorland route throughout its 250-mile length from Edale in the Peak District of Derbyshire to Kirk Yetholm on the Scottish border, always returning from its brief forays down to the civilization of valley towns and villages to sweeping miles of remote upland moor where loneliness and a (usually mucky) struggle against wind and weather are the keynotes. This twenty-mile stretch of the Pennine Way from the Brontë moors to Littleborough runs counter to the usual south-to-north direction of travel, but doing it this way round puts hill crests and far ridges constantly in front of the walker as an incentive, rather than the official direction's long, blank views of brown and black moor slopes. The roll of the hills gives you an effortless sense of momentum as they lead from the walled sheep-farming highlands of Yorkshire down to the first of those Lancashire cotton towns that run together to melt into the gigantic sprawl of the Manchester–Bolton conurbation.

From the stark ruins of Top Withens farmhouse (Emily Brontë's 'Wuthering Heights'), the Pennine Way turns its back on a twenty-mile panorama over the moors each side of the valley of the River Worth, and runs south-west along the length of Walshaw Dean reservoir to cross the head of the Hebden Water into a wild stretch of moorland beyond. Here I parted company with the Way, preferring the beautiful path under the trees beside the Hebden Water and below the

knobby outcrops of Hardcastle Crags. Dippers were bobbing their white breasts and flirty tails on stones in the middle of the rushing water as I walked down past the abandoned bulk of Gibson Mill, at one period in its eventful history a dance-and-dine bolthole for Hebden Bridge folk.

Hebden Bridge was a smoky old hole only a few years ago, its cloth factories lying at the bottom of the Calder Valley beside road, railway and canal under a permanent pall of smoke. But times have moved on. These days the gritstone of the buildings, oxidized to black through the years, has been cleaned up, and the town sparkles in creamy-white salubrity. Suddenly it has become the place to settle for fresh air and a country atmosphere, many of its old-fashioned shops and mill buildings converted into smart restaurants and boutiques.

Above the mills and the four-storey terraces piled one above another up the hillsides is a steep climb through trees to the farm at Old Chamber, where semi-derelict barns in unregenerate black gritstone look down on the town from blank windows and empty, arched doorways. These high farmsteads, clinging to the sharp edges of the moors, were the setting for fervid scenes of instant religious conversion in the eighteenth century, when an unquenchable flame of Methodism swept across the Yorkshire hills. Itinerant preachers would gather congregations into barns and out-houses all over the area, and whip them into religious ecstasy – 'I'm saved, brothers, I'm saved!' – with scorching oratory. Though the barnfuls of workers entering grace on their knees are long gone, there is still nothing of compromise about these remote settlements, many of them recently driven out of business and into dereliction by the harshness of conditions up here in the teeth of weather that still bites ferociously in winter.

A paved cart track between stone walls leads past Kilnshaw Farn, where every window and shed door frames a snarling dog. Strangers don't belong in this plateau on Erringden Moor; they hurry past the dour black farms as quickly as they can, keeping their ankles beyond the stretch of the dog chains, to climb up the hillside to the monument on Stoodley Pike. Shaped like a blunt black candle in a squat holder, the monument is a rather premature symbol of victory over Napoleon, put up as it was to commemorate his abdication in 1814, before his last great come-back. It dominates the forward view from the Pennine Way in both directions. I stopped to drink a long draught of ice-cold, sweet water from a spring by the path before reaching the monument and climbing its interior spiral steps in pitch darkness to the viewing platform. From here there is a stunning view to every point of the compass: long moors to the east and south, high hillsides patched with stone walls above the huddle of Todmorden to the west, and back to the north the lonely plateau of Erringden Moor with its widely separated farms and its parallel ribs of stone walls running together to dip into the top level of the Calder Valley.

There is no mistaking the course of the Pennine Way from the monument. It has been beaten out flat between the gritstone boulders by a million hiking boots, a sparkling white pedestrian high road that skirts a long escarpment looking down on Todmorden before striking off into broad, bare moorland. The shoulder of Coldwell Hill has been grooved by those tramping feet into a deep gully, and on the far side there are tall black standing stones to point the way forward to Warland Drain. This concrete channel brings water off the moors through a network of pipes, to fill the string of reservoirs built up here between the wars to serve the industrial valley towns of Lancashire. Along their rims – Warland Reservoir, Light Hazzles Reservoir, Blackstone Edge Reservoir – runs the Pennine Way in a windy silence broken only by bleat of sheep and clack of wheatears flashing their white rumps from stone to stone. Stoodley Pike and its monument slip out of sight behind a shoulder of Langfield Common, and ahead the far view is filled with the million red brick walls and grey slate roofs of giant Manchester. Somewhere here you cross the boundary from Yorkshire into Lancashire. No fortifications or border posts to mark the meeting of the two old enemies of the White and Red Roses – just white cotton grass and black outcrops of rock where rocking stones, undercut by rain and wind, perch on their parent cliffs.

The White Horse inn stands at the crossing point of

Pennine Way footpath and A58 trans-Pennine trunk motor road. 'Earned it?' smiled the landlord, glass poised under beer pump, as he surveyed my dusty boots and pack. I took my reward gratefully, and climbed on under Blackstone Edge where more weathered outcrops of gritstone make a jagged curve on the skyline. Here the Aiggin Stone, an ancient marker now tumbled beside the path, shows the meeting point of tracks from every direction. 'Roman Road' the map names the east–west track, a hollow in the grass paved with squared-off stones. Down the middle of the old moor road the builders – possibly Romans, more likely medieval engineers helping the trains of wool-laden packhorses over the hills – laid a gutter of shaped stones to carry storm water clear of the travellers' feet and hooves. It is a beautiful and lasting piece of workmanship, which leads down the hill and into the flanks of the Roch Valley. A path travels over fields and along a shady dingle to an old mill house sunk deep among overhanging oak trees at the bend of a lane, its water channel choked with yellow marigolds and purple rosebay willowherb. This is as perfect a remote country scene as one could imagine. But along the lane in Littleborough are the canal, the railway, the terraced houses and industrial mill buildings, still overlooked by high green hillsides, but bringing the first hint of the manufacturing monsters inter-twined just round the curve of the valley.

As with the country of the White Rose, so with that of the Red – man and his industries dominant in the south, moorland and rock outcrop striking ever wilder chords as one travels north. John Seymour paints a memorably stark picture of the industrial waste country near Wigan to get us on our way, while at the other end of Lancashire's landscape spectrum Edmund Vale steers us towards the Cumbrian mountains through a nineteenth-century Forest of Bowland virtually untouched by the outside world. In between are excursions westward to the pre-Industrial Revolution coast north of Liverpool, and to the 'Windmill Land' of the Fylde peninsula behind Blackpool, whose gentle charms Allen Clarke stoutly champions against the more impressive impact of mountain scenery. Phoebe Hesketh takes us hunting over the Rivington moors, a world away from the roaring bustle of the surrounding cotton towns, and we wallow with Harrison Ainsworth in the gothic demonology of accursed Pendle Hill.

BLACKBURN TO WIGAN, SOUTH LANCASHIRE

117. John Seymour, *Sailing Through England* (1956)

After leaving Blackburn one drops down six big locks and quickly comes into a very strange but beautiful countryside: what I remember as the 'Johnson's Hillock' country. (Johnson's Hillock is a flight of seven locks.) This is a country of small hills, but wild-looking. There are no stone walls; it is hedge country, and strangely stunted, wind-bent trees grow up among the hedges, and also stand about by themselves in the meadows. Occasionally one sees a ploughed field, a sight to which one has become unaccustomed in travelling over the Pennines; but most of the country is still grass. There are many copses and woods about, particularly in the steep little valleys, and often one sees an old, abandoned mill with its tall chimney, standing in solitude in some little bushy valley. A strange oasis of wild countryside among the mill towns: it reminded me more of some undeveloped country rather than of England. But of course, close to the northward, over the Ribble, was the Forest of Bowland: one of the fairly extensive areas of really wild country left in England . . .

The country remained much the same, and still beautiful in a wild, wind-swept way, until we began to get near Wigan. We then came into a landscape quite unearthly: it was as though we were on another planet, and a dead planet, perhaps Jupiter. As far as we could see clearly, down below us on our starboard hand was 'open cast' coal working. Giant draglines had pulled the ground into enormous heaps: heaps as big as natural hills, and of different colours, depending on whether it was top-soil or sub-soil overburden or what it was. The scale of the thing was colossal: the gashes made by the monsters were like Grand Canyons, the hills and valleys were like fantasic erosion in a desert. Beyond this gigantic upheaval of the earth, but in the far distance, we could see, through the smoke haze, a backcloth of chimneys, pit-head gears, strange erections of steel. We had arrived at the Wigan coal field.

Then we could see Wigan itself. It lay below us, on our starboard hand, stretching away to the westward down a gentle slope. Right at the bottom of the built-up area we could see the cooling towers of a great power-house, very high and yet well below our level. In between were thousands of streets of little brick-built terraced houses: thousands upon thousands of them. Wigan. Industrialism with the kid gloves off . . .

We called the country between Manchester and Wigan 'the flash country', because it is featured by huge shallow lagoons called 'flashes'. These are caused by subsidence brought about by extraction of coal under-ground, plus the pumping up of water from the mines. One sometimes sees the ruins of farmhouses or villages, sticking out of the water. The country was originally flat, but is now hilly in places owing to slag heaps: ancient slag heaps that have been eroded by the rains of a century or two. The canal is a phenomenon. It is raised high above the countryside by slag banks. But really high: one looks far down at the strange, coaly-looking, flashes, and the barren ground in between. The reason for this height is that the ground has sunk to that extent owing to subsidence, but the canal has been unable to sink. A level of water had of course to be maintained. And so barges are constantly at work carrying waste from the mines and dumping it on the canal banks, raising them ever higher to keep pace with the sinking land, and also dumping waste into the water! The latter process is necessary, because other-wise the walls of the canal would become too thin and high and would collapse.

From this high vantage point we looked over this wasted landscape, barren land and barren water, to the occasional clump of mine head gears, and mine buildings, with little pit villages nearby them, like villages out in some rocky desert. We stopped in one such mining village, and Sally did a drawing, while I went to the pub and found the same rough, kindly welcome from the off-shift miners that I had found in the Fox at Wigan. We carried on, and got to the Fox just after dark, and very pleasant it was to go in there too, and have a place made for me again by the cheerful coal fire, and be smiled at again by the lovely large landlady with the big ear-rings!

CROSBY, LANCASHIRE COAST

118. John Aiken, *A Description of the Country from 30 to 40 Miles Round Manchester* (1795)

The fea-fhore all along this coaft is remarkable for its flatnefs and number of large fand banks, highly dangerous to fhipping in ftrong wefterly winds, which are very prevalent here. The fea is fuppofed to abound with fifh, but few are taken, and thofe only with hook and line, the fifhermen either not poffeffing boats to go out to fea, or not chufing to truft themfelves on fuch a boifterous coaft. The kinds taken are chiefly cod, ray or fkaite, and flounders. The fhore is protected by a barrier of fand hills, held together by the *ftar* or fea-reed, the roots of which penetrate deep into the fands, and offer a fixed point round which they may collect. This ftar is ufeful for making mats, befoms, thatch, &c. but the law is very ftrict with regard to cutting it, fince when it is deftroyed, the hills are prefently blown away, and the lands behind overwhelmed by a moving fand. Thefe hills are in fome places half a mile broad, with feveral large openings or flats of land between them; and when in the midft of them, no defarts of Arabia can appear more dreary. There is little or no timber growing on the coaft; and a perfon, from obferving that all the trees to a great diftance up the country are, as it were, fhorn on the weft fide, and bent the oppofite way, would be apt to conclude that none would grow; yet it is certain that the country was once very woody, for in the mofs lands, large quantities of oaks are often found within a foot or two of the furface, lying with their heads all one way, as if blown over by a violent weft wind, or overthrown by a fudden irruption of the fea. A gentleman in this parifh got up near fifty loads out of one field, the wood moftly ordinary, and fit only for fuel. Sometimes trees of value are met with. The wood is ufually dark-coloured and of little durability, though often ufed for pofts and fencing. Many of the mofs lands are fo full of it that they are with difficulty ploughed. Along the fea-fhore, and near the Grange land-mark, are the ftumps of feveral large trees, which, by being in a line and at equal diftances, were undoubtedly planted: whence it would feem as if formerly either the climate was not fo rough, or the fea did not advance fo far, fince there would now be no poffibility of raifing trees in the fame fituation. It appears, however, as if the fea had formerly overrun a good deal of this country, from the ftrata of fea-flutch, mofs, fand, and fhells found in various parts; and the fea now again feems retiring.

FYLDE

119. Allen Clarke, *Windmill Land* (1916)

It is a pleasant walk on a fine day, in any season, to Staining. For after you leave Newton Drive – on the left are fields, part of Layton Hawes, two thousand acres of 'common land' once extending halfway to what is now St Annes, belonging to the people and 'enclosed' (plain English, 'stolen') by Act of Parliament in the eighteenth century, when so much common land was 'annexed' by the landed proprietors; and on the right the green upland on the crest of which is Whinney Heys Farm (scene of the last Sunday ramble I had through the fields with a certain little lad whose face I now see no more, and therefore precious in my memory) – you are in a prettily typical Windmill Land or Fylde lane: not the most beautiful sample of a Fylde lane, I admit; you must get farther afield for the fairest; but still one possessing the happy Fylde characteristics of green joy and azure benediction, and, above all, that delectably soothing magic, which you find nowhere else (anyhow, I don't), that emparadises the heart with restfulness and blesses the soul with peace. Because of this holy healing spell I call it the Felicitous Fylde. Not the Sublime Fylde, nor the Grand Fylde, for there is no wondrous wild nor romantic scenery, but the Felicitous Fylde, because it fills one with a quiet celestial feeling that mighty mountains with gorges and torrents, souvenirs of the violent volcanic epochs when the earth's crust was subject to tremendous and dreadful fiery agitations and earthquake disturbances, can never give. For all scenery retains more or less the character of its origin, and though the great mountains are now as still as statues, they mysteriously impress the soul of the beholder with vague thoughts and wonders of the turmoil in which they had birth, while such level pastoral plains as the Fylde, this Windmill Land, the gentle result of ages of sedimentary deposit, enchant the heart with the deliciously drowsing lullaby of musical waters and the droning murmur of tender tides.

Not that I would belittle the mountains. I love them, too, and enjoy them when in the mood for mountains, which have their thrill and glory for the climbing, adventurous soul. I love Lakeland, which is next door to Windmill Land – Lakeland magnificent for mountains, wonderful for waters, and dear to me in memories of steamer trips from Fleetwood and the beautiful railway ride from Barrow to Lakeside. But one does not wish to be climbing and toiling always, not even up the sublime ascents to Lakeland's cloud-capped peaks. There are times when one craves repose and daydream, and for such times there is no region like Windmill Land, with its green blossom-broidered leas, and flowery lanes, and level ways, and the easy-going windmills, eloquent preachers in their way – has it ever struck you how many parsons, with their arms going in

251

the pulpit, are like windmills? – of the gospel of country contentment and rural tranquillity.

RIVINGTON, LANCASHIRE MOORS

120. Phoebe Hesketh, *Rivington* (1972)

All this while hounds were in full cry. Tingling with excitement I galloped alongside the second whip. 'Game pony!' he shouted as we cleared a stream together. Halfway up the next hill they checked outside a spinney. Richard, flushed and elated, cantered up a few moments before the Master who roared at us: 'What d'you mean pushing in front like that? If those ponies are uncontrollable, they can damn well go home!'

Colonel Darley in the hunting field was not the same person as the well-bred and genial host of Moorside. At this moment, blotched with anger, he looked ready to burst with the effort of restraining himself from shouting 'Bloody Hell!' which, I suppose, is what we deserved.

Hounds were feathering, but they'd lost the scent. The huntsman ordered the whips to call them in; he'd decided to draw the side of the moor above Picaddilly – our countryside rejoices in resounding names – an extension of Rivington Moor and typical of the area: bumping miles of bracken and bent interrupted by peat-bogs and dashing streams. Unfeatured country crossed by the familiar walls of millstone-grit. Obediently we trotted behind with the stragglers; on the road now, through the village of White Coppice, last outpost on the fringe of a desolate moorland. The stony track rose steeply from the valley where rowan and birch trees border the stream. Up here only a scrubby oak or two and a scatter of thorns scratch a living.

Above and behind us to the left was a patch of forbidden country, about five hundred acres belonging to the Marshalls of Hailstorm Hall. Forbidden to the Hunt because Gerald Marshall, the only son, had once been ordered off the field. This incident had occurred the season his mother turned out on an aged police-horse guaranteed to display the maximum mettle with the minimum risk. Though terrified of hunting, Mrs Marshall wore the full regalia of top hat and veil with side-saddle habit. Violets, artificial eyelashes, and a wig completed her get-up. For her, a fall would have been unthinkable. Nevertheless, the unthinkable happened. (The Marshalls were generous subscribers.) Several gentlemen, including the Master, dismounted in their concern to smooth over the débâcle, and shield its indignity from curious eyes. After the two incidentes the Hunt took every possible precaution of avoiding Marshall territory.

For some reason on this particular day the hare made Hailstorm Hall her centre. Round and round the garden she ran, exuberant hounds on her scent – the first three couples soon to be joined by the whole pack which took up the line in unison. In vain, huntsman and whips strove to whip them off; helpless, Master and Field watched from the valley. Beyond recall they streamed around the threatening shoulder of Hailstorm Hill. The crescendo of hound-music, mounting to a Wagnerian chorus of triumph thrilled us who heard it with horrid foreboding. Suddenly, like a whip, a shot cracked the air. 'Now we're for it!' the Master spoke to Aubrey who had just ridden up. Three more shots in rapid succession were followed by ominous silence. Rigid in our saddles we stared up the bleak hillside.

After a long interval three red coats bobbing in the midst of the pack were to be seen moving down the fell. The huntsman rode up to the Master and mumbled a few words in his ear. He whistled in dismay and turned to a knot of us gathered anxiously nearby. 'Old Marshall's shot three hounds. Killed two.' Enormous consternation moved the Field. To injure hounds in any way was sacrilege unheard of. 'I'll call up the RSPCA!' he hissed, grinding his teeth. 'Do him in for cruelty to hounds.'

Richard, who had been listening intently, turned to the impeccably plaited maiden beside him. 'But the

RSPCA is for cruelty to *all* animals. Couldn't we be had up for cruelty to hares?' The Plaited One who wore a Pony Club badge (she was a niece of the Master) stiffened her back. 'Don't be silly,' she replied sharply, 'hunting's quite different; it's a sport. To shoot hounds deliberately – well, I never heard of anything so revolting in my life!'

121. Phoebe Hesketh, *No Time for Cowards* (1952)

Northern Stone

Sap of the sullen moor is blood of my blood.
A whaleback ridge and whiplash of the wind
Stripping the branches in a rocking wood –
All these are of my lifestream, scoured and thinned.

Lack-leaf spring, monotonous days of wet
And grudging acres where the sheep live hard;
Unfeatured country where no weed can set
A yellow eye to light reluctant sward;
The untamed fell, spreading a matted mane,
Gold as a lion below the dying sun,
And cat-o'-nine-tails of the scourging rain
Companion me when every friend has gone.

And now the grape-bloom of a night-blue hill
Surrounds my spirit with a deep content;
O, profligate with stars, the night is still
Regenerate of all that day has spent.

Lurks no concession in this northern stone
And stubborn soil and shock-haired tufts of reed?
The few who thrive here feed upon the bone;
None look for plenty in the famished seed.

Yet, breath of my breath, they have me by the throat,
These dark, indifferent moors that take no care
For life resurgent in the starving root
And love undaunted by the hostile air.

Pendle Hill, North Lancashire

122. Harrison Ainsworth, *The Lancashire Witches* (1848)

By this time the sky was comparatively clear, but small clouds were sailing across the heavens, and at one moment the moon would be obscured by them, and the next, burst forth with sudden effulgence. These alternations produced corresponding effects on the broad, brown, heathy plain extending below, and fantastic shadows were cast upon it, which it needed not Richard's heated imagination to liken to evil beings flying past. The wind, too, lay in the direction of the north end of Pendle Hill, whither Richard was about to shape his course, and the shadows consequently trooped off towards that quarter. The vast mass of Pendle rose in gloomy majesty before him, being thrown into shade, except at its crown, where a flood of radiance rested.

Like an eagle swooping upon his prey, Richard descended into the valley, and like a stag pursued by the huntsman he speeded across it. Neither dyke, morass, nor stone wall checked him, or made him turn aside; and almost as fast as the clouds hurrying above him, and their shadows travelling at his feet, did he reach the base of Pendle Hill.

Making up to a shed, which, though empty, luckily contained a wisp or two of hay, he turned Merlin into it, and commenced the ascent of the hill on foot. After attaining a considerable elevation, he looked down from the giddy heights upon the valley he had just traversed. A few huts, forming the little village of Barley, lay sleeping in the moonlight beneath him, while further off could be just discerned Goldshaw, with its embowered church. A line of thin vapour marked the course of Pendle Water, and thicker mists hovered over the mosses. The shadows were still passing over the plain.

Pressing on, Richard soon came among the rocks protruding from the higher part of the hill, and as the

255

path was here not more than a foot wide, rarely taken except by the sheep and their guardians, it was necessary to proceed with the utmost caution, as a single false step would have been fatal. After some toil, and not without considerable risk, he reached the summit of the hill.

As he bounded over the springy turf, and inhaled the pure air of that exalted region, his spirits revived, and new elasticity was communicated to his limbs. He shaped his course near the edge of the hill, so that the extensive view it commanded was fully displayed. But his eye rested on the mountainous range on the opposite side of the valley, where Malkin Tower was situated. Even in broad day the accursed structure would have been invisible, as it stood on the further side of the hill, overlooking Barrowford and Colne; but Richard knew its position well, and while his gaze was fixed upon the point, he saw a star shoot down from the heavens and apparently alight near the spot. The circumstance alarmed him, for he could not help thinking it ominous of ill to Alizon.

Nothing, however, followed to increase his misgivings, and erelong he came in sight of the beacon. The ground had been gradually rising, and if he had proceeded a few hundred yards further, a vast panorama would have opened upon him, comprising a large part of Lancashire on the one hand, and on the other an equally extensive portion of Yorkshire. Forest and fell, black moor and bright stream, old castle and stately hall, would have then been laid before him as in a map. But other thoughts engrossed him, and he went straight on. As far as he could discern he was alone on the hilltop; and the silence and solitude, coupled with the ill report of the place, which at this hour was said to be often visited by foul hags, for the performance of their unhallowed rites, awakened superstitious fears in his breast.

Slaidburn

123. Edmund Vale, *The North Country* (1937)

If you study maps of the Pennines which are above a quarter inch in scale you will probably be struck by the number of successive districts marked on them as forests. Although the map perpetuates these names, most of them are obsolete, though not all. Blackburnshire was one of the royal forests, and it contained several lesser ones such as Rossendale, Trawdon, Bowland, and Amounderness. These are still shown on the map as names. Most of them are now bare moorland, but there is little doubt that in the nineteenth century the treed area in and about there was much greater. The Forest of Bowland is a semi-detached mass of the western Pennines which has escaped mention elsewhere.

It is a strange and desolate area with a singularly beautiful heart – at Slaidburn. I have vivid early recollections of this place when my father was rector of it for a short time. It was then reckoned to be the second largest parish in England. The fells stand round it on every side. To the north they range for about fourteen miles and there is no road through. To the west there is a long road to Lancaster (about twenty miles) through that sinister moorland pass called the Trough of Bowland about which, when I was a boy, tales of highwaymen were still alive, and folk-memory still dwelt on the herd of wild cattle that used to roam the old forest. Our nearest way out into the world was by a nine-mile drive over the fells in the rectorial wagonette which took two hours (for there were no motors anywhere then). What with sitting exposed in the eye of the weather while the wind howled over the moors and the sleet and rain swept upon you, and what with walking all the hills and then climbing back into wet seats, the journey was a grim undertaking in the winter-time.

But Slaidburn was a fairyland in the summer. The river Hodder poured into the village over a fantastic limestone staircase of petrified corals and then wound smoothly through green lawns and parklands. And it went on winding and winding through splendid country where the true wild maidenhair, the lily-of-the-valley, and the globe-flower grew, till it found a way through the wall of the fells by the wooded gorge of Whitewell. But in spite of its isolation (or because of it) Slaidburn was a hearty village in those days. The church was packed on a Sunday with the exception of the bell-ringers, who used their ancient prerogative to retire as soon as their work was done to the Hark-to-Bounty inn, in spite of all my father could say. And the village retained all its crafts of carpentry, smithing, knitting, and weaving. The silent, hardy man, Rushton the carrier, made a bi-weekly journey over the fells to Clitheroe with a wagon and team in all weathers to replenish the supplies of the village. Newspapers came with the mail-cart, but it was local gossip which counted for more than anything else. The outside world had very little to do with Slaidburn except at the time of a general election, and I believe one of the greatest sensations that had been known for a long time was caused through my father refusing to preach in a black gown in spite of the expressed wishes of the patron of the living that this Cromwellian custom should still be adhered to.

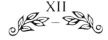

To the Lake District

They cancelled the train that was to have taken me from Lancashire to Lakeland. A two-hour gap yawned in the timetable. 'What's up?' shouted the lady with holiday suitcases to the railwayman on the opposite platform in Carnforth station. He shrugged, raised his eyes to heaven and scuttled back into his hutch. It set a costive tone for that evening's journey on the Furness Railway – stop, start, stop again and shrug. But with views as absorbing as those that spread outside the carriage windows, I did not in the least mind jerking along till sunset.

The looping railway round the foothills and estuaries of southern Cumbria was never intended for passengers. For several years after its opening in 1846 it dragged iron ore and other minerals out of the Lakeland hills to the iron foundries in the east. Only when tourism began to take off in a big way did the directors wake up to the enormous potential profits slipping year by year through their fingers. From Carnforth station on Morecambe Bay the trains of the Furness Railway rattled their way down, round and along the entire west-ward bulge of the Cumbrian coastline, hurdling the three great estuaries of Kent, Leven and Duddon on viaducts and embankments, creeping west and then north on an epic journey to such unglamorous, uncelebrated Lakeland outposts as Barrow-in-Furness, Corkickle, Whitehaven, Workington and Aspatria. The tourists kept clear of these coastal regions with their coal and iron mines, their un-prettified harbours, slag heaps and scars. That's very much the way things are today, though those who ignore this unfashionable fringe of the Lake District are missing half the flavour of Cumbria.

The replacement train that eventually limped into Carnforth was a filthy old thing, a thirty-year-old relic dug out of some back yard to make up the roster. I sat on a dusty seat by the smeared window and was thankful for our sluggish progress. Past the window in a slowly wheeling disc revolved mile behind mile of dead flat sand, glinting along its furthest edge with the tide now ten miles out and still retreating. Morecambe Bay uncovers one hundred and seventeen square miles of sand at low tide, and most of it was in view. Uncountable numbers of gulls and waders were busy at their evening feed, probing the sand banks, squabbling over shellfish in the pools and scanning the quickly flowing channel of the River Kent from the air. The bay is one vast, silver-streaked plate of sand, its edge below the railway track a bright green skirt of marsh dimpled with rounded hollows empty of water. At the apex of the bay Holme Island lies joined to the mainland by a grassy neck of marsh, its couple of acres smothered in trees and surrounded by a stout stone wall. A boy was fishing on one of the sandbanks, foolhardily far from the shore: the tide was at its lowest, but only the rash take chances with the treacherous tides of Morecambe Bay. Hundreds of travellers have been drowned down the years as they tried to make the crossing between Lancashire and Cumbria, losing their way among sinking sands that can swallow a horse and cart, or failing to pick the right crossing place of the Kent which is capable of switching its course from one side of the bay to the other. As I gazed out of the train window I remembered crossing the sands with the flamboyant and admirable official guide, Cedric Robinson, bare-footed and high-spirited, who shepherds adventurers across. Cedric surveys his route the day before a crossing, marking it with the traditional 'brobs' or little sprigs of laurel. Suffering fools gladly is just one of his many qualities – though not the fools who try the crossing on their own.

Silverdale and Arnside stations went by, shabby and unpainted, done down by years of neglect. Grange-over-Sands is a different case, though – neat little benches with squirrels and fruit clusters worked into their cast-iron ends, a packed platform of elderly couples and a chubby-faced teenage guard chaffing the old ladies and waving his green flag fit to burst. Grange is respectable above all, carefully preserved in Victorian gentility for devoted holidaymakers and residents who like it like that, a place that's proud of its total lack of similarity to fun-and-frolics Morecambe across the bay. What on earth would the immaculately capped and polished station masters of nineteenth-century Grange have made of the railway employee on the opposite platform who watched an old lady stagger by with a heavy bag in each hand without lifting a finger to help her, his belly bulging from an untucked shirt, scuffed trainers on his feet? He was whistling happily to himself, in a way Victorian railwaymen would never have dared to do.

Grange's immaculate houses peeped out among the trees as the train groaned away from a platform laden with disembarkers. At Kent's Bank station just along the line, no one came and no one went – the Adlestrop of Morecambe Bay. That empty platform had held the red-sweatered brass band of the *Lancashire Evening Post* when I had made the sands crossing with Cedric Robinson, trumpeting ashore the sponsored walkers who had been in the party to the blare of 'Oh We Do Like to be Beside the Seaside'.

Now the train crept across the waist of the Cartmel Peninsula, where (legend says) Irish monks landed in the Dark Ages looking for a place to settle. They had divine instructions to search until they found a valley that contained water flowing south. It was only after months of diligent searching that they thought of the place where they had originally come ashore. The remains of Cartmel Priory were hidden from the train, but the monks' retreat on Chapel Island out in Cartmel Sands stood bravely among its trees as we nosed out on to the viaduct across the twisting River Leven. The town of Ulverston lies on the far bank of this second broad estuary, a busy town with big square industrial buildings and tall works chimneys, well away from the shore and never properly in touch with tourism. There was a glimpse back to flocks of dunlin swooping over the Leven's sand banks, and then the train was running across the wide green interior of the Furness Peninsula that separates Leven and Duddon. In times past Furness was the political and financial centre of far-flung areas of the north-west of England, thanks to the influence of the monks of Furness Abbey. The Abbey ruins still stand, right beside the railway, tall dusky-red sandstone walls, arches and empty windows seen flickering by behind the trees; but these days all the power in the peninsula is wielded down at the southern end in the shipyards and engineering works of Barrow-in-Furness.

My view of Barrow from the carriage window was one of impressive strength – great cranes seen towering beyond the reservoir that holds water for the docks – and of sad squalor in the ranks of derelict, graffiti-daubed terraced houses that presented empty faces to the train. The Vickers yards and works are still going strong, said the Barrow-born lady in the next seat, but parts of the town are falling down through neglect. It had been built complete in twenty years between 1850 and 1870, bounced into being on a wave of optimism in shipbuilding and in steelmaking from ore dug locally at Dalton-in-Furness. A worker's town, provided with a handful of dignified civic buildings and fine wide streets, always struggling with the problems caused by its isolated position.

I learned more about Barrow from the taxi driver who took me north along the shore of the River Duddon's wide, curving estuary. The Furness Railway had delivered its final blow in Barrow station, from which my connecting train, tired of waiting for the straggler from Carnforth, had departed five minutes before we pulled in. The taxi driver, a Barrow man to his fingertips, was brusquely humorous about his home town, its neglect by successive governments, the decline in skill of its shipyards and the pride taken by the townspeople in their unfashionable, close-knit way of life outside the tourist orbit. 'If you haven't lived here all your life,' he told me emphatically, 'and served your time in that yard – well, you'll not understand the Barrovians'.

The River Duddon's shoreline of wading birds, green marshes and sand banks, backed by low hills, echoes those of both Kent and Leven. There is the same wide-roving view down to immensities of bare brown sand, the same feeling of spaciousness and openness. But the Duddon estuary is the place where coastal Cumbrian industry and Lake District majesty of landscape come together. To the south in Barrow loom enormous sheds housing the half-built skeletons of Trident nuclear submarines. At Askam-in-Furness a mile-long, jagged-spined peninsula of consolidated slag from former iron-smelting activities pokes a scabby finger out into the estuary – Askam Pier, the locals call it wryly, and the map solemnly records the name. But to the north as we drove up to Broughton-in-Furness the sharp blue waves of the southern fells of Lakeland filled half the sky, a truly exciting and heart-lifting prospect. Wordsworth's River Duddon at my side, and Wordsworth's Lake District peaks before my eyes. The taxi driver smiled, not entirely sardonically, at my gasp of pleasure and fixed, foolish grin. I gave inward thanks to the Furness Railway for its inefficiency. From a railway carriage window you can only look sideways. If I'd caught my connection in Barrow, I would have missed that wonderful great northward sweep from the workaday to the sublime.

No landscape in Britain has sharpened – or blunted – so many poetical nibs as the mountains of the Lake District. In the two centuries since people learned to see these tremendous heights and depths as magnificent, rather than as terrifying, everyone – from superbly gifted poets to those barely capable of stringing two rhymes together – has had a go at the Lake District. And all Lake poets, past and present, creep about under the shadow of William Wordsworth, which has stifled as many as it has inspired. I found myself hopelessly bogged down in a mass of poetry, sublime, competent, pedestrian and plain awful when I tried to pick the best gems from this over-stuffed treasure chest. So Lakeland poetry is represented here by just two of its finest practitioners: Wordsworth himself, of course, and from our own times the Millom poet Norman Nicolson, one of the very few fitted to share the stage with the master.

No influence as overpowering as William Wordsworth's is at work on the prose writers whom the Lake District has inspired, though their work is all shot through with the same passion for this landscape as fires the poets. Wordsworth has his say in this medium, too; a fine head of steam let off against the planting of intrusive larches on the fellsides. His sister Dorothy contributes a typically tender and ecstatic entry from her Journal on the glory of Grasmere under snow, while the modern Cumbrian writer Melvyn Bragg races away with the hunt across the Buttermere fells. Thomas de Quincey slows the pace with a leisurely view from the windows of Wordsworth's predecessor as Poet Laureate, Robert Southey, and the indefatigable seventeenth-century traveller Celia Fiennes rides away from the Lakeland mountains with one of her stream-of-consciousness commentaries on a landscape not yet romanticized in travellers' eyes.

A breezy blast of 1930s superiority comes from H. H. Symonds, Varsity-learned and proud of it, glad to grit his teeth and plunge into an icy pool or squelch the fell tops in the rain. Lake District buffs with their local knowledge can make mere ramblers feel knee-high. You're either 'one of us' or you're entirely beyond the pale. Symonds is right in there with those who *belong* – and doesn't he let you know it!

RIVER DUDDON, SOUTH-WEST CUMBRIA

124. William Wordsworth, *River Duddon Sonnets*
(1820)

Child of the clouds! remote from every taint
Of sordid industry thy lot is cast;
Thine are the honours of the lofty waste:
Not seldom, when with heat the valleys faint
Thy handmaid Frost with spangled tissue quaint
Thy cradle decks; – to chant thy birth, thou hast
No meaner Poet than the whistling Blast,
And Desolation is thy Patron-saint!
She guards the ruthless Power! who would not spare
Those mighty forests, once the bison's screen,
Where stalked the huge deer to his shaggy lair
Through paths and alleys roofed with darkest green;

Thousands of years before the silent air
Was pierced by whizzing shaft of hunter keen!

125. Norman Nicolson, *Five Rivers* (1943)

To the River Duddon

I wonder, Duddon, if you still remember
An oldish man with a nose like a pony's nose,
Broad bones, legs long and lean but strong enough
To carry him over Hardknott at seventy years of age.
He came to you first as a boy with a fishing-rod
And a hunk of Ann Tyson's bread and cheese in his pocket,
Walking from Hawkshead across Walna Scar;
Then as a middle-aged Rydal landlord,
With a doting sister and a pension on the civil list,
Who left his verses gummed to your rocks like lichen,
The dry and yellow edges of a once-green spring.
            . . . Wordsworth wrote:
'Remote from every taint of sordid industry'.
But you and I know better, Duddon lass.
For I, who've lived for nearly thirty years
Upon your shore, have seen the slagbanks slant
Like screes sheer into the sand, and seen the tide
Purple with ore back up the muddy gullies
And wiped the sinter dust from the farmyard damsons.
A hundred years of floods and rain and wind
Have washed your rocks clear of his words again,
Many of them half-forgotten, brimming the Irish sea.
But that which Wordsworth knew, even the old man
When poetry had failed like desire, was something
I have yet to learn, and you, Duddon,
Have learned and re-learned to forget and forget again.
Not the radical, the poet and heretic,
To whom the water-forces shouted and the fells
Were like a blackboard for the scrawls of God,
But the old man, inarticulate and humble,
Knew that eternity flows in a mountain beck –
The long cord of the water, the shepherd's numerals
That run upstream, through the singing decades of dialect.
He knew beneath mutation of year and season

Flood and drought, frost and fire and thunder,
The frothy blossom on the rowan and the reddening
   of the berries,
The silt, the sand, the slagbanks and the shingle,
And the wild catastrophes of the breaking mountains,
There stands the base and root of the living rock,
Thirty thousand feet of solid Cumberland.

BUTTERMERE, WESTERN LAKE DISTRICT

126. Melvyn Bragg, *The Hired Man* (1969)

John looked around him. Everywhere the fells rose,
their yellow-green winter grass cut across by the dark
bracken, the scree grey, a dull glint of mineral which
would later glitter under the sun. Even under such
canopied cloud, the air seemed to leap at your flesh and
bark its shins on your skin. Farms and cottages sat along
the valley bottom and on the lower slopes as easily as
rock-pools left by the tide; and from the intent scarlet
face of Isaac to the top of the Mellbreak itself, the day
was made for sport such as this.

Holme Wood yielding nothing, they moved on to a
small planting at the foot of Little Dodd. The hounds
clamoured – but for no more than a hare, and John
laughed at the electric hopping of that animal as its
white tail flashed up the fell-side. Hardisty called the
dogs back to him and they went up the Mosedale Beck,
right into the fells, their sides rising steeply. This was
the time for conserving talk and energy and the two or
three dozen men tramped steadily through the peaty
bottoms, skirted the bouldering outcrops, said little,
intent on Hardisty, scarlet, at their head. Before them
the hounds fanned out until the bare hillsides seemed to
breed dogs out of those cavities and clefts which pocked
them. Heads to the ground, feet padding ceaselessly,
long tails swaying gently, the brown, black-white
patched dogs muzzled for the scent. They went the
length of that climbing valley without raising more
than a crow. Even the sheep seemed unimpressed,

merely scattering a few yards distant and then standing to look on the procession, rigidly still.

It was after midday that the fox was raised – down towards Burtless Wood beside Buttermere. It turned immediately and ran back the way the men had come and John had a view – the fox racing across a skyline, clinging to the ground it seemed, tail straight up in the air to leave no scent. But the hounds had the view as well, and they were after it.

It gave them a hard run, into Mosedale bottom where it crossed the beck three times, around Hen Comb, behind Little Dodd, back the other direction towards Kirkstile. They lost it for a few minutes there until someone halloed they had seen it slipping up the beck – and they were off again.

John seemed to swoop and roll among the fells as he followed the chase. The field spread out, the hounds themselves strung along a quarter of a mile, two or three of them off on a scent of their own – lost to the day's sport: one hound cut its paw so badly on a wall that it dropped out, the terriers scurried along, the tied pair, like a diminutive canine monster. There were halloos every few minutes and the men themselves became hunters, climbing the heights in anticipation of a vantage which would give them a total view and enable them to race down when the kill was near, cutting up the loose screes and perhaps finding that the valley they reached was already clear of the chase, making for the badger sets down at High Nook which the fox itself could be expected to make for (they had been blocked the previous night), suddenly, by the action of that lush red-brown fox, spread out over a full range of hills and valleys.

KESWICK, NORTHERN LAKE DISTRICT

127. Thomas de Quincey, *Recollections of the Lake Poets* (1839)

Southey's library, in both senses of the word, was placed at the service of all the ladies alike. However, they did not intrude upon him, except in cases where they wished for a larger reception room, or a more interesting place for suggesting the topics of conversation. Interesting this room was, indeed, and in a degree not often rivalled. The library – the collection of books, I mean, which formed the most conspicuous part of its furniture within – was in all senses a good one. The books were chiefly English, Spanish, and Portuguese; well selected, being the great cardinal classics of the three literatures; fine copies, and decorated externally with a reasonable elegance, so as to make them in harmony with the other embellishments of the room. This effect was aided by the horizontal arrangement upon brackets, of many rare manuscripts – Spanish or Portuguese. Made thus gay within, this room stood in little need of attractions from without. Yet, even upon the gloomiest day of winter, the landscape from the different windows was too permanently commanding in its grandeur, too essentially independent of the seasons or the pomp of woods, to fail in fascinating the gaze of the coldest and dullest of spectators. The lake of Derwent Water in one direction, with its lovely islands – a lake about ten miles in circuit, and shaped pretty much like a boy's kite; the lake of Bassinthwaite in another; the mountains of Newlands arranging themselves like pavilions; the gorgeous confusion of Borrowdale just revealing its sublime chaos through the narrow vista of its gorge; all these objects lay in different angles to the front; whilst the sullen rear, not fully visible on this side of the house, was closed for many a league by the vast and towering masses of Skiddaw and Blencathara – mountains which are rather to be considered as frontier barriers, and chains of hilly ground, cutting the county of Cumberland into great chambers and different climates, than as insulated eminences; so vast is the area which they occupy; though there *are* also such separate and insulated heights, and nearly amongst the highest in the country. Southey's lot had therefore fallen, locally considered, into a goodly heritage. This grand panorama of mountain scenery, so varied, so expansive, and yet having the delightful feeling about it of a deep seclusion and dell-like sequestration from the world – a feeling which, in the midst of so expansive an area, spread out below his windows, could not have been sustained by any barriers less elevated than Glaramara, Skiddaw, or (which could be also descried) 'the mighty Helvellyn and Catchedicam'; this congregation of hill and lake, so wide, and yet so prison-like, in its separation from all beyond it, lay for ever under the eyes of Southey.

BORROWDALE, CENTRAL LAKE DISTRICT

128. H. H. Symonds, *Walking in the Lake District*
     (1933)

Saturday, 8 August   Heavy rain all night; wet morning. Afternoon: Dale Head, past Hindscarth, and down the shoulder of Robinson to the Buttermere foot of Honister; views magnificent.

Sunday 9   Heavy rain all night: river up two feet six. Fine aft.: Lobstone Band, Scawdel Fell, Maiden Moor; down into Borrowdale through screes and bracken to below the Birches.

Monday 10   Walked in continuous rain by Stonethwaite and the Stake to Pike o' Stickle (reached it at 1.45 p.m., rain blazing). Back by High White Stones and Greenup Edge: the clouds had lifted, an afternoon in a thousand along this ridge.

Gray or no Gray, if that was not Borrowdale, I should like to know what is! For this is the true Borrowdale August – fitful and magnificent with storm and sun, and a clear sky at last above the waving fields of blue-green bracken. For Borrowdale has not only a great name but a great position, lying under the big fells, on the side where the rain falls – mountains high enough, Scafell and the Gable, to catch the clouds from the long Atlantic and so bring them down on the lee side in blessings on your bended neck; and it is these fells, and not 'wadd' mines, which give to-day to 'Seawhaite' its just repute – the highest rain-fall (150 inches in a year) of any place inhabited in Great Britain. None the less, if you can avoid August there, you may disagree with the rain gauge; for on our N.W. seaboard there is in this month a proved sag in the Atlantic's character. But for all that, give me thirty-six hours of Borrowdale rain, when the clouds follow one another down on to the white houses of Seatoller, thrusting upon each other in black succession from the V-shaped opening of the 'Stee', and you may have your thirty-six hours on some rainless East Anglian beach, and I shall not envy you.

For do you know Seatoller? and Seatoller House? and did you know Moses Pepper? – stern Rechabite, quarry-man, and, by the loyal aid of wife and daughters, master of the most famous place of lodging in all Cumberland – and the family maintains it still. The visitors' book of that house, more than of any dalehead house, is a piece of history. Cabinet Ministers, undergraduates, profes-sors, publicists, walkers, lawyers, runners – you will find them in that book. All King's and Trinity[1] used to sleep there – all of them that could walk: did you never hear of the 'Lake Hunt' of past days? – when there were no motor coaches, and the day's letters jogged up in a pony cart, something after twelve, and there were no hot-baths there (Oxford's entreaties led to those), nor cold baths either, but the same Elysian pool under the big rock, where there is a foot-bridge to-day and curious eyes? In those great days of old, men *ran* upon the fells, chasing paper and fleet long-distance champions and high hopes of dinner in the evening. And Seatoller is a

---

[1]There is a celebrated witticism in this book, the entry 'A. B. Smith; Trinity' which a man wrote, and left, and came again next year and found it annotated thus: 'Not known at Trinity. Try Trinity College, Oxford.'

270

grand place still to be in – but for all the high hours of a fine day now you must be away, well up above reversing motor coaches. In the evening the sunset lights scatter high colour, as before, on High Knotts and the ridge of Chapel Fell, and the snails walk abroad stoutly in the garden.

129. Wordsworth (1818)

*Composed upon an evening of extraordinary
splendour and beauty*

I

Had this effulgence disappeared
With flying haste, I might have sent,
Among the speechless clouds, a look
Of blank astonishment;
But 'tis endued with power to stay,
And sanctify one closing day,
That frail Mortality may see –
What is? – ah no, but what *can* be!
Time was when field and watery cove
With modulated echoes rang,
While choirs of fervent Angels sang
Their vespers in the grove;
Or, crowning, star-like, each some sovereign
    height,
Warbled, for heaven above and earth below,
Strains suitable to both. – Such holy rite,
Methinks, if audibly repeated now
From hill or valley, could not move
Sublimer transport, purer love,
Than doth this silent spectacle – the gleam –
The shadow – and the peace supreme!

II

No sound is uttered, – but a deep
And solemn harmony pervades
The hollow vale from steep to steep,
And penetrates the glades.
Far-distant images draw nigh,
Called forth by wondrous potency

Of beamy radiance, that imbues
Whate'er it strikes with gem-like hues!
In vision exquisitely clear,
Herds range along the mountain side;
And glistening antlers are descried;
And gilded flocks appear.
Thine is the tranquil hour, purpureal Eve!
But long as god-like wish, or hope divine,
Informs my spirit, ne'er can I believe
That this magnificence is wholly thine!
– From worlds not quickened by the sun
A portion of the gift is won;
An intermingling of Heaven's pomp is spread
On ground which British shepherds tread!

III

And, if there be whom broken ties
Afflict, or injuries assail,
Yon hazy ridges to their eyes
Present a glorious scale,
Climbing suffused with sunny air,
To stop – no record hath told where!
And tempting Fancy to ascend,
And with immortal Spirits blend!
– Wings at my shoulders seem to play;
But, rooted here, I stand and gaze
On those bright steps that heaven-ward raise
Their practicable way.
Come forth, ye drooping old men, look abroad,
And see to what fair countries ye are bound!
And if some traveller, weary of his road,
Hath slept since noon-tide on the grassy ground,
Ye Genii! to his covert speed;
And wake him with such gentle heed
As may attune his soul to meet the dower
Bestowed on this transcendent hour!

IV

Such hues from their celestial Urn
Were wont to stream before mine eye,
Where'er it wandered in the morn

Of blissful infancy.
This glimpse of glory, why renewed?
Nay, rather speak with gratitude;
For, if a vestige of those gleams
Survived, 'twas only in my dreams.
Dread Power! whom peace and calmness serve
No less than Nature's threatening voice,
If aught unworthy be my choice,
From THEE if I would swerve;
Oh, let thy grace remind me of the light
Full early lost, and fruitlessly deplored;
Which, at this moment, on my waking sight
Appears to shine, by miracle restored;
My soul, though yet confined to earth,
Rejoices in a second birth!
– 'Tis past, the visionary splendour fades;
And night approaches with her shades.

130. William Wordsworth, *Guide to the Lakes*
     (5th ed., 1835)

It must be acknowledged that the larch, till it has
outgrown the size of a shrub, shows, when looked at
singly, some elegance in form and appearance, especially in spring, decorated, as it then is, by the pink tassels
of its blossoms; but, as a tree, it is less than any other
pleasing: its branches (for *boughs* it has none) have no
variety in the youth of the tree, and little dignity, even
when it attains its full growth; *leaves* it cannot be said
to have, consequently neither affords shade nor shelter.
In spring the larch becomes green long before the native
trees; and its green is so peculiar and vivid, that finding
nothing to harmonize with it, wherever it comes forth,
a disagreeable speck is produced. In summer, when all
other trees are in their pride, it is of a dingy lifeless hue;
in autumn of a spiritless unvaried yellow, and in winter
it is still more lamentably distinguished from every
other deciduous tree of the forest, for they seem only to
sleep, but the larch appears absolutely dead. If an
attempt be made to mingle thickets, or a certain

proportion of other forest-trees, with the larch, its horizontal branches intolerantly cut them down as with a scythe, or force them to spindle up to keep pace with it. The terminating spike renders it impossible that the several trees, where planted in numbers, should ever blend together so as to form a mass or masses of wood. Add thousands to tens of thousands, and the appearance is still the same – a collection of separate individual trees, obstinately presenting themselves as such; and which, from whatever point they are looked at, if but seen, may be counted upon the fingers. Sunshine or shadow has little power to adorn the surface of such a wood; and the trees not carrying up their heads, the wind raises among them no majestic undulations. It is indeed true, that in countries where the larch is a native, and where, without interruption, it may sweep from valley to valley, and from hill to hill, a sublime image may be produced by such a forest, in the same manner as by one composed of any other single tree, to the spreading of which no limits can be assigned. For sublimity will never be wanting, where the sense of innumerable multitude is lost in, and alternates with, that of intense unity; and to the ready perception of this effect, similarity and almost identity of individual form and monotony of colour contribute. But this feeling is confined to the native immeasurable forest; no artificial plantation can give it.

GRASMERE, CENTRAL-SOUTHERN LAKE DISTRICT

131. Dorothy Wordsworth, *Journal* (1800)

14 May 1800 [Wednesday]   Wm. and John set off into Yorkshire after dinner at ½ past 2 o'clock, cold pork in their pockets. I left them at the turning of the Lowwood bay under the trees. My heart was so full that I could hardly speak to W. when I gave him a farewell kiss. I sate a long time upon a stone at the margin of the lake, and after a flood of tears my heart was easier. The lake looked to me, I knew not why, dull and melancholy, and the weltering on the shores seemed a heavy sound. I walked as long as I could amongst the stones of the shore. The wood rich in flowers; a beautiful yellow, palish yellow, flower, that looked thick, round, and double, and smelt very sweet – I supposed it was a ranunculus. Crowfoot, the grassy-leaved rabbit-tooth-ed white flower, strawberries, geranium, scentless violets, anemones two kinds, orchise, primroses. The heckberry very beautiful, the crab coming out as a low shrub. Met a blind man, driving a very large beautiful Bull, and a cow – he walked with two sticks. Came home by Clappersgate. The valley very green; many sweet views up to Rydale head, when I could juggle away the fine houses; but they disturbed me, even more than when I have been happier; one beautiful view of the Bridge, without Sir Michael's. Sate down very often, though it was cold. I resolved to write a journal of the time till W. and J. return, and I set about keeping my resolve, because I will not quarrel with myself, and because I shall give Wm. pleasure by it when he comes home again.

Windermere to Ullswater, Eastern Lake District

132. Celia Fiennes, *Journal* (1698)

I rode in sight of this Winander Water as I was saying up and down above 7 mile; afterwards as I was ascending another of those barren fells – which tho' I at last was not halfe way up, yet was an hour going it up and down, on the other side going only on the side of it about the middle of it, but it was of such a height as to shew one a great deale of the Country when it happens to be between those hills, else those interposeing hinders any sight but of the clouds – I see a good way behind me another of those waters or mers but not very bigge; these great hills are so full of loose stones and shelves of rocks that its very unsafe to ride them down . . .

Here I came to villages of sad little hutts made up of drye walls, only stones piled together and the roofs of same slatt; there seemed to be little or noe tunnells for their chimneys and have no morter or plaister within or without; for the most part I tooke them at first sight for a sort of houses or barns to fodder cattle in, not thinking them to be dwelling houses, they being scattering houses here one there another, in some places there may be 20 or 30 together, and the Churches the same; it must needs be very cold dwellings but it shews something of the lazyness of the people; indeed here and there there was a house plaister'd, but there is sad entertainment, that sort of clap bread and butter and cheese and a cup of beer all one can have, they are 8 mile from a market town and their miles are tedious to go both for illness of way and length of the miles.

I cross'd one of the stone bridges that was pretty large which entred me into Cumberlandshire: this river together with the additional springs continually running into it all the way from those vaste precipices comes into a low place and form a broad water which is very cleer and reaches 7 mile in length, Ules water [Ullswater] its called, such another water as that of

Wiander mer [Windermere], only that reaches 10 mile in length from Ambleside to the sea, and this is but 7 such miles long; its full of such sort of stones and slatts in the bottom as the other, neer the brimm where its shallowe you see it cleer to the bottom; this is secured on each side by such formidable heights as those rocky fells in same manner as the other was; I rode the whole length of this water by its side sometyme a little higher upon the side of the hill and sometyme just by the shore and for 3 or 4 miles I rode through a fine forest or parke where was deer skipping about and haires, which by meanes of a good Greyhound I had a little Course, but we being strangers could not so fast pursue it in the grounds full of hillocks and furse and soe she escaped us.

XIII

To the North-East

For wonderfully varied walking, and a real sense of shifting, always changing landscape, these long miles over fellside and moor can't be beaten. Dramatically impressive mountain scenery sends you marching out of Lakeland, and pastorally beautiful river valley scenery greets your entry into the upland wilds of the north-east. In between are lonely miles over peat moors and along deserted drovers' roads with hilltops, tucked away valleys and tiny stone-built villages as a backdrop.

In the course of linking up Lakeland and Teesdale, one pathfinder above all others has forged a memorable route. Alfred Wainwright devised his 190-mile Coast-to-Coast Walk from St Bees Head to Robin Hood's Bay long after his meticulously hand-drawn and written guides to the Lake District had made him famous among walkers, but this walk will be the one to carry his name on to future generations of hikers. Halfway along, at Keld in Upper Swaledale, the Coast-to-Coast Walk meets the Pennine Way on its great 250-mile slog up from Edale in Derbyshire to Kirk Yetholm over the Scottish Border. Wainwright dominates the Pennine Way, too. His *Pennine Way Companion*, compiled back in the late 1960s, is still the definitive guide. Chatty, informative, didactic, admonitory, Wainwright holds your hand the whole way.

I walked the Pennine Way in 1976/7 and the Coast-to-Coast Walk in 1981, on both occasions in the company of Alfred Wainwright (on the page) and my father (in the flesh). My father is a formidable long-distance walker whose enthusiasm I shrugged off in hurtful teenage before coming to share in later years. The relevant entries in the diaries I kept of those two marathon walks can tell the tale from here on.

1981 – Wainwright's Coast-to-Coast Walk

Monday, 3 August: Grasmere to Patterdale – eight miles
We left the Traveller's Rest after a good but fairly expensive night (£16 B&B) and turned north-east up a stony path which gradually gained height above Tongue Gill. Cloudy and with a chilly breeze – occasional spoonfuls of mist slopped over the shoulder of St Sunday Crag looming in front of us, but just high enough not to obscure things. A few other hikers around, some in shorts and plimsolls, others heavy laden like us.

At the top of Grisedale Pass above a series of waterfalls we came out by Grisedale Tarn, whose steely waters were whipped by the wind in wavelets towards the rim, looking as if they were about to spill over and tumble down into Patterdale.

Helvellyn was out because of the mist, but Dad went off to tackle St Sunday Crag while I nursed my flu down the long descent into Patterdale, stumbling over stones in the path. Dad, a speck of orange and white a thousand feet above me, waved every now and then before disappearing into the low cloud . . .

Tuesday, 4 August: Patterdale to Bampton Grange –
fifteen miles
Bright sun and blue sky when we set off from Braesteads Farm, but a band of mist at about one thousand feet stayed all day, obscuring the tops. We had a long, undulating and stony walk along the southern shore of beautiful Ullswater, backed by the fells and dotted with water-skiers and sailing boats. It must be marvellous to live in one of those Victorian houses among the trees above the lake.

We passed pony-trekkers (no acknowledgement), sturdy bearded he-men ('how-do'), young couples out for a stroll ('hello') and middle-aged mums and dads with kids ('good morning').

At Howtown we stopped at the hotel for ginger-beer shandy in a bar for locals only – strictly segregated from the tourist part. We ate Mrs Kitchen's huge Leicester-and-lettuce doorstep sandwiches by the lake, watching the water-skiers, and then plodded on to Pooley Bridge. Here we were right at the top of Ullswater, having walked its entire length.

Climbed up a dusty, stony old cart track on to the moor and had a nice stroll on high ground with cloud-enveloped High Street and its Roman road away to the right, before descending into Bampton Grange at five-thirty. Behind us are the Lakeland fells – in front, more pastoral scenery. Outside the Crown and Mitre the church clock lingeringly strikes the quarter-hours in a minor key: whether deliberately or not, I don't know.

Wednesday, 5 August: Bampton Grange to
Newbiggin-on-Lune – eighteen miles

Lovely, hot day of blue sky and far cloud. We left Bampton Grange just as the church clock was atonally striking ten, and walked beside the River Lowther, crossing stiles and squeezing through gaps to go down-hill into Shap.

The A6 is now pretty quiet compared with its hectic heyday before the M6 was opened in 1970, but nothing can make Shap picturesque in spite of the fells all round. It's strung out along the road, still dirty and desolate, with a huge quarry at the southern end and a forest of pylons.

Over the fells to Oddendale – Wainwright admonishing us to keep away from its 'sequestered privacy' – and a climb up to the winter pasture and walled enclosure and barn of Potrigg. Now on limestone, with attendant flowers and soft grass underfoot. Robin Hood's Grave just a heap of stones about three feet high in a dry gully – disappointing.

Beacon Hill carried a cross commemorating Queen Victoria's Golden Jubilee among the limestone outcrops that made this section hard going. We pressed on uphill to Castle Folds, an ancient settlement on a grassy knoll surrounded by ankle-cracking limestone pavement. Here we abandoned Wainwright and slithered steeply down the contours to Sunbiggin Tarn, a mass of reeds and wildfowl.

Both pairs of feet feeling it by now, but we girded our loins for the last few miles over heather, following sheep tracks to a road and the last interminable mile down to Newbiggin. The village has been bypassed by the new road, a quiet hamlet of grey stone houses. Friendly, welcoming Mrs Law at Oddfellow's House. A huge meal, and a lift from Mr Law to the King's Head at Ravenstonedale a mile down the road, a whitewashed old inn by the river. I sketched it from the bridge. Relays of art critics from the pub came to look – the landlord wanted to buy the drawing to frame for his wall. I sold it to him for a pint – a fair bargain.

Thursday, 6 August: Newbiggin to Keld – seventeen miles

The rain began as we left the best night's lodgings so far, and didn't let up all day. My new anorak was penetrated within an hour, so for most of these long miles I walked in a watery wonderland!

A stony lane led us to Swaledale Bridge, a nice old humpback over a beck. Then beside a wall, up on to Limekiln Hill and down into Kirkby Stephen. KS an unspoilt little market town along the main road to Blackpool, full of cramped shops and inns, where farmers and locals mixed with sopping hikers in the street. We had a cup of coffee in a café and left the town by a steep, narrow road dominated by lorries from the clattering limestone quarry near the top of Hartley Fell.

We decided to put in a few miles on the high fells in spite of the grey cloud cover, mist-shrouded tops all round and the incessant rain. Laboriously gained one thousand feet of height, passing old open-cast mines on the banks of becks – they must have been hell to work a hundred years ago, miles from the nearest settlement and served by a single rutted cart track.

Downhill through limestone clints to the lonely fell

road to Keld. From here on it was head-down, one-foot-in-front-of-the-other stuff, walking directly into the weather, with barren fell-sides all around. At one point we could see the road ahead for a good two miles, and it was all uphill.

At long last we dipped downhill and came squelching and sniffing into Keld, past the Youth Hostel where a group of hikers were stripping off their steaming rain gear in the garage. Miss Calvert at Woodside hasn't changed much in five years – still chatty and giggly. We gradually got warm and dry, though the rain is still belting down outside (nine o'clock in the evening).

We chatted with Miss Calvert about Keld – a dying village. She's lived here or hereabouts all her life. She thinks the first chink in the wall of Keld's community life was when the old lady who ran the pub couldn't get any of her relations to take it on. Eventually a teetotal Methodist bought it and stopped the licence. He had a few of his windows broken, but no one really appreciated the importance of the loss of the village's main meeting place. Then the shop closed, and the school about eight years ago. The village hall, built by local people as a co-operative effort in the 1920s and often packed for concerts and dances in those days, can't be filled now and has fallen out of use – 'it doesn't pay'.

Townsfolk have bought up some of the cottages at prices the local young couples can't afford, but only use them as summer homes, so there is no new blood in the place. Lowland farmers won't move here to farm, as hill-farming skills are reckoned to be accessible only to those 'born to it'.

The chapel has closed (I think), and for shopping, a drink, church, entertainment and schooling people have to go at least three and often many more miles.

Yet in summer Keld is thronged with visitors who constantly ask for shops and pub. When the few old folk are gone (present population is twenty-four) Keld may become completely a holiday cottage village – this change having happened all in the space of thirty years.

1976 – Pennine Way

Thursday, 5 August: Keld to Bowes – fourteen miles
Three-mile walk back to Miss Calvert's from the pub at Muker last night. Had a short lift from a man who had been playing Beethoven sonatas on the cello with the Vicar of Muker.

We left Keld and walked up on to the moors above – stunning view looking back over Keld, Swaledale and other dales and fells, stretching away below us.

Up and up through the Swaledale sheep, by peat hags and old mine shafts with a flat but very wide prospect of mountains to the north and west. An old miners' track led to the Tan Hill inn (1732 feet), the highest pub in England; once a buzzing meeting place of pack-train leaders, miners and travellers, now a Pennine Way stopping place. They ought to give Wainwright free drinks for life for his suggestive 'Never was a pint better earned' at the foot of the page in the guide book.

We drank and moved on, another five miles on springy peat between heather moors – ruined sheep-folds, shooting butts, grouse. A sunny day and a monotonous slog – obviously terrible in rain, as shown by the maze of boot-prints round boggy patches.

The bright green fields and buildings of Sleighthome Farm appeared ahead at last. We crossed a beck and went on by drystone walls. A huge bull was sniffing the hindquarters of one of his concubines with the air of a connoisseur of rare old brandy, and let us pass without challenge. Some men were wall-building: an oldster on a tractor throwing off the flat slabs which young men in industrial mittens laid quickly along the growing wall. We crunched along stony farm paths, with the abandoned Barnard Castle–Kirkby Stephen railway running on the left. Tortoiseshell butterflies in clouds on the stone walls.

Bowes a long, grey street on a hill, with juggernaut problems. Fifty-foot monsters blew a gale round our shoulders and whipped us along the street to the Grove guest house. A grey town, a grey evening, that gave both of us the blues.

Friday, 6 August: Bowes to Middleton-in-Teesdale –
twelve miles

We shook the dust of Bowes from our feet early this
morning, blown like feathers by lorry slip-stream to our
side road up on to the moors, just opposite Dickens's
'Dotheboys Hall'. A heavy sky over Tute Hill where the
skeletons of MOD huts, long abandoned in a grassy
wasteland, rot slowly. We walked past an abandoned
farm and outbuildings, sprouting bushes from roof and
windows. Across heather and barren grass – a really
desolate scene dotted with sheep. Some asleep in the dry
drainage ditches. Not another soul in sight, a chilly
wind and dark clouds.

Goldsborough – a lump of gritstone sticking up above
the moor. Baldersdale an area of huge reservoirs and
green fields, inspiration for pages of sententious
sermonizing by Wainwright:

No bank of flowers now . . . concrete runways.
No more exhilarating days of joyous spate and leaping
    waters . . .
Life has gone from it.
A river has died.
Been killed
By the hand of man . . .

Lunedale was a patchwork of green fields – welcome
to the jaded eye after so many miles of sedge and brown
grass. We crossed the neck of the reservoir at Grass-
holme and bumped up and down through stiles and
gates on a rutted track that led finally to a wonderful
prospect over Middleton and the valley of the Tees – the
first wide view all day. Down thankfully through
bracken into Middleton and the Cleveland Arms. Opposite stood the low, dark, dingy King's Arms, where last
year Dad was offered an oil rub by a twenty-stone lady
from Birmingham. No such adventures this time – just a
bath and a pint of beer from a wooden barrel.

The appearance of Durham and Northumberland shifts between a coal-bearing landscape of pale, scrubby grass, pit heaps and geometrical red-brick mining villages, the heavy industry of ironworking and shipbuilding (now all but dead) that scars the mouths and throats of the rivers Tyne and Wear, and the wide moors and uplands behind and beyond, some of the loveliest and loneliest scenery in Britain. The moors of the north-east form a winding highway to the Scottish Border, running from the limestone delights of Upper Teesdale through the gritstone of the lower Tyne valley and back to the limestone again in the Northumbrian highlands.

John Hillaby continues his Journey with a celebration of the Teesdale flora and a condemnation of the dark, dank coniferous forests north of Hadrian's Wall. A. Wainwright, best and saltiest by far of Pennine Way companions, stamps 'approved' on the waterfall of High Force as it plunges over the Whin Sill, a shelf of hard, volcanic dolerite which outcrops in several places along our way. The banks of the River Tyne west of nineteenth-century Newcastle are a refuge for Thomas Bewick, as are the hunting moors north of the city for Henry Tegner's twentieth-century pitman. David 'Dippie' Dixon, the enthusiastic chronicler of life before the motor car in Upper Coquetdale, brings us with hearts in mouths on to the flanks of the Cheviot and within sight of Scotland.

Upper Teesdale, County Durham

133. John Hillaby, *Journey Through Britain* (1968)

Upper Teesdale is remarkable for an outcrop of black rock called dolerite, curious stuff which hangs over the river like the ramparts of a medieval fortress. It is lava, squeezed out through cracks in the limestone by volcanic action. The river pours over the top of the rampart at Cauldron Snout and gushes down towards Middleton in a series of waterfalls. When the dolerite was originally squeezed out, hot, it baked the sedimentary rocks into coarse crystalline stuff aptly called sugar limestone, the home, now, of many rare plants.

No botanical name-dropping can give an adequate impression of the botanical jewels sprinkled on the ground above High Force. Here you find the little Teesdale violet, smaller and more downy than the bankside flower, also asphodel, sandworts, alpine meadow-rue, lady's mantle, and high slopes bright with spring gentians.

In this valley a tundra has been marvellously preserved; the glint of colour, the reds, deep purples, and blues have the quality of Chartres glass. For me Teesdale was more beautiful than I could have imagined; certainly more strange and evocative than I could have foreseen.

There are marked differences in the posture of some of the plants found on those fell-sides. They lie close to the ground, as if still cowering from Arctic winds. Here are lineal descendants of flowers which, like the Celts, took to the hills when the islands were invaded by hosts of new plants. The invasion took place when the ice retreated and the valleys became clothed in forest and blankets of acid bog. This explains many of the similarities between plants of the high, treeless places and those found near the seashore. Both are places of refuge for the dispossessed.

HIGH FORCE

134. A. Wainwright, *Pennine Way Companion* (1968)

High Force is not the highest waterfall in the country, but it is the biggest. No other creates such a profound impression on the senses, no other has such a dramatic yet beautiful setting. The thunderous crash of its waters can be heard from afar: they fall without grace, in a furious rage. It is a spectacle all should see. A great many do, for this is a showplace. A convenient hotel and car park, by the side of the Alston road, and a good path (entered upon payment of a toll) down through the woods ensure a crowded patronage on the Durham side of the river.

High Force occurs where the Tees, after a long restless journey through wild moorlands from its source on Cross Fell, suddenly plunges over a seventy-foot drop in its rocky bed into a wooded gorge buttressed by huge vertical walls. It is a transition in seconds from one extreme to another. Normally there is one fall only; after heavy rain it is usual for a supplementary fall to appear on the right; in times of rare spate the full width of the gorge can become a tumult of thrashing water. The scene is enhanced by the dolerite formations and by deep pools overhung by rich foliage.

This is the Tees' finest moment.

TEESDALE

135. Sir Walter Scott, *Rokeby* (1813)

I

The sultry summer day is done,
The western hills have hid the sun,
But mountain peak and village spire
Retain reflection of his fire.
Old Barnard's towers are purple still
To those that gaze from Toller-hill;
Distant and high, the tower of Bowes
Like steel upon the anvil glows;
And Stanmore's ridge, behind that lay,
Rich with the spoils of parting day,
In crimson and in gold array'd,
Streaks yet a while the closing shade,
Then slow resigns to darkening heaven
The tints which brighter hours had given.
Thus aged men, full loth and slow,
The vanities of life forego,
And count their youthful follies o'er,
Till Memory lends her light no more.

II

The eve, that slow on upland fades,
Has darker closed on Rokeby's glades,
Where, sunk within their banks profound,
Her guardian streams to meeting wound.
The stately oaks, whose sombre frown
Of noontide made a twilight brown,
Impervious now to fainter light,
Of twilight make an early night.
Hoarse into middle air arose
The vespers of the roosting crows,
And with congenial murmurs seem
To wake the Genii of the stream;
For louder clamour'd Greta's tide,
And Tees in deeper voice replied,
And fitful waked the evening wind,
Fitful in sighs its breath resign'd.

RIVER TYNE, NORTHUMBERLAND

136. Thomas Bewick, *A Memoir* (1887)

To be placed in the midst of a Wood in the night, in
whirlwinds of snow, while the tempest howled above
my head, was sublimity itself & drew forth aspirations
to Omnipotence such as had not warmed my imagination so highly before – but indeed without being
supported by extacies of this kind, the spirits, so beset,
would have flagged & I should have sunk down – As
soon as the days began to lengthen & the sprouting
herbage had covered the ground, I often stopped with
delight by the sides of Woods, to admire the dangling
Woodbine & Roses & the grasses, powdered, or spangled
with pearly drops of dew – & also week after week the
continued succession of plants & wild flowers – the
Primrose, the wild Hyacinths the Hare bell, the daisey,
the cowslip & these altogether I thought no painter ever
could imitate – I had not at that time ever heard of the
name of the great & good Linnaeus & knew only plants

by their common English Names – While admiring these beautifully enamelled spots on my way, I was also charmed with the equally beautifull little songsters which were constantly pouring out their various notes to proclaim the Spring – While this exhilerating Season glided on by imperceptable degrees unfolding its blossoms 'till they faded into summer & as the days lengthened, my hours of rising became more & more early – I have often thought that not one half of mankind knew any thing of the beauty, the serenity & the stillness of the summer mornings, in the country, nor ever witnessed the rising Sun's shining forth upon the new day – I had often listned with great pleasure & attention to my fathers description of the morning – with his remarks upon the various wild quadrupeds & the strange birds he had seen or heard in these still hours throughout the year, for he left his bed very early in summer & seldom later than 4 or 5 oclock in the Winter – The Autumn I viewed as the most interesting season & in its appearance the most beautiful of the varied year – it is then that the yellow harvest of the fields & the produce of the orchards are gathered in as the rewards of the labours of the Year – While the picturesque beauties & varying foliage of the fading woods – with their falling leaves & the assembling, in flocks, of the small Birds put me in mind of the gloomy months with which the year is closed.–

This is the short account of many years of great & uninterrupted health, buoyant spirits & of great happiness to me – I had begun betimes & by degrees, to habituate myself to temperance & exercise, which hardened the constitution to such a pitch that no wet, nor cold had any bad effect upon me – on setting out upon my weekly pedestrian *flights* up the Tyne, I never looked out to see whether it was a good day or a bad one – the worst that ever fell from the skies never deterred me from undertaking my journey – on setting out I always waded through the first pool I met with & had sometimes the River to wade at the far end – I never changed my cloaths, however they might be soaked with wet & though they might be stiffened by the Frost, on my returning home at night 'till I went to bed – I had inured myself to this hardihood, by always sleeping with my windows open, where a thorough air, as well as the snow blew through my room – in this I lay down, stripped into *bare buff* except being rolled in a blanket, upon a mattrass as hard as I could make it – Notwithstanding this mode of treating myself, I never had any ailment, even in the shape of a cold.

Hadrian's Wall

137. G. M. Boumphrey, *Along the Roman Roads* (1935)

Another mile or two (26 from Newcastle now) and at last the road bore away to the south-west and left me to follow the Wall alone where it ran out across the moor and climbed up for Sewingshields Crags straight ahead. The next 10 miles were the best of all. The formation of the ground is curious. Seen from the south, it looks like ordinary rather desolate moorland rising to a ridge running east and west. When you climb to the top of this, you find to your surprise that you are on the edge of precipitous grey crags which fall abruptly down to the moors, sometimes 200 or 300 feet below. This is the Great Whin Sill of north England and it is along the very brink of it that Hadrian's Wall runs. And it is just this part of the wall that is best preserved, the full width and often 5 or 6 feet high.

As you leave the road you see ahead of you the sheer edge of Sewingshields with the Wall running along the brink. There was a medieval castle here and it is said that King Arthur and his Knights still sit there, in an underground hall, wrapped in a magic sleep, waiting the coming of one who shall break the spell. From the top of the Crags the view is wonderful – north over the Wastes, as the moors are called, with Broomlee Lough at your feet, or south to the Tyne valley – or east or west for that matter – in fact it is one of the places of England. It must have looked very different to the Roman sentries at times, when the grey mist swirled down, blotting out everything, and they gazed into it until their eyes burned, seeing everywhere shapes that might have moved the second before. A grim place then!

Wark Forest

138. John Hillaby, *Journey Through Britain* (1968)

Towards noon I returned to *Vercovicium* and slipped out through the chariot gate. Within a mile you enter a forest as dark as any that ever sheltered a painted Pict. The transition is sudden, dramatic. Behind are the towering cliffs. In front is a close-planted arboreal slum. This is a man-made forest, the biggest in Britain and by far the most unpleasant I encountered. It stretches from the Wall to the Border and beyond, an area of nearly three hundred square miles. Throughout this great tract of country the Forestry Commission has planted young trees, mostly Canadian spruce planted so close that, apart from the forest rides, it is impossible to get between them. The eye craves for variety, for something less monotonous than the endless corduroy of conifers. Although the Pennine Way runs through only a very small section of the forest – in all perhaps no more than about four miles – in that distance the walker is likely to get lost, misguided by signposts that point in the wrong direction and pulled up short by rides blocked by brushwood. It rained, hard, as it so often did on those occasions and I went round and round like a rat in a laboratory maze. Wet through and annoyed that one could be so badly treated by a public authority, I managed to get out of the Christmas trees near an isolated farmhouse.

Instant hospitality. When had I last eaten? asked the young farmer. Would I care for a bath? Everett of Watergate had been at home for two days, entertaining the children while his wife was in hospital having a baby, their third or fourth. The place looked upside-down and everyone seemed extraordinarily happy. My host even phoned up a local schoolmaster so that we could have a bit of a party that night. We talked for hours. I slept, eventually, on the kitchen floor between the open fire and the table, marvelling again at the unpredictable oscillations of Fortune.

NORTH OF NEWCASTLE-UPON-TYNE

139. Henry Tegner, *A Border County* (1955)

One Boxing Day I came across the little man, away out near North Bavington, with three much younger cyclists whom he was apparently initiating into the niceties of hunting by bike. North Bavington is a good eighteen miles from Seaton Burn, where the little grey man lives. Seaton Burn is a village of coal mines on the outskirts of Newcastle, a dreary place of little attraction. Passing through it on my daily visits to the city, I often meet the pitman on his cycle facing a gale of wind from the north as he slowly pedals his way to the meets out in the Northumbrian countryside. Sometimes these meets are well over twenty miles from his home, so that he must cover an immense mileage during his day's hunting.

It was not, however, until I went out one day to follow hounds on a cycle myself that I realized his amazing knowledge of the game. Armed with an old pair of opera glasses, he saw, and graciously showed me, more of the sport of foxhunting than ever I saw from the back of a horse.

By now we had got to know each other and he told me of his earlier experiences in the coal pits as a young miner. The confinement and lack of sunshine were hard for him to bear, but he stuck it out until, in late middle age, his lungs gave out and he was forced to the surface.

During the summer he laboured on the land, giving a hand to the local farmers, and during the winter he hunted three days a week and usually managed to put in a couple of days as a beater in the surrounding shoots.

The last time I saw him he was standing at the gates

of Blagdon Hall with a number of beaters who were waiting for the guns. Neat as a new pin, with his polished gaiters and his old grey mackintosh rolled and slung over his back, he was leaning on his stripped willow stick with a look of anticipation in his eyes at the sport the day held in store.

The Cheviot

140. David 'Dippie' Dixon, *Upper Coquetdale* (1903)

A friend of the writer was once overtaken by a violent thunderstorm when alone on the heights of Cheviot. Being of a philosophical turn of mind, he quietly descended from the crest of the hill, and lying prone amongst the heather for safety, viewed the storm in all its terrific grandeur around and beneath him with no small enjoyment, but at the penalty of being thoroughly soaked by the deluge of rain. This he soon remedied so soon as the storm was over, by stripping off his clothes, sitting patiently half clad until they were somewhat dried in the scalding sunshine. This same gentleman, who was an ardent botanist and entomologist, was once pursuing a very rare moth on the summit of Cheviot, when, paying more attention to the specimen on the wing than to his footsteps, he never knew until he found himself up to the waist in the middle of a 'moss-hag'. Scrambling out as best he could, his underparts wet, not with pure water, but with a thick muddy coating of a black peaty substance. As he could not very well present himself to civilized society in such a plight, he took off his nether garments, and having washed them in a pool of water, spread them out to dry on a large rock, behind which he sat himself down, never thinking for a moment but that he was perfectly safe from intrusion on such a lonely spot as the 'tap o'Cheevut'. Presently he heard voices, and on peering cautiously round the corner of his rocky shelter, he was much disconcerted at seeing a party of ladies and gentlemen approaching the spot where he lay. Whether they had observed the 'washing' laid out to dry, or had caught sight of the unfortunate naturalist, one cannot say; but, greatly to his relief, the unwelcome visitors turned aside and disappeared over the brow of the hill. Once we accompanied this dear good man on a botanizing tour around the hills of Cheviot, and intent on finding a rare plant, a specimen of which both of us were eager to possess, we, with all the foolhardiness of botanists, climbed and edged our way along the face of a steep hillside, alive to nothing but the coveted plant, when, to our dismay, we found we were on the brink of a declivity some hundreds of feet above the valley. To return was almost impossible; so telling me to 'lie close to the hill and mind my feet', after a somewhat perilous few minutes we gained a place of safety, with a feeling of thankfulness that we had escaped harm, and a resolve to be more careful in our future ramblings after flowers.

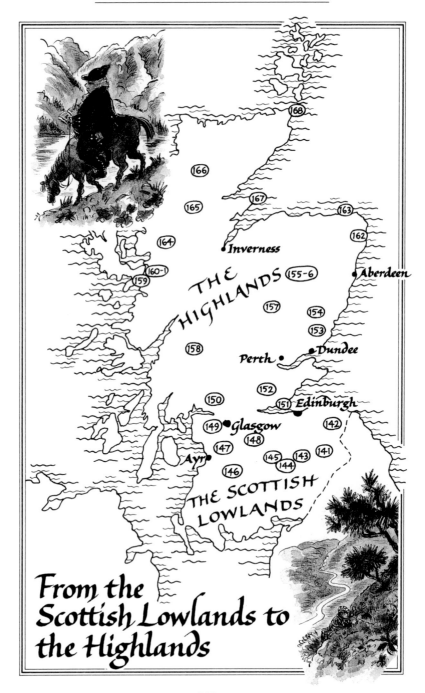

168

166

167

165 163

162

164

Inverness

160-1
159

THE
HIGHLANDS 155-6

Aberdeen

157
154
153

158

Perth Dundee

152

150 151 Edinburgh

149 Glasgow 142

147 148

Ayr 145 143 141
144

146

THE SCOTTISH
LOWLANDS

From the
Scottish Lowlands to
the Highlands

298

XIV

To the Scottish Lowlands

The Cheviot hills roll in green billows across the remote borderlands between Northumberland and Scotland. This is wild, wet country where sodden peat sucks your boots at every step and black rain clouds sweep up from behind a hill to soak you without warning. It's all too easy to find yourself marooned on a featureless hilltop with miles of unidentifiable hills and valleys in view all round, the compass telling you one thing, the map another and your fast-failing sense of direction a third. Individually the Cheviot hills are tame things compared with the mountains of North Wales and the Scottish Highlands. There are no sky-piercing peaks or plunging screes, no awe-inspiring naked rock masses to make the walker's blood run hot or cold. But collectively, rolling smoothly away to the horizon in an unvarying succession of wet green waves, they give a more powerful sense of loneliness than many far grander stretches of mountain country. In sunshine they can show a stunning, unadorned beauty, particularly when looking down from a height into one of the deep valleys cut by a steeply falling burn whose water only sparkles for the couple of hours a day when the sun reaches to the valley bottom. Alto-cumulus clouds look whiter and taller over a sunny Cheviot than anywhere else along the Border. But when the weather takes a turn for the worse and chilly shadows darken those hilltops, the Cheviots put on a grim and daunting character suited to the history of clan ambushes, Border battles, murder and revenge that was acted out for so many centuries in and around their loneliest heights and depths. They have been fought over, disputed and snatched back and forth between English and Scots, and between Border families fighting and feuding amongst themselves. They are full of corners and crannies ideal for concealment of armed men and stolen cattle, perfect landscape for guerrilla warfare and surprise attack. Farms are few and far between, villages fewer and farther, towns of any size absent from all but the fringes of the hills. Among the moody Cheviots, you can feel more completely on your own than almost anywhere else in lowland Britain.

Alwinton lies in Upper Coquetdale, at the feet of the Cheviots, towards the head of the River Coquet. There is a great yearly sheep fair here, and sheep farming dominates the area. No other form of farming really suits these grassy, easy-sloped hills, from which came the Roman-nosed, large white Cheviot sheep that replaced so many clansmen on the big estates of the Scottish Highlands during the Clearances of the eighteenth and nineteenth centuries. Alwinton's few grey stone houses and barns are soon left behind as you strike out on the strip of tarmac road that winds with the Coquet up the ever-narrowing valley. There are many roads climbing through the rolling Cheviots from England into Scotland, few of them tarred. Clennell Street, Salter's Road, Gamel's Path, Dere Street – they cross and re-cross the Border as stony cattle trods or sodden, peaty tracks through the grass. Monks on their way to and from their abbeys and grange farms used them: so did cattle thieves, sheep rustlers, builders of Iron Age forts, salt merchants, raiding parties of one family going to or returning from massacre of another. The Street, as the road up the valley from Alwinton is called, bends by Quickening Cote and Shillmoor, sometimes beside and sometimes above the shallow river. Either side curve the green Cheviot slopes, big acreages of grassland separated for the most part not by the stone walls characteristic of northern hill country, but by fences. Shillmoor Farm makes a strikingly lonely and remote picture, seen from a crest of the Street, lying in a bend of the meeting place of River Coquet and Usway Burn with the 1500-foot swell of Shillhope Law at its back.

At Windyhaugh there is a tiny school for the few children of Upper Coquetdale. Here the Street sheds its tarmac and climbs north-west up the hillsides and along the ridges for many miles into Scotland. Leaving the Street and the River Coquet to follow the Rowhope Burn up a northward-winding valley, a path climbs across the cheek of Ward Law above an outlying plantation of the sprawling coniferous forest of Kidland to the east. In the sunshine it's a pathway over gold and green billows. In wet weather it becomes a slippery, sticky slog up the slope, splashing across a burn; on and up into a blanket of mist, lying over the bare heart of the Cheviots, that shrouds the course of the Pennine Way long-distance footpath as it crosses the summit of Windy Gyle near the end of its 250-mile journey from the English Midlands. On this crest at over two thousand feet the wind blows mist drops from the backs of the sheep and chills a soaked walker to the marrow. And here on this sombre height England meets Scotland at the Border. A post-and-wire fence marks the line of the boundary today, a matter-of-fact barrier in a place steeped in bloody history.

Before the Act of Union between the old enemies, Truce Days were regularly declared when grievances could be aired and reparation made without the usual battle and blood-shed. Windy Gyle was recognized as a de-militarized zone where these negotiated settlements could be hammered out, but that didn't stop one of the Scottish contingent from shooting Sir Francis Russell up here in 1585. Russell was one of the deputy wardens of the Middle Marches, charged with policing the Border; and his murder – he was son of the Earl of Bedford into the bargain – brought England and Scotland almost to blows. A heap of stones at Windy Gyle, probably in fact a Bronze Age burial heap, is named Russell's Cairn in recognition of the victim's social and political status. But if every man, woman and child done to death in these hills had a cairn to their memory, the Cheviots would be under stones, not grass.

If William Wordsworth is a hard act to follow for would-be Lake Poets, those wanting to celebrate the rolling hills and rivers of the Scottish Borders in verse have Robert Burns to set their sights on. For wit, humour, free-flowing skill and feeling, Burns has no equal or near rival. Not that this has prevented a host of admirers from chancing their pens. Their representative here, the 'Ayrshire Volunteer' and his 'Ode to Carmel Water', is included in no spirit of mockery, but as a token of the esteem – veneration would be more accurate – felt for Burns everywhere on the Borders down the years since his death in 1796 at the age of thirty-seven, worn out by hard work and by earlier exertions with bed and bottle. Burns lived recklessly, thought radically, stirred up laughter and sadness, died young – eminently qualified to be the Scottish national poet.

What Robert Burns did for Border poetry, Sir Walter Scott did for Border prose, and also for poetry of a very different sort from that of Burns. Both kinds of writing find a place here – Scott's prose depictions of the landscape and its features near Moffat and up north of Glasgow on the road to Loch Lomond, and his lovely chilly poem 'November on Tweedside'.

Another Scott – Lady John – does her level best to keep up with her namesake in her breathless 'Ride over Lammermuir', showing at any rate a detailed knowledge of that countryside gained through many such rides. There's a touch of the genuine article from the Ettrick Shepherd, James Hogg, and a good bloody Border Ballad of 1593 from Annandale (in which a lot of stout lads cut each other to ribbons in true Border style), notable for the number of hills, streams and paths named by the balladeer that can still be identified on today's maps.

North of the Glasgow–Edinburgh line poetry gives way to prose, most of it direct and homely stuff. Local rambler Richie Bernard celebrates his native Ochil hills, James Simson recollects a nineteenth-century childhood on the shores of a Forth estuary nowadays far too polluted and built-up for such innocent pleasures, and the erstwhile gypsy Betsy Whyte recalls her young days near Kirriemuir in fertile Angus, north of the Tay. Here in Angus, too, we follow

J. M. Barrie's poachers up the South Esk River towards the
Cairngorm mountains and the final stretch of our journey.

Ashiestiel, Selkirkshire (Borders)

141. Sir Walter Scott, *Marmion* (1808)

November on Tweedside

November's sky is chill and drear,
November's leaf is red and sere:
Late, gazing down the steepy linn
That hems our little garden in,
Low in its dark and narrow glen
You scarce the rivulet might ken,
So thick the tangled greenwood grew,
So feeble trilled the streamlet through;
Now, murmuring hoarse, and frequent seen
Through bush and briar, no longer green,
An angry brook, it sweeps the glade,
Brawls over rock and wild cascade,
And foaming brown, with doubled speed,
Hurries its waters to the Tweed.
No longer Autumn's glowing red
Upon our Forest hills is shed:
No more, beneath the evening beam,
Fair Tweed reflects their purple gleam;
Away hath passed the heather-bell
That bloomed so rich on Neidpath Fell;
Sallow his brow, and russet-bare
Are now the sister-heights of Yair.
The sheep, before the pinching heaven,
To sheltered dale and down are driven,
Where yet some faded herbage pines,
And yet a watery sunbeam shines;
In meek despondency they eye
The withered sward and wintry sky,
And, far beneath their summer hill,
Stray sadly by Glenkinnon's rill;
The shepherd shifts his mantle's fold,
And wraps him closer from the cold;

His dogs no merry circles wheel,
But, shivering, follow at his heel;
A cowering glance they often cast,
As deeper moans the gathering blast.
My imps, though hardy, bold, and wild
As best befits the mountain child,
Feel the sad influence of the hour,
And wail the daisy's vanished flower;
Their summer gambols tell, and mourn,
And anxious ask – Will Spring return,
And birds and lambs again be gay,
And blossoms clothe the hawthorn spray?

LAMMERMUIR, EAST LOTHIAN (LOTHIAN)/ BERWICKSHIRE (BORDERS)

142. Lady John Scott, *A Ride Over Lammermuir* (1904)

A Ride Over Lammermuir

They are sweeping over the Earnscleuch hill,
Where the silver mist hangs thin and still.
Their horses' hoofs from the heather flowers
Scatter the bloom in purple showers,
The moor-cock flies with sudden spring
From their swift approach on his startled wing,
Onwards they rush – far to the right
Edgarhope's dark forests fringe the height.
And now they wind their rapid way
Down a rocky pathway worn and grey
Which brings them to the mossy side
Of Blythe's wild water, dark and wide.
A hollow plunge and the struggling shock
Of the iron on the slippery rock,
And their horses spring on the grassy ledge
That slopes to the water's southern edge.
With drooping head and slackened rein
Up the steep mountain side they strain,
Each sinew stretched, each nostril wide,
Impatient in their fiery pride,
Gasping with eagerness they stop

At length upon its craggy top.
One moment's pause and their riders' gaze
Has marked the track through the glittering haze,
And with noiseless tread o'er the marshy plain,
And the measured ring of the bridle chain,
They bound with motion light and free
As the dancing waves on a summer sea.
They have crossed the moss, they are standing now
On Gairmoor Edge, whose rugged brow
Frowns on those shadowy hills, that stand
The boundary of a stranger land.
They little know on Cheviot's side,
Who mark that barrier dark and wide,
What fairy scenes its bleak crags hide.
Oh, many a vale lies calm and fair
With peaceful waters murmuring there,
And many a wild and lonely wood
Where the old grey-hen leads forth her brood,
And many a green and sunny glade
Where in the tall fern's fragant shade
The fox and hare their homes have made.
Even as they reached the Gairmoor's side,
The veil of mist, that far and wide
Hung dimly over hill and lea,
Rose slowly upwards – they could see
From woodland green and moorland grey
T'was stealing silently away,
Till over Cheviot's wildest height
It vanished from their dazzled sight.
A glorious scene beneath them spread
A flood of golden light was shed
On all the valley wide and green
That stretched those distant hills between;
And waves of sunshine seemed to roll
O'er tangled wood and mossy knoll.
Long was the rapturous gaze they cast
In silence round – too bright to last,
That glittering light was fading fast,
Mellowed and softened down and still,
It settled over glen and hill.

ETTRICK FOREST, SELKIRKSHIRE (BORDERS)

143. James Hogg, *The Queen's Wake* (1813)

Now, my loved Harp, a while farewell;
　　I leave thee on the old gray thorn;
The evening dews will mar thy swell,
　　That waked to joy the cheerful morn.

Farewell, sweet soother of my woe!
　　Chill blows the blast around my head;
And louder yet that blast may blow,
　　When down this weary vale I've sped.

The wreath lies on Saint Mary's shore;
　　The mountain sounds are harsh and loud:
The lofty brows of stern Clokmore
　　Are visored with the moving cloud.

But Winter's deadly hues shall fade
　　On moorland bald and mountain shaw,
And soon the rainbow's lovely shade
　　Sleep on the breast of Bowerhope Law;

Then will the glowing suns of spring,
　　The genial shower and stealing dew,
Wake every forest bird to sing,
　　And every mountain flower renew.

But not the rainbow's ample ring,
　　That spans the glen and mountain grey,
Though fanned by western breeze's wing,
　　And sunned by summer's glowing ray,

To man decayed, can ever more
　　Renew the age of love and glee!
Can ever second spring restore
　　To my old mountain Harp and me!

But when the hue of softened green
　　Spreads over hill and lonely lea,
And lowly primrose opes unseen
　　Her virgin bosom to the bee;

When hawthorns breathe their odours far,
　　And carols hail the year's return;
And daisy spreads her silver star
　　Unheeded by the mountain burn;

Then will I seek the aged thorn,
　　The haunted wild and fairy ring,
Where oft thy erring numbers borne
　　Have taught the wandering winds to sing.

Devil's Beef Tub, Dumfriesshire (Dumfries and Galloway)

144. Sir Walter Scott, *Redgauntlet* (1824)

'We were to halt for breakfast at Moffat. Well did I
know the moors we were marching over, having hunted
and hawked on every acre of ground in very different
times. So I waited, you see, till I was on the edge of
Errickstane brae – Ye ken the place they call the
Marquis's Beef-stand, because the Annandale loons
used to put their stolen cattle in there?'

Fairford intimated his ignorance.

'Ye must have seen it as ye cam this way; it looks as if
four hills were laying their heads together, to shut out
daylight from the dark hollow space between them. A
d—d deep, black, blackguard-looking abyss of a hole it
is, and goes straight down from the road-side, as
perpendicular as it can do, to be a heathery brae. At the
bottom, there is a small bit of a brook, that you would
think could hardly find its way out from the hills that
are so closely jammed round it.'

'A bad pass indeed,' said Alan.

'You may say that,' continued the Laird. 'Bad as it
was, sir, it was my only chance; and though my very
flesh creeped when I thought what a rumble I was going
to get, yet I kept my heart up all the same. And so, just
when we came on the edge of this Beef-stand of the
Johnstones, I slipped out my hand from the handcuff,

cried to Harry Gauntlet, "Follow me!" – whisked under
the belly of the dragoon horse – flung my plaid round me
with the speed of lightning – threw myself on my side,
for there was no keeping my feet, and down the brae
hurled I, over heather and fern, and blackberries, like a
barrel down Chalmers's Close in Auld Reekie. G——, sir, I
never could help laughing when I think how the
scoundrel redcoats must have been bumbazed; for the
mist being, as I said, thick, they had little notion, I take
it, that they were on the verge of such a dilemma. I was
half way down – for rowing is faster wark than rinning –
ere they could get at their arms; and then it was flash,
flash, flash – rap, rap, rap – from the edge of the road; but
my head was too jumbled to think any thing either of
that or the hard knocks I got among the stones. I kept
my senses thegither, whilk has been thought wonderful
by all that ever saw the place; and I helped myself with
my hands as gallantly as I could, and to the bottom I
came. There I lay for half a moment; but the thoughts of
a gallows is worth all the salts and scent-bottles in the
world, for bringing a man to himself. Up I sprung, like a
four-year-auld colt. All the hills were spinning round
with me, like so many great big humming-tops. But
there was nae time to think of that neither; more
especially as the mist had risen a little with the firing.
I could see the villains, like sae mony craws on the
edge of the brae; and I reckon that they saw me; for
some of the loons were beginning to crawl down the
hill, but liker auld wives in their red-cloaks, coming
frae a field-preaching, than such a souple lad as I was.
Accordingly, they soon began to stop and load their
pieces. Good-e'en to you, gentlemen, thought I, if that
is to be the gate of it. If you have any farther word
with me, you maun come as far as Carriefraw-gauns.
And so off I set, and never buck went faster ower the
braes than I did; and I never stopped till I had put
three waters, reasonably deep, as the season was rainy,
half-a-dozen mountains, and a few thousand acres of
the worst moss and ling in Scotland, betwixt me and
my friends the redcoats.'

ANNANDALE, DUMFRIESSHIRE (DUMFRIES AND GALLOWAY)

145. Traditional, *Scott's Minstrelsy of the Scottish Border* (1802–3)

The Lads of Wamphray

'Twixt Girth-head and the Langwood end,
Lived the Galliard, and the Galliard's men;
But and the lads of Leverhay,
That drove the Crichton's gear away.

It is the lads of Lethenha',
The greatest rogues among them a':
But and the lads of Stefenbiggin,
They broke the house in at the rigging.

The lads of Fingland, and Helbeck-hill,
They were never for good, but aye for ill;
'Twixt the Staywood-bush and Langside-hill,
They steal'd the brokit cow and the branded bull.

It is the lads of the Girth-head,
The deil's in them for pride and greed;
For the Galliard and the gay Galliard's men,
They ne'er saw a horse but they made it their ain.

The Galliard to Nithsdale is gane,
To steal Sim Crichton's winsome dun,
The Galliard is unto the stable gane,
But instead of the dun, the blind he has ta'en.

'Now Simmy, Simmy of the Side,
Come out and see a Johnstone ride!
Here's the bonniest horse in a' Nithside,
And a gentle Johnstone aboon his hide.'

Simmy Crichton's mounted then,
And Crichtons has raised mony a ane;
The Galliard trow'd his horse had been wight,
But the Crichtons beat him out o' sight.

As soon as the Galliard the Crichton saw,
Behind the saugh-bush he did draw:
And there the Crichtons the Galliard hae ta'en,
And nane wi' him but Willie alane.

'O Simmy, Simmy, now let me gang,
And I'll never mair do a Crichton wrang!
O Simmy, Simmy, now let me be,
And a peck o' gowd I'll give to thee!

'O Simmy, Simmy, now let me gang,
And my wife shall heap it with her hand.' –
But the Crichtons wadna let the Galliard be,
But they hang'd him hie upon a tree.

O think then Willie he was right wae,
When he saw his uncle guided sae;
'But if ever I live Wamphray to see,
My uncle's death avenged shall be!'

Back to Wamphray he is gane,
And riders has raised mony a ane;
Saying – 'My lads, if ye'll be true,
Ye shall a' be clad in the noble blue.' –

Back to Nithsdale they have gane,
And awa' the Crichton's nowt hae ta'en;
But when they cam to the Wellpath-head,
The Crichtons bade them 'light and lead.

And when they cam to Biddes-burn,
The Crichtons bade them stand and turn;
And when they cam to the Biddes-strand,
The Crichtons they were hard at hand.

But when they cam to the Biddes-law,
The Johnstones bade them stand and draw;
'We've done nae ill, we'll thole nae wrang,
But back to Wamphray we will gang.'

And out spoke Willie of the Kirkhill,
'Of fighting, lads, ye'se hae your fill.' –
And from his horse Willie he lap,
And a burnish'd brand in his hand he gat.

310

Out through the Crichtons Willie he ran,
And dang them down baith horse and man;
O but the Johnstones were wondrous rude,
When the Biddes-burn ran three days blood!

'Now, sirs, we have done a noble deed;
We have revenged the Galliard's bleid,
For every finger of the Galliard's hand,
I vow this day I've kill'd a man.' –

As they cam in at Evan-head,
At Ricklaw-holm they spread abroad;
'Drive on, my lads, it will be late;
We'll hae a pint at Wamphray gate.

'For where'er I gang, or e'er I ride,
The lads of Wamphray are on my side;
And of a' the lads that I do ken,
A Wamphray lad's the king of men.'

RIVER COYLE, AYRSHIRE (STRATHCLYDE)

146. Robert Burns, *Poems Chiefly in the Scottish Dialect* (1787)

To William Simpson, Ochiltree May 1785
I gat your letter, winsome Willie;
Wi' gratefu' heart I thank you brawlie;
Though I maun say't, I wad be silly,
          An' unco vain,
Should I believe, my coaxin billie,
          Your flatterin strain.

But I'se believe ye kindly meant it,
I sud be laith to think ye hinted
Ironic satire, sidelins sklented,
          On my poor Musie;
Through in sic phraisin terms ye've penn'd it,
          I scarce excuse ye.

My senses wad be in a creel,
Should I but dare a hope to speel,

Wi' Allan or wi' Gilbertfield,
   The braes o' fame;
Or Ferguson, the writer-chiel,
    A deathless name.

(O Ferguson! thy glorious parts
Ill-suited law's dry, musty arts!
My curse upon your whunstane hearts,
   Ye E'nbrugh gentry!
The tythe o' what ye waste at cartes
    Wad stow'd his pantry.)

Yet when a tale comes i' my head,
Or lasses gie my heart a screed,
As whyles they're like to be my dead,
   (O sad disease!)
I kittle up my rustic reed;
   It gies me ease.

Auld Coila, now, may fidge fu' fain,
She's gotten poets o' her ain,
Chiels wha their chanters winna hain,
   But tune their lays,
Till echoes a' resound again
    Her weel-sung praise.

Nae Poet thought her worth his while,
To set her name in measur'd stile;
She lay like some unkend-of isle,
   Beside New Holland,
Or whare wild-meeting oceans boil
    Besouth Magellan.

Ramsay an' famous Ferguson
Gied Forth an' Tay a lift aboon;
Yarrow an' Tweed to monie a tune,
   Owre Scotland rings,
While Irwin, Lugar, Ayr, an' Doon,
    Naebody sings.

Th' Ilissus, Tiber, Thames, an' Seine,
Glide sweet in mony a tunefu' line!
But, Willie, set your fit to mine,

An' cock your crest,
We'll gar our streams and burnies shine
Up wi' the best.

We'll sing auld Coila's plains an' fells,
Her moors red-brown wi' heather bells,
Her banks an' braes, her dens an' dells,
Where glorious Wallace
Aft bure the gree, as story tells,
Frae southron billies.

At Wallace' name, what Scottish blood
But boils up in a spring-tide flood!
Oft have our fearless fathers strode
By Wallace' side,
Still pressing onward, red-wat-shod,
Or glorious died.

O, sweet are Coila's haughs an' woods,
When lintwhites chant amang the buds,
And jinkin hares, in amorous whids,
Their loves enjoy,
While through the braes the cushat croods
Wi' wailfu' cry!

Ev'n winter bleak has charms to me,
When winds rave through the naked tree:
Or frosts on hills of Ochiltree
Are hoary gray;
Or blinding drifts wild-furious flee,
Dark'ning the day!

O Nature! a' thy shows an' forms
To feeling, pensive hearts hae charms!
Whether the summer kindly warms,
Wi' life an' light,
Or winter howls, in gusty storms,
The lang, dark night!

The Muse, nae Poet ever fand her,
Till by himsel he learn'd to wander,
Adown some trottin burn's meander,
An' no think lang;

313

O sweet, to stray an' pensive ponder
> A heart-felt sang!

The warly race may drudge an' drive,
Hog-shouther, jundie, stretch, an' strive,
Let me fair Nature's face descrive,
> And I, wi' pleasure,
Shall let the busy, grumbling hive
> Bum owre their treasure.

Fareweel, 'my rhyme-composing brither!'
We've been owre lang unkenn'd to ither:
Now let us lay our heads thegither,
> In love fraternal:
May Envy wallop in a tether,
> Black fiend, infernal!

While Highlandmen hate tolls an' taxes;
While moorlan' herds like guid, fat braxies;
While terra firma, on her axis
> Diurnal turns,
Count on a friend, in faith an' practice,
> In Robert Burns.

CARMEL WATER

147. 'An Ayrshire Volunteer' (William Lamberton),
Poems and Songs (1878)

> *Ode to Carmel Water*
Pleasant Carmel, bounteous stream,
Here let youthful poets dream,
Where all things rejoicing seem,
May ever on thy banks be seen;
Flocks and herds and pastures green,
And groves which happy lovers screen;
Bosky dells and fruits and flowers,
Happy homes and gladsome bowers;
And stalwart men and faithful wives,
Who show their virtues in their lives;
And gentle maids, divinely fair,
May they be Heaven's peculiar care;

And may each noble, generous youth,
Be ever valiant for the truth;
And nightly from each humble dwelling
May songs of praise be sweetly swelling,
Showing the Saviour's love and worth
Is still acknowledged on the earth.

Here's peace, blest rest, and silence deep,
When holy men the Sabbath keep;
When Sabbath bells the echoes wake
Mankind, of Eden's bliss partake:
Long has it been, long may it be,
The poor man's weekly jubilee.

Sweet peace has long thy banks possessed,
Where in deep pools thou lov'st to rest,
With Heaven reflecting on thy breast.
There timid wild-fowl lightly skim,
And there my hardy boys will swim;
And there the quick-eyed trouts arise,
And oft his art the angler tries
To catch secure the tempting prize.

May Spring send here her fairest flowers,
And Summer bring the sultry bowers,
And Autumn wave the yellow corn,
And Winter with its snow return,
To bind thy stream with icy chains,
While he again as monarch reigns.
But other scenes appear to view,
When hunters pass with wild halloo,
And savage hounds the fox pursue;
When brought to bay and killed at last,
Its carcase forms a rich repast
For hungry hounds to break their fast.

Say, was thy stream oft tinged with blood
In the old days, misnamed 'the good;'
When men and times were dark and rude,
And barons castles, grim and strong,
Beheld thy waters rush along?
No greater day to thee hast been
Since Robert bore away his queen
From Allan's towers to palace fair;

They were indeed a royal pair:
And left behind thy little stream,
Where she enjoyed life's morning dream.
Where happy homes thy banks adorn,
May future heroes yet be born,
And future bards inspired rehearse
Their glorious acts in deathless verse.

I hear the marksman's rifle crack,
Which thy banks do echo back;
And the deep booming cannon's roar
Is heard from batteries on the shore;
All manned by British Volunteers,
The nation's guard in future years.

LANARK, LANARKSHIRE (STRATHCLYDE)

148. Stuart Lewis (1756–1817)

Lanark Mills

Adieu! romantic banks of Clyde,
Where oft I've spent the joyful day;
Now, weary-wand'ring on thy side,
I pour the plaintive, joyless lay.
To other lands I'm doomed to rove,
The thought with grief my bosom fills;
Why am I forced to leave my love,
And wander far from Lanark Mills?

Can I forget th' ecstatic hours,
When ('scaped the village evening din)
I met my lass 'midst Braxfield bowers,
Or near the falls of Corhouse Linn!
While close I clasp'd her to my breast,
(Th' idea still with rapture thrills!)
I thought myself completely blest,
By all the lads of Lanark Mills!

Deceitful, dear, delusive dream,
Thou'rt fled – alas! I know not where,
And vanish'd is each blissful gleam,
And left behind a load of care.

Adieu! dear winding banks of Clyde,
A long farewell, ye rising hills;
No more I'll wander on your side,
Though still my heart's at Lanark Mills.

While Tintock stands the pride of hills,
While Clyde's dark stream rolls to the sea,
So long my dear-loved Lanark Mills,
May Heaven's best blessing smile on thee.
A last adieu! my Mary dear,
The briny tear my eye distils;
While reason's powers continue clear,
I'll think of thee, and Lanark Mills.

Glasgow and Paisley Canal, Renfrewshire (Strathclyde)

149. Hugh MacDonald, *Rambles Round Glasgow* (1854)

The banks of the canal between Glasgow and Paisley, artificial though they be, are as rich in natural beauty as the winding margin of many a river. In various places they are finely wooded, while throughout their entire length they are fringed with a profusion of our sweetest wild flowers. Every here and there, also, glimpses of the surrounding country are obtained – in some cases extending for many miles around, and embracing scenes of great fertility and loveliness. As we pass along, the reapers in picturesque groups are busy in the bright yellow fields. Occasionally, also, the voices of juvenile strollers from the purlieus of the city are heard on the tangled and bosky banks, where they come in search of the hips and haws and the blackboyds, which, however, have scarcely yet attained the necessary degree of ripeness. At intervals, 'few and far between', one of the Company's boats passes lazily to its destination; while every now and again a solitary angler gazes despairingly at his float, and mutters 'Nothing doing' to our passing inquiries concerning his piscatorial success.

About four miles from the city, the Cart approaches within a few feet of the canal. At this point of the stream we find the yellow water-lily (*nuphar lutea*) growing abundantly, with its broad cordate leaves and bright golden flowers covering the surface of the water. A number of other fine plants also are thickly strewn along the alluvial margin. Among these are the handsome wood crane's-bill (*geranium sylvaticum*), several stately species of thistle, flinging their snowy locks to the passing breeze, and the rough burr-reed with its green sword-like leaves guarding the shallows of the streamlet, and forming an impervious shade for the water-hen. A dense wood on the opposite side of the Cart at this place forming part of the extensive estates of Sir John Maxwell of Pollok, seems to be well stocked with game and other wild birds, and we have often heard with delight their peculiar cries and notes while lingering at the spot during the spring and summer gloamings. Here, too, we have observed for several successive seasons a pair of those sweet, though in this part of the country somewhat rare songsters, the black-cap warblers (*curruca atricapilla*), which seem to have bred in the vicinity, although with all our skill (and in our school-days it was famous) we have failed to discover the well screened nest.

FROM GLASGOW TOWARDS LOCH LOMOND, DUNBARTONSHIRE (STRATHCLYDE)

150. Sir Walter Scott, *Rob Roy* (1817)

The road which we travelled, while diverting the way with these discussions, had become wild and open, as soon as we had left Glasgow a mile or two behind us, and was growing more dreary as we advanced. Huge continuous heaths spread before, behind, and around us in hopeless barrenness, now level and interspersed with swamps, green with treacherous verdure, or sable with turf, or, as they call them in Scotland, peat-bogs and now swelling into huge heavy ascents, which wanted the dignity and form of hills, while they were still more toilsome to the passenger. There were neither trees nor bushes to relieve the eye from the russet livery of absolute sterility. The very heath was of that stinted imperfect kind which has little or no flower, and affords the coarsest and meanest covering, which, as far as my experience enables me to judge, mother Earth is ever arrayed in. Living thing we saw none, except occasionally a few straggling sheep of a strange diversity of colours, as black, bluish, and orange. The sable hue predominated, however, in their faces and legs. The very birds seemed to shun these wastes, and no wonder, since they had an easy method of escaping from them; at least I only heard the monotonous and plaintive cries of the lapwing and curlew, which my companions denominated the peasweep and whaup.

At dinner, however, which we took about noon, at a most miserable alehouse, we had the good fortune to find that these tiresome screamers of the morass were not the only inhabitants of the moors. The goodwife told us, that 'the gudeman had been at the hill'; and well for us that he had been so, for we enjoyed the produce of his *chasse* in the shape of some broiled moor-game, a dish which gallantly eked out the ewe-milk cheese, dried salmon, and oaten bread, being all besides that the house afforded. Some very indifferent two-penny ale, and a glass of excellent brandy, crowned our repast; and as our horses had, in the meantime, discussed their corn, we resumed our journey with renovated vigour.

I had need of all the spirits a good dinner could give, to resist the dejection which crept insensibly on my mind, when I combined the strange uncertainty of my errand with the disconsolate aspect of the country through which it was leading me. Our road continued to be, if possible, more waste and wild than we had travelled in the forenoon. The few miserable hovels that showed some marks of human habitation, were now of still rarer occurrence; and at length, as we began to ascend an uninterrupted swell of moorland, they totally disappeared. The only exercise which my imagination received was, when some particular turn of the road gave us a partial view, to the left, of a large assemblage of dark-blue mountains stretching to the north and north-west, which promised to include within their recesses, a country as wild perhaps, but certainly differing greatly in point of interest, from that which we now travelled. The peaks of this screen of mountains were as wildly varied and distinguished as the hills which we had seen on the right were tame and lumpish; and while I gazed on this Alpine region, I felt a longing to explore its recesses, though accompanied with toil and danger, similar to that which a sailor feels when he wishes for the risks and animation of a battle or a gale, in exchange for the insupportable monotony of a protracted calm. I made various enquiries of my friend Mr Jarvie respecting the names and positions of these remarkable mountains; but it was a subject on which he had no information, or did not choose to be communicative. 'They're the Hieland hills – the Hieland hills – Ye'll see and hear eneugh about them before ye see Glasgow Cross again – I downa look at them – I never see them but they gar me grew. – It's no for fear – no for fear, but just for grief, for the puir blinded half-starved creatures that inhabit them – But say nae mair about it – it's ill speaking o' Hielandmen sae near the line.'

PORT LAING, FIFE

151. James Simson, *A Childhood at Inverkeithing, or Life at a Lazaretto* (1882)

Port Laing sands was our favourite resort. There we would amuse ourselves in many ways, and among others by picking up oyster shells and skimming them along the surface of the sea. Sometimes we would climb the face of the ground to the level of the plateau on which the cattle were grazing, and, if they were at some distance from us, make for the old farm-house; or take the narrow path along the steep coast line past Caroline's Nose till we came to the Ferry. Attractive as Port Laing was considered, I do not remember ever having seen anyone there but ourselves and those with us; and I was very often there. I certainly never saw anyone bathing at the place. The Ferry does not seem to have been much resorted to at the time alluded to, as a summer residence; or it had its own facilities for sea-bathing without resorting to Port Laing sands. The distance between the two was not great, although there was a little climbing to be done on both sides. It was at Port Laing I first learned that crabs (called 'partans') hid themselves in the sand, for I dug them out of it, near the salmon stake-nets that were there.

Between the sand proper and the hill there was what geologists call a 'raised beach', of a very little elevation, on which I have seen very fair crops reaped by old Adam ——, who made or used a very good road from the hill down to it. Between the cultivated ground and the sand there were some stones of considerable size and irregular shape, that could hardly be considered a fence made by the hand of man, although they served that purpose, but as if they had almost been left there by nature. Immediately near these stones, on the side facing the sea, yet not washed by it, there were some pretty specimens of what are to be found in such a place, that is, tall and stout stalks, with few leaves, bearing flowers of a delicate pink-like colour.

This sandy beach is associated in my memory with an adventure with two boys, a very little older than myself, getting a boat at Inverkeithing and leaving the bay in it. My first care was to lie down in the boat till it passed our pier, when we pulled along the shore in the direction of Port Laing, and out of what current there might have been. It was a small boat and easily managed, one oar being on one side near the bow, and two on the other side nearer the stern. We were wretched rowers, taking 'spoonful about' with our oars. The other boys insisted on passing the sands, but I got

321

frightened at the idea of going beyond the first head-
land into a sea unknown to me, and refused to pull
another stroke, when we returned, and got home in
safety.

OCHIL HILLS, CLACKMANNAN (CENTRAL)/ PERTHSHIRE (TAYSIDE)

152. Richie Bernard, *Walks in the Ochils* (1984)

On a clear, sunlit day the tractor-marked hilltop
pathway descending gently to the distant Frandy is a
joy to be tramping along. The Perthshire giants heave
their alluring heights in the north, and on all sides are
the rounding Ochil tops with their myriad glens and
endless rippling burns. With a sharp descent, the
junction of two of these burns, the Grodwell and the
Broich, was reached, and I could see by the big linn
where they met that the water level had risen since my
last trip. The plant life too had developed, and the hill
pansies, the only blooms then visible, were accompanied now by pink campion, marsh marigold, meadow-
sweet and ragged robin in the damp stretches at the
hillfoot, while the rocks by the burn carried white
sprays of mossy saxifrage, yellow dandelion-like
hawk-heads, and the slender, blue-flowered stems of
butterwort, their basal leaves clinging starfish-like to
the wet rock slabs.

I was caught empty handed, the camera in the
haversack, when a long, sleek-coated water vole
cruised upstream, to wheel abruptly into one of its
subterranean hidy-holes as I dithered into action. The
photographer's motto should definitely be that of the
scouts.

The excitement occasioned by this incident had
barely subsided when the long, fiord-like arm of the
Upper Glendevon Reservoir became visible, with which
the Broich, that I'd followed for a good two miles, has
an anonymous merger.

I leaned on the bridge leading to the present day Back-hills Hoose for a bit, mentally reconstructing the landscape before the deluge. The dam-head is butted on its far side to a high cliff where kestrels once had an impregnable ancestral nest-site, for it was only by a risky stomach-prone squint into the depths that the chocolate-blotched eggs could be spied. The picturesque series of rock-enfiladed, fern hung, foam splashed falls that terminated in the immense fish-haunted linn at the cliff-foot have gone before the need to provide Fife folk with a sufficiency of flush-toilets. No winter winds howl now round the once sturdy gables of the original Back-hill Hoose. With man's instigation, a dozen burns have ganged up to inter it fathoms deep. Long gone are the days of the legendary home-made scones, and the milk straucht frae the coo, that were in constant supply to famished travellers who came rapping at its weather-beaten door. The replacement bungalow up the steep, stoney track bore an air of aloofness, which the right-of-way people had failed to dispel by diverting walkers loch-wards short of the house and so preventing casual communication with the occupants.

A period of stile-climbing and gulley crossing and I was on the pebbly shore of the loch. Nostalgic affection for that lost and lovely mile of winding Devon had instilled an umbrage in me towards the liquid mass that enveloped it, but I now admit, with reluctance, that the loch has introduced a new and desirable element into the area, that is, if it remains at its present water-level – the wide pebbly beaches, the machair-like stretches, and maritime plant life, the piping of the sandpipers, redshanks and oystercatchers, the vociferous gullery on a rocky islet, and most of all the presence of the rare ringed plover which, otherwise, I'd never have met up with. The birds had instinctively chosen the remote end of the loch for their activities, and after a traverse of boulder-strewn reaches and peat-sided gulleys the now familiar alarm-call was heard once more. I made a quick search while the birds scurried like mice along the shoreline, but again with no success. Remnants of nests there were but nowt with eggs. I was disappointed, but not deeply so, for there remained the incentive for future excursions in another summer.

It was westward then with the loch narrowing until the Devon finally took shape and the right-o-way bridge was reached. Around two miles of rough going have been added to the Blackford trip, compared with the old direct path to Glen Bee before the loch's intervention. The large, peat-hued pools in the river invited a fly but, in my rod-less state, I was a penniless bairn with a nose brizzed wistfully against the sweetie-shop window. Three burns feed the Devon up here near its source, all from a southerly direction, and I intended to follow the first of them, the Greenhorn, to its start on the north side of Ben Cleuch. I'd bet on it being the windingest burn in the Ochils, and involved me in an endless series of corner cutting water-jumps in its two miles of 'meandering in a mazy motion'. I halted to 'snap' a dozen white butterflies on a crimson bank of thyme, and again in a futile attempt to pull out a dead sheep stuck in a narrow bit of the burn. When clear of the burn and high among the peat-hags I once more saw a figure on the skyline. No shepherd this time, for he seemed to be studying a map and looking around indecisively, so I waved and we approached each other. A middle-aged man hailing from Grangemouth, he'd started at Dollar aiming for Blackford, but inaccurate map-reading had landed him miles off the route. He was grateful for my help in setting him right, to the extent of a handshake when we parted, an emotional outburst infrequent among us Scots.

I watched him wend his way down into the glen then turned to make the long, gradual ascent of the Cleuch, looking forward to the relaxing descent of the sun-bright homeward slopes.

GLAMIS, ANGUS (TAYSIDE)

153. Betsy Whyte, *The Yellow on the Broom* (1979)

The laughing of children and the barking of a puppy greeted us as we reached the camp.

We had a barricade up. This is a bit added on to the sleeping quarters – but much higher, allowing standing room. It was built with long sticks of hazel or birch and covered with any kind of covering to be had – old sacks, tarpaulins, or what have you. There was a hole left in the top centre to let the smoke out. The fire, often an old dup tin made into a brazier, was in the middle and we could all sit around it, sheltered from the cold.

Mother had been very busy. She had a huge pot of broth ready and another pot filled with swedes and potatoes, mashed together with a knob of butter and pepper and salt. Another pot full of boiled rice, to which she always added one or two beaten eggs, was also ready.

After our bellies were filled the men would lie back and smoke and chat, while the women got on with the rest of the work. Some went for water which had to be carried in pails – some half mile easily. Others went to gather sticks for the fires. Sometimes the men would do this, but more often it was left to the women. Then there were the children to be washed and bedded, all the dishes and pots to be washed, and clothes to be washed out.

Mary wanted to do the dishes, but Mother didn't trust her with this chore. Although we often went about a bit ragged and even dirty, we were very particular where food and dishes are concerned. Travellers still are.

A big enamel basin was kept for washing dishes and dishcloths in. Nothing else was allowed to be washed in it. Food was kept in a box away from folks' breaths and if anyone coughed or sneezed over food it would have to be thrown away.

Mother had once broken two lovely little bowls

because Mary had stepped over them. 'Have you no sense at all, lassie?' she had said. 'You don't step with your petticoats out over dishes. You could have lifted them up instead.' It had been some of the men who had left the bowls on the ground – had it been a girl or woman she would have been reprimanded for it, but men were different.

'You do the dishes, Bessie,' Mother told me. She knew that I hated dish-washing and waited for my rebellious reply. But I was still a bit worried lest the gentry would send a policeman or, worse still, a Cruelty man up because I had begged the tobacco. So I just went to do as Mother asked.

I heard her outside the tent saying to one of the others 'Bessie's surely going to die. She's actually doing the dishes!'

SOUTH ESK RIVER, ANGUS (TAYSIDE)

154. J. M. Barrie, *Auld Licht Idylls* (1888)

Life in the bothies is not, I should say, so lonely as life at the schoolhouse, for the hands have at least each other's company. The hawker visits them frequently still, though the itinerant tailor, once a familiar figure, has almost vanished. Their great place of congregating is still some country smiddy, which is also their frequent meeting-place when bent on black-fishing. The flare of the black-fisher's torch still attracts salmon to their death in the rivers near Thrums; and you may hear in the glens on a dark night the rattle of the spears on the wet stones. Twenty or thirty years ago, however, the sport was much more common. After the farmer had gone to bed, some half-dozen ploughmen and a few other poachers from Thrums would set out for the meeting-place.

The smithy on these occasions must have been a weird sight; though one did not mark that at the time.

The poacher crept from the darkness into the glaring smithy light; for in country parts the anvil might sometimes be heard clanging at all hours of the night. As a rule, every face was blackened; and it was this, I suppose, rather than the fact that dark nights were chosen that gave the gangs the name of black-fishers. Other disguises were resorted to; one of the commonest being to change clothes or to turn your corduroys outside in. The country folk of those days were more superstitious than they are now, and it did not take much to turn the black-fishers back. There was not a barn or byre in the district that had not its horseshoe over the door. Another popular device for frightening away witches and fairies was to hang bunches of garlic about the farms. I have known a black-fishing expedition stopped because a 'yellow-yite', or yellow-hammer, hovered round the gang when they were setting out. Still more ominous was the 'péat' when it appeared with one or three companions. An old rhyme about this bird runs – 'One is joy, two is grief, three's a bridal, four is death.' Such snatches of superstition are still to be heard amidst the gossip of a north-country smithy.

Each black-fisher brought his own spear and torch, both more or less home-made. The spears were in many cases 'gully-knives', fastened to staves with twine and resin, called 'rozet'. The torches were very rough-and-ready things – rope and tar, or even rotten roots dug from broken trees – in fact, anything that would flare. The black-fishers seldom journeyed far from home, confining themselves to the rivers within a radius of three or four miles. There were many reasons for this: one of them being that the hands had to be at their work on the farm by five o'clock in the morning; another, that so they poached and let poach. Except when in spate, the river I specially refer to offered no attractions to the black-fishers. Heavy rains, however, swell it much more quickly than most rivers into a turbulent rush of water; the part of it affected by the black-fishers being banked in with rocks that prevent the water's spreading. Above these rocks, again, are heavy green banks, from which stunted trees grow aslant across the river. The effect is fearsome at some points where the trees run into each other, as it were, from opposite banks. However, the black-fishers thought nothing of these things. They took a turnip lantern with them – that is, a lantern hollowed out of a turnip, with a piece of candle inside – but no lights were shown on the road. Everyone knew his way to the river blindfold; so that the darker the night the better. On reaching the water there was a pause. One or two of the gang climbed the banks to discover if any bailiffs were on the watch; while the others sat down, and with the help of the turnip lantern 'busked' their spears; in other words, fastened on the steel – or, it might be, merely pieces of rusty iron sharpened into a point at home – to the staves. Some had them busked before they set out, but that was not considered prudent; for of course there was always a risk of meeting spoil-sports on the way, to whom the spears would tell a tale that could not be learned from ordinary staves. Nevertheless little time was lost. Five or six of the gang waded into the water, torch in one hand and spear in the other; and the object now was to catch some salmon with the least possible delay, and hurry away. Windy nights were good for the sport, and I can still see the river lit up with the lumps of light that a torch makes in a high wind. The torches, of course, were used to attract the fish, which came swimming to the sheen, and were then speared. As little noise as possible was made; but though the men bit their lips instead of crying out when they missed their fish, there was a continuous ring of their weapons on the stones, and every irrepressible imprecation was echoed up and down the black glen. Two or three of the gang were told off to land the salmon, and they had to work smartly and deftly. They kept by the side of the spearsman, and the moment he struck a fish they grabbed at it with their hands. When the spear had a barb there was less chance of the fish's being lost; but often this was not the case, and probably not more than two-thirds of the salmon speared were got safely to the bank. The takes of course varied; sometimes, indeed, the black-fishers returned home empty-handed.

To the Highlands

No one really knows the point at which Lowlands meet Highlands. But to catch a definitive shift of landscape and atmosphere from richly fertile to elementally barren, travel up the South Esk River from the Angus cornlands into the Grampian mountains. The South Esk River flows through Glen Clova, and this long valley sounds a wilder, harder note the further north and west you go. The sides rise, close in and begin to change their smooth greenery for stony screes and sharp edges of bare rock. At the top the glen divides like the fork of a fish's tail, Glen Clova running north and the side valley of Glen Doll curving to the west. Looking up Glen Doll to the great corrie or bowl-shaped lip closing it off like a wall at the upper end, you can sense – almost smell – the towering Cairngorm range behind.

Jock's Road runs up Glen Doll, an old whisky-smuggler's and cattle-drover's route that linked the Lowland fattening meadows and markets with the Highland breeding grounds. Above the shallow, rushing White Water Burn it humps and flattens for a couple of miles between the Forestry Commission spruce, pines and larches, before slanting up the open hillside at the head of the glen.

Walking with me along Jock's Road was an old friend, a botanist, bird-watcher and musician, who had himself seen both golden eagles and peregrines on the mountains around Glen Doll. None were about this day, but through binoculars we made out an eagle's nest, a whitened bundle of sticks, jammed into a crack of the rock wall opposite. On the hillside by the zig-zagging, dusty path were more wild

flowers than I could identify; but my companion seemed
never lost for a name – milkwort with flattened, blade-like
blue petals; feathery *equisetum sylvaticum* or wood horse-
tail; tiny blue gentians; white eyebright like minature
daisies starring the grass; green-flowered alpine lady's
mantle; saxifrage flowers with green and yellow spokes.

A kestrel called in an echoing shriek from up ahead over
the rim of the corrie, to which Jock's Road climbed across
burns that poured in cold needles of water down slimy mats
of brown moss. Looking back from the top of the pass we saw
the old drover's road as a dusty white scar wavering away
down the side of the glen towards the stream a thousand feet
below. Behind were blue hills descending to the hidden, fat
Lowlands; ahead and above the starved, rocky Highlands. A
saddle of peaty, water-sodden ground led us to Davy's
Bourach beside the path, a dark little stone shelter where
benighted travellers would find no comfort – just the bare
essentials of a few sticks of wood for a fire, and four rough
walls against snow, rain or wind. Close to this place, a
memorial tablet on a rock told us, five members of the
Universal Hiking Club of Glasgow had died at New Year,
1959, falling or freezing to death. Somewhere up that flowery
path we had crossed a boundary, invisible but unmistakable.
From this beautiful and threatening pass it is Highland
Scotland all the way.

Where the Scottish Highlands actually separate from the
Lowlands is a matter of personal feeling. You know when
you're in the Highlands, though the hills may be no higher
than those Lowland ones you have been travelling through.
As with Wales, there is overwhelming grandeur of landscape, though dispersed over a much larger area – particularly in the central and western regions. Here on the last leg
of our journey we climb through the heights of the Cairngorms, celebrating their hill burns and their deep corries,
and runs west with R. L. Stevenson's David Balfour over
forlorn Rannoch Moor to the beautifully remote coast that
looks across to the Isle of Skye. Here Gavin Maxwell and Mij
the otter delight in the freedom of 'Camusfeàrna' (Sandaig),

while Dr Samuel Johnson gets on his high horse in nearby Glenelg.

Not all of the Highland region rears up in craggy splendour, however. Up in the north-eastern cornlands of Buchan we travel across gentle braesides to Aikey Fair and along a rocky coast to the fishing villages of the Moray Firth. Then a return to the wild west, with John Hillaby losing his way on Ben More Assynt, and Hamish Brown finding secret joy in the roadless country south-east of Ullapool. To cap it, a couple of high views more in the mind than the eye, over this whole remote and rugged tip of Scotland.

This literary ramble has brought us straggling, snaking and meandering a couple of thousand miles through every kind of landscape – pastoral, industrial, shoreline, valley and hill, moor and mountain – from the south-western to the north-eastern ends of the land. We have done the mammoth journey in the company of every kind of writer – serious, humorous, perceptive, opinionated, lyrical, blunt, ecstatic, cynical. The last word goes to the writer with whom we began the journey back at Land's End, and who has popped up at intervals all the way along – John Hillaby, coming in 1965 to the end of his own journey through Britain as he guides us to the final stopping place at John o'Groats.

CAIRNGORM HILLS, ABERDEEN/BANFF (GRAMPIAN)/INVERNESS (HIGHLAND)

> 155. Janet M. Smith in ed. Hamish Brown, *Poems of the Scottish Hills* (1982)
>
> *Corries*
> Corries are like pots of transmutation,
> Eerie vessels, magic cauldrons
> Of ancient tales; boiling vapour,
> Mist, rain, snow, hail into roots.
> Roots of grasses, of flowers, of trees,
> (Alpine birch and creeping willow);
> Rivers' roots, life sap
> Ready for spring.

For fifty years I have loved corries
But have not praised them. Stupid. Dumb.
Feet can worship, eyes can adore,
But words – dear, plaguey, illusive words
Are not to mind when spirit needs them.
There is only the silence of corries.
Maybe a plover's cry.

Yet I have loved them: Coire Lagan
Where once a friend heard alien singing
From deep water, and so was drawn
To the water's edge, in the mist, by the singing,
An won back late, by a friend below.
Perhaps she knew, perhaps now she knows
The corrie's secret – that womb of the hill,
The pot, the depth of life.

Coir'a'Ghrunnda has the wide slabs,
The sun's anvil to beat out eyes
In extreme heat. Coire Mhic Fhearchair
Of the huge shoulders like Norway's sea cliffs
Could swallow most others. Coire Etchachan
Dear and familiar, is studded with cushion pinks
Coral on grey granite. And the little corries,
Coireachan beaga of hundred hillsides
Are for everyday use.

Now if some words have fifty years
Can join in praise, it is praise of deep things.
Springs, streams and water, the hills' own life.

156. Nan Shepherd, *In the Cairngorms* (1934)

The Hill Burns

So without sediment
Run the clear burns of my country,
Fiercely pure,
Transparent as light
Gathered into its own unity,
Lucent and without colour;
Or green,

Like clear deeps of air,
Light massed upon itself,
Like the green pinions,
Cleaving the trouble of approaching night,
Shining in their own lucency,
Of the great angels that guarded the Mountain;
Or amber so clear
It might have oozed from the crystal trunk
Of the tree Paradisal,
Symbol of life,
That grows in the presence of God eternally.
And these pure waters
Leap from the adamantine rocks,
The granites and schists
Of my dark and stubborn country.
From gaunt heights they tumble,
Harsh and desolate lands,
The plateau of Braeriach
Where even in July
The cataracts of wind
Crash in the corries with the boom of seas in anger;
And Corrie Etchachan
Down whose precipitous
Narrow defile
Thunder the fragments of rock
Broken by winter storms
From their aboriginal place;
And Muich Dhui's summit,
Rock defiant against frost and the old grinding of ice,
Wet with the cold fury of blinding cloud,
Through which the snow-fields loom up, like ghosts
    from a world of eternal annihilation,
And far below, where the dark waters of Etchachan
    are wont to glint,
An unfathomable void.
Out of these mountains,
Out of the defiant torment of Plutonic rock,
Out of fire, terror, blackness and upheaval,
Leap the clear burns,
Living water,

335

Like some pure essence of being,
Invisible in itself,
Seen only by its movement.

FALLS OF BRUAR, PERTHSHIRE (TAYSIDE)

157. Robert Burns (1787)

The
Humble Petition of Bruar Water[1]
To the Noble Duke
of Athole.

My Lord, I know your noble ear
    Woe ne'er assails in vain:
Emboldened thus, I beg you'll hear
    Your humble slave complain,
How saucy Phœbus' scorching beams,
    In flaming summer-pride,
Dry-withering, waste my foamy streams,
    And drink my crystal tide.

The lightly-jumpin glowrin trouts,
    That through my waters play,
If, in their random, wanton spouts,
    They near the margin stray;
If, hapless chance! they linger lang,
    I'm scorching up so shallow,
They're left the whitening stanes amang,
    In gasping death to wallow.

Last day I grat wi' spite and teen,
    As Poet Burns came by,
That to a Bard I should be seen
    Wi' half my channel dry:
A panegyric rhyme, I ween,
    Even as I was he shored me;
But had I in my glory been,
    He, kneeling, wad adored me.

---

[1]Bruar Falls in Athole are exceedingly picturesque and beautiful; but their effect is much impaired by the want of trees and shrubs. R.B.

Here, foaming down the shelvy rocks,
   In twisting strength I rin;
There, high my boiling torrent smokes,
   Wild-roaring o'er a linn:
Enjoying large each spring and well
   As Nature gave them me,
I am, although I say't mysel,
   Worth gaun a mile to see.

Would then my noble master please
   To grant my highest wishes,
He'll shade my banks wi' tow'rin trees,
   And bonie spreading bushes.
Delighted doubly then, my Lord,
   You'll wander on my banks,
And listen monie a grateful bird
   Return you tuneful thanks.

The sober laverock, warbling wild,
   Shall to the skies aspire;
The gowdspink, Music's gayest child,
   Shall sweetly join the choir:
The blackbird strong, the lintwhite clear,
   The mavis mild and mellow;
The robin pensive Autumn cheer,
   In all her locks of yellow:

This too, a covert shall ensure,
   To shield them from the storm;
And coward maukin sleep secure,
   Low in her grassy form:
Here shall the shepherd make his seat,
   To weave his crown of flowers;
Or find a sheltering safe retreat,
From prone-descending showers.

And here, by sweet endearing stealth,
   Shall meet the loving pair,
Despising worlds with all their wealth
   As empty, idle care:
The flowers shall vie in all their charms
   The hour of heaven to grace,

And birks extend their fragrant arms,
  To screen the dear embrace.

Here haply, too, at vernal dawn,
  Some musing bard may stray,
And eye the smoking, dewy lawn,
  And misty mountain, grey;
Or, by the reaper's nightly beam,
  Mild-chequering through the trees,
Rave to my darkly-dashing stream,
  Hoarse-swelling on the breeze.

Let lofty firs, and ashes cool,
  My lowly banks o'erspread,
And view, deep-bending in the pool,
  Their shadows' wat'ry bed!
Let fragrant birks in woodbines drest
  My craggy cliffs adorn;
And, for the little songster's nest,
  The close embow'ring thorn.

So may old Scotia's darling hope,
  Your little angel band,
Spring, like their fathers, up to prop
  Their honoured native land!
So may through Albion's farthest ken,
  To social-flowing glasses,
The grace be – 'Athole's honest men,
  And Athole's bonie lasses!'

RANNOCH MOOR, ARGYLL (STRATHCLYDE)/
PERTHSHIRE (TAYSIDE)

158. Robert Louis Stevenson, *Kidnapped* (1886)

'Well, then, east, ye see, we have the muirs,' said Alan.
'Once there, David, it's mere pitch-and-toss. Out on yon
bald, naked, flat place, where can a body turn to? Let
the redcoats come over a hill, they can spy you miles
away; and the sorrow's in their horses' heels, they
would soon ride you down. It's no good place, David;

and I'm free to say, it's worse by daylight than by dark.'

'Alan,' said I, 'hear my way of it. Appin's death for us; we have none too much money, nor yet meal; the longer they seek, the nearer they may guess where we are; it's all a risk; and I give my word to go ahead until we drop.'

Alan was delighted. 'There are whiles,' said he, 'when ye are altogether too canny and Whiggish to be company for a gentleman like me; but there come other whiles when ye show yoursel' a mettle spark; and it's then, David, that I love ye like a brother.'

The mist rose and died away, and showed us that country lying as waste as the sea; only the moorfowl and the peewees crying upon it, and far over to the east, a herd of deer, moving like dots. Much of it was red with heather; much of the rest broken up with bogs and hags and peaty pools; some had been burnt black in a heath fire; and in another place there was quite a forest of dead firs, standing like skeletons. A wearier-looking desert man never saw; but at least it was clear of troops, which was our point.

We went down accordingly into the waste, and began to make our toilsome and devious travel towards the eastern verge. There were the tops of mountains all round (you are to remember) from whence we might be spied at any moment; so it behoved us to keep in the hollow parts of the moor, and when these turned aside from our direction to move up in its naked face with infinite care. Sometimes for half an hour together, we must crawl from one heather bush to another, as hunters do when they are hard upon the deer. It was a clear day again, with a blazing sun; the water in the brandy bottle was soon gone; and altogether, if I had guessed what it would be to crawl half the time upon my belly and walk much of the rest stooping nearly to the knees, I should certainly have held back from such a killing enterprise.

'CAMUSFEÀRNA' (SANDAIG), INVERNESS (HIGHLAND)

159. Gavin Maxwell, *Ring of Bright Water* (1960)

We arrived at Camusfeàrna in early June, soon after the beginning of a long spell of Mediterranean weather. My diary tells me that summer begins on 22nd June, and under the heading for 24th June there is a somewhat furtive aside to the effect that it is Midsummer's day, as though to ward off the logical deduction that summer lasts only for four days in every year. But that summer at Camusfeàrna seemed to go on and on through timeless hours of sunshine and stillness and the dapple of changing cloud shadow upon the shoulders of the hills.

When I think of early summer at Camusfeàrna a single enduring image comes forward through the multitude that jostle in kaleidoscopic patterns before my mind's eye – that of wild roses against a clear blue sea, so that when I remember that summer alone with my curious namesake who had travelled so far, those roses have become for me the symbol of a whole complex of peace. They are not the pale, anaemic flowers of the south, but a deep, intense pink that is almost a red; it is the only flower of that colour, and it is the only flower that one sees habitually against the direct background of the ocean, free from the green stain of summer. The yellow flag irises flowering in dense ranks about the burn and the foreshore, the wild orchids bright among the heather and mountain grasses, all these lack the essential contrast, for the eye may move from them to the sea beyond them only through the intermediary, as it were, of the varying greens among which they grow. It is in June and October that the colours of Camusfeàrna run riot, but in June one must face seaward to escape the effect of wearing green-tinted spectacles. There at low tide the rich ochres, madders and oranges of the orderly strata of seaweed species are set against glaring, vibrant whites of barnacle-covered rock and shell sand, with always beyond them the elusive, changing blues and purples of the moving water, and somewhere in the foreground the wild roses of the north.

Into this bright, watery landscape Mij moved and took possession with a delight that communicated itself as clearly as any articulate speech could have done; his alien but essentially appropriate entity occupied and dominated every corner of it, so that he became for me the central figure among the host of wild creatures with which I was surrounded. The waterfall, the burn, the white beaches and the islands; his form became the familiar foreground to them all – or perhaps foreground is not the right word, for at Camusfeàrna he seemed so absolute a part of his surroundings that I wondered how they could ever have seemed to me complete before his arrival.

GLENELG, INVERNESS (HIGHLAND)

160. Dr Samuel Johnson, *A Journey to the Western Islands of Scotland* (1775)

We left *Auknasheals* and the *Macraes* in the afternoon, and in the evening came to *Ratiken*, a high hill on which a road is cut, but so steep and narrow, that it is very difficult. There is now a design of making another way round the bottom. Upon one of the precipices, my horse, weary with the steepness of the rise, staggered a little, and I called in haste to the Highlander to hold him. This was the only moment of my journey, in which I thought myself endangered.

Having surmounted the hill at last, we were told that at *Glenelg*, on the sea-side, we should come to a house of lime and slate and glass. This image of magnificence raised our expectation. At last we came to our inn weary and peevish, and began to inquire for meat and beds.

Of the provisions the negative catalogue was very copious. Here was no meat, no milk, no bread, no eggs,

341

no wine. We did not express much satisfaction. Here however we were to stay. Whisky we might have, and I believe at last they caught a fowl and killed it. We had some bread, and with that we prepared ourselves to be contented, when we had a very eminent proof of Highland hospitality. Along some miles of the way, in the evening, a gentleman's servant had kept us company on foot with very little notice on our part. He left us near *Glenelg*, and we thought on him no more till he came to us again, in about two hours, with a present from his master of rum and sugar. The man had mentioned his company, and the gentleman, whose name, I think, is *Gordon*, well knowing the penury of the place, had this attention to two men, whose names perhaps he had not heard, by whom his kindness was not likely to be ever repaid, and who could be recommended to him only by their necessities.

We were now to examine our lodging. Out of one of the beds, on which we were to repose, started up, at our entrance, a man black as a Cyclops from the forge. Other circumstances of no elegant recital concurred to disgust us. We had been frighted by a lady at Edinburgh, with discouraging representations of Highland lodgings. Sleep, however, was necessary. Our Highlanders had at last found some hay, with which the inn could not supply them. I directed them to bring a bundle into the room, and slept upon it in my riding coat. Mr Boswell being more delicate, laid himself sheets with hay over and under him, and lay in linen like a gentleman.

161. James Boswell, *The Journal of a Tour to the Hebrides (1785)*

We rode on well, till we came to the high mountain called the Rattakin, by which time both Dr. Johnson and the horses were a good deal fatigued. It is a terrible steep to climb, notwithstanding the road is formed slanting along it; however, we made it out. On the top of it we met Captain M'Leod of Balmenoch (a Dutch officer who had come from Sky) riding with his sword slung across him. He asked, 'Is this Mr Boswell?' which was a proof that we were expected. Going down the hill on the other side was no easy task. As Dr. Johnson was a great weight, the two guides agreed that he should ride the horses alternately. Hay's were the two best, and the Doctor would not ride but upon one or other of them, a black or a brown. But, as Hay complained much after ascending the *Rattakin*, the Doctor was prevailed with to mount one of Vass's greys. As he rode upon it down hill, it did not go well; and he grumbled. I walked on a little before, but was excessively entertained with the method taken to keep him in good humour. Hay led the horse's head, talking to Dr. Johnson as much as he could; and (having heard him, in the forenoon, express a pastoral pleasure on seeing the goats browzing) just when the Doctor was uttering his displeasure, the fellow cried, with a very Highland accent, 'See such pretty goats!' Then he whistled, *whu!* and made them jump. – Little did he conceive what Doctor Johnson was. Here now was a common ignorant Highland clown imagining that he could divert, as one does a child, – Dr. *Samuel Johnson!* – The ludicrousness, absurdity, and extraordinary contrast between what the fellow fancied, and the reality, was truly comick.

It grew dusky; and we had a very tedious ride for what was called five miles; but I am sure would measure ten. We had no conversation. I was riding forward to the inn at Glenelg, on the shore opposite to Sky, that I might take proper measures, before Dr Johnson, who was now advancing in dreary silence, Hay leading his horse, should arrive. Vass also walked by the side of his horse, and Joseph followed behind: as therefore he was thus attended, and seemed to be in deep meditation, I thought there could be no harm in leaving him for a little while. He called me back with a tremendous shout, and was really in a passion with me for leaving him. I told him my intentions, but he was not satisfied, and said, 'Do you know, I should as soon have thought of picking a pocket, as doing so.' – *Boswell.* 'I am diverted with you, sir.' – *Johnson*. 'Sir, I could never be diverted with incivility. Doing such a thing, makes one lose confidence in him who has done it, as one cannot tell what he may do next.' – His extraordinary warmth confounded me so much, that I justified myself but lamely to him; yet my intentions were not improper . . .

We came on to the inn at Glenelg. There was no provender for our horses; so they were sent to grass, with a man to watch them. A maid shewed us up stairs into a room damp and dirty, with bare walls, a variety of bad smells, a coarse black greasy fir table, and forms of the same kind; and out of a wretched bed started a fellow from his sleep, like Edgar in King Lear, *'Poor Tom's a cold.'*

This inn was furnished with not a single article that we could either eat or drink; but Mr. Murchison, factor to the Laird of Macleod in Glenelg, sent us a bottle of rum and some sugar, with a polite message, to acquaint us, that he was very sorry that he did not hear of us till we had passed his house, otherwise he should have insisted on our sleeping there that night; and that, if he were not obliged to set out for Inverness early next morning, he would have waited upon us. – Such extraordinary attention from this gentleman, to entire strangers, deserves the most honourable commemoration.

Our bad accommodation here made me uneasy, and almost fretful. Dr. Johnson was calm. I said, he was so from vanity. – *Johnson*. 'No, sir, it is from philosophy.' – It pleased me to see that the *Rambler* could practise so well his own lessons.

I resumed the subject of my leaving him on the road, and endeavoured to defend it better. He was still violent upon that head, and said, 'Sir, had you gone on, I was thinking that I should have returned with you to Edinburgh, and then have parted from you, and never spoken to you more.'

I sent for fresh hay, with which we made beds for ourselves, each in a room equally miserable. Like

Wolfe, we had a *'choice of difficulties'*. Dr. Johnson made things easier by comparison. At M'Queen's, last night, he observed, that few were so well lodged in a ship. To-night he said, we were better than if we had been upon the hill. He lay down buttoned up in his great coat. I had my sheets spread on the hay, and my clothes and great coat laid over me, by way of blankets.

Old Deer, Aberdeen (Grampian)

162. William Alexander, *Notes and Sketches Illustrative of Northern Rural Life in the Eighteenth Century* (1877)

Seventy or eighty years ago Aikey Fair, which is still held annually on Aikey Brae, in the parish of Old Deer, in Buchan, was the largest fair in the north of Scotland. A legendary account of its origin is to the effect that a packman of unknown antiquity, Aul' Aikey by name, in crossing the river Ugie, on stepping stones, a mile west of the ancient 'Abbey of Deir', dropped his pack. On fishing it out of the water, then slightly flooded, he proceeded some three hundred yards farther on to what is now known as Aikey Brae, which was then, as it still is, covered with short grass and heath. Here he spread out his goods to dry. The contents of the pack consisted of prints and woollens, some of them being of gaudy colours. A good many people passed during the day, and being attracted by his stock bought up all the articles in it. Aul' Aikey was charmed with the success which followed what he had regarded as a calamity – the accidental soaking of his pack. Apologizing to his purchasers for the meagreness of his stock he promised to show them something better worth looking at if they would meet him next year at the same time and place. He kept his word, while the report of his gains brought others with goods for sale to the same place, and so traffic gradually increased year by year till Aikey Brae, from its central position, became a general mart for the large and populous district of Buchan . . .

Aikey Fair day was regarded as the great summer holiday; and both old and young flocked to it. Indeed, it was the boast to have seen so many fairs. 'Old Cairnadaillie', who died at the age of ninety-six, affirmed that he had been at ninety-one successive fairs at Aikey Brae, having been first carried there in his mother's arms. As many as 10,000 persons are said to have been sometimes present, all attired in their Sunday best. The men appeared in the old-fashioned, home-spun, woven, and tailored coat and vest, with big pockets and big buttons, knee breeches and hose, all made of the wool of sheep reared at home. They wore shoes with large buckles; and some of the rustic dandies came dressed in white trousers and vest. The women also were in their 'braws', and those of the fair sex who could afford it appeared in white. They generally wore high-crowned gipsy mutches. Then, as now, in matters of dress, the common folk trode on the heels of the gentry. The latter made a point of attending the fair, and several carriages might always be seen at it. The traffic at Aikey Fair, as at other annual fairs of the period, included cattle, horses, sheep, merchandise, and chap-book literature of no very pretentious character. There was always a wonderful supply of 'carvy' and coriander sweeties wherewith the lads might treat the lasses. The shows and amusements at the fair were of a very simple kind. The pipers from the country around assembled, and often a dance would be improvised on the green-sward. As time wore on there appeared the 'slicht o' han' men' to divide the attention of the idle and curious.

GARDENSTOUN, BANFF (GRAMPIAN)

163. Rev. John B. Pratt, *Buchan* (1858)

We descend by a winding path to the village of *Gardenston* or *Gamrie*, which, like Pennan, is built on the margin of the Moray Firth, at the base of a steep hill. The road, following its turnings and windings down the face of the brae, cannot be far short of a mile, the direct descent probably not exceeding a sixth of the distance. In making our way to it, we descend from terrace to terrace, and look down, as it were, into the very chimneys of the houses below. The situation is singularly striking. The houses are perfect eyries, built on ledges, and in the recesses of the cliff. The lower and older part of the village is close upon the sea. The harbour was crowded with boats, and two small sailing craft were receiving their cargo of fish. Men with the loose sailor-jacket, red woollen nightcap, and huge boots peculiar to their craft; women with the national serge petticoat, short wrapper, and head-gear – consisting of a handkerchief fastened under the chin – all familiar to a Scottish eye, gave a pleasing animation to the scene.

At the *Ironsides Inn* we had comfortable accommodations. And what a scene presented itself from the windows! Perched on a sort of plateau, some ten or twelve feet above the sea-level, we had a full view of the broad expanse of the Moray Firth. A little to the left, the Mhor-head, a stupendous cliff rising abruptly from the sea, and casting its deep shadow across the sleeping waters of the rock-bound bay. On the near shoulder of this bluff headland, and in the 'glack' of the hill, halfway up its rugged sides, the old church of Gamrie, standing, where it has stood for eight centuries and a half, in desolate objectiveness! Such a sight as this is neither to be seen with indifference, nor easily to be forgotten . . .

Leaving Gardenston by a westerly path along the beach, we come to another ravine between the village and the Mhor-head.

The rocks, always grand and picturesque, are rendered the more striking on this part of the coast, by huge masses, standing out here and there in the water, like an advanced guard against the assaults of the sea on the solid rocks behind. And hard service they have seen, being worn perfectly smooth by the constant action of the waves, and owing their preservation to the hardiness of their constitution; their less durable companions, sandstone rocks, having, one after another, yielded to the fury of the onset. The storms, as we were told, rage here with indescribable fury, of which there is sufficient evidence.

A tiny rivulet races down this rock-girt ravine towards the sea, and is shortly lost in the shingly beach, as though its heedless course had been suddenly arrested at the sight of that mighty wonder of creation!

The steep sides of the glen rise to the height of a hundred and fifty or two hundred feet. After crossing the mouth of the gorge we pass along its western verge till we reach a point at which the ravine files off in two different directions, severally stretching away among the neighbouring uplands. At this point the path takes a sudden bend to the right, leading through a mazy confusion of wild-roses and other flowering shrubs, directly to the old church of Gamrie, already mentioned as standing on a sort of plateau or shelf in the hill, and overlooking the bay and village of Gardenston, far below.

STRATH CARRON, ROSS AND CROMARTY (HIGHLAND)

164. Alasdair Alpin MacGregor, *The Goat Wife* (1939)

One Sunday morning, when I was about fourteen, I set off with Dick on what, up to that time, was the longest solitary expedition upon which I had embarked. I climbed to the summit of Carn Bhren. To achieve this had been one of the dreams of my young life. When I used to gaze across to its twin peaks from the higher part of our own moorland, or from the peat-moss in the valley, it seemed almost unattainable. But the ambition to conquer its summit never waned in me. I often have thought since how trifling an achievement this really was in comparison with my adventures, in later years, among the Coolins of Skye, and with my solitary wanderings through the stony, watery wastes of the Outer Hebrides. And, yet, I wonder whether my perspective as a boy of fourteen was quite so ridiculously out of proportion as I sometimes imagine it to have been? At that age, I certainly regarded a journey to Carn Bhren as a colossal undertaking. It was as an adventure into another realm. An expedition of this magnitude demanded of me a good deal of serious forethought and preparation. I often asked myself very privately whether, physically, I was able for it! Against storm and starvation, against fatigue, I prepared myself, as though I had been setting out on a thousand miles' journey, with the prospect of being absent for a year or more! On browsing over all this now, I am amused when I find that, today, I could attain the peaks of Carn Bhren comfortably in a forenoon from Cnocnamoine.

Be this as it may, Dick and I conquered Carn Bhren. And I often ruminate on that Sunday I sat on the very top of it, with Dick lying at my feet, his long tongue hanging out, and he panting with heat and excitement. There he lay, while I divided with him my lunch of sandwiches and homemade scones, and then gave him the juicy bone Aunt Dorothy had stuffed into my pocket on leaving. Down below us, and to the west, ran a strip of the road linking Alness and Ardross with the head of Strath Carron. Far beyond, I could see the Hebrides and the serrated Coolins of the Misty Isle – the scene upon which I used to gaze so fondly in early childhood. To the north lay Ben Klibreck. Grouped in the far north-west were Ben More Assynt, Quinag, Canisp, Suilven, and all the other weird peaks of Sutherland, rising mysteriously from the peat-hags bestrewn upon the Archæan rocks – one of the oldest fragments of the world.

Seana Bhraigh, Ross and Cromarty (Highland)

165. Hamish Brown, *Hamish Brown's Scotland* (1988)

A glimpse at the map to find some of Scotland's really remote Munros would lead the searcher to some splendid 'wilderness areas': rugged, isolated and often exceptionally beautiful.

By *really remote* I mean areas which are perhaps climbed with a night or two away from roads and civilization. Any and every Munro could be done and back in a day; but there are some defended by terrain and time, which would make this more of an endurance test than a pleasure. This is the criterion then . . .

Seana Bhraigh, to begin. Impecunious student days saw us first exploring this direction. Malcolm and I were based on a tent by Loch Droma between the Fannichs and the Beinn Dearg hills, over the dam from the road which runs across westwards to Ullapool – or past An Teallach of the sunset spires. We used cycles, ranging widely east and west. But as our time ran on, Seana Bhraigh still remained unreached. It took nineteen miles of cycling and eighteen on foot to secure it.

It is hidden away behind the Beinn Dearg hills which are rocky and steep and grand themselves. It is surrounded by great expanses of wild country with no public roads . . .

> 'Something lost behind the Ranges. Lost and waiting for you. Go! . . . Anybody might have found it, but – His Whisper came to Me!'

These odd words which I could not then trace (they are Kipling; *The Explorer*) kept going through my mind. Pictures of perfection that day – the dog dancing through blowing bog cotton puffs – a figure perched high above the precipices of the Luchd Choire, haloed with light above the blue depths – a lingering lunch by the

351

cairn with the peaks right up to Sutherland in view – a
tingling dip in a high pool with a plover calling its woes
around – a thunder of hooves on dried peat bog as a
hundred head of deer stormed past – the wheeling
motion of a wing-set eagle . . .

Is there anything to beat Scotland's soft and secret
pageant? Alps? Andes? Antarctica? I doubt it. Subtle it
is, the combination of all the senses, sharp in sun or
snow, pulsing with life. It was good to be young on
Seana Bhraigh.

BEN MORE ASSYNT, SUTHERLAND (HIGHLAND)

166. John Hillaby, *Journey Through Britain* (1968)

About six o'clock that night a loch loomed up far down
in the gorge-like valley and I worked down to it, slowly.
I felt excessively tired. The water was far from where I
expected to see it, but I imagined, hopefully, that I had
swung round towards the eastern end of Shin. Hope
changed to apprehension when the water appeared to
curl away in the wrong direction, to the west.

I scrambled down to within two hundred yards of
the shore. A flock of seabirds flapped off. I looked at
them in utter dejection. Instead of Loch Shin, I had
dropped down to the sea-loch Glencoul, on the coast.
There was no way out, for the cliffs were precipitous,
and I had no alternative but to go back.

A bad night that. The grey shawl of mist still hung
round the top of the gorge. The rocks I scrambled down
earlier, hopefully, seemed twice as steep on the way
back. I recall only a few landmarks: one, a prostrate
pine, its bone-white roots sticking up in the air like a
petrified octopus; another, an enormous waterfall, the
famous *Chual Aluinn*, the biggest uninterrupted drop in
Britain. It fell down with the noise of escaping steam. It
seemed to fall out of the sky, for the crest was hidden in
the mist.

How I had managed to stray down to Glencoul

became compass-clear far too late for comfort. The sweep of the gorge had beguiled me away from harder going, over the wall of the valley. There, as in Glen Ling and elsewhere, a wrong decision at a critical point had led to hours of arduous and unnecessary scrambling. That particular point in the gorge isn't even graced with a Gaelic name, but for those who may stray there, the formal map reference of the point of decision is 305245. From there it took me another three hours to get down to Loch Shin.

Once down from those heights there are no *creags* or chasms. Only manure-coloured water and olive-grey bog gently rising and falling for miles and miles. I squelched along. Two more of my six remaining toe-nails fell off. Not painfully. New pink ones appeared, miraculously, underneath.

The red ribbon of the northern night lay low along the west. Scarcely any mist, but almost dark now, the silence heavy and the sense of loneliness profound. No jubilation when the long-sought loch appeared, for in the dark I could scarcely see what I had sought for so long.

Moray Firth, North-Eastern Scotland

167. Neil Gunn, *Highland River* (1937)

Looking back on his childhood, Kenn finds, is looking back on a small figure in a sunny valley. The birch and hazel trees that clothe the sides of the valley are in full leaf; the green river-flats, widening and narrowing and disappearing round bends, are moss-soft to noiseless feet. The white scuts of the rabbits disappear in bracken clumps or sandy burrows or up under the foliage of trees. A hawk sails from one side of the valley to the other; inland, a buzzard circles high up over a gulch where rock faces stare.

A shot is heard faintly towards the high ground and the small figure stops and listens. That must be Gordon the keeper working the low ground in towards Con na Craige. Wild cats had been coming in from the Sutherland mountains and he had been setting traps for them. He also had traps for the hawks and the eagles.

All of which meant that Gordon was not on the river that day!

The strath is emptied of his presence, drained of the fear of him, and the little figure takes a small run, full of eagerness and the thrill of freedom.

He wanders, he stops, he peers into pools, he pokes under stones, he examines rabbit burrows, he listens, he looks about him, he wanders on.

From high overhead the river in its strath must look like a mighty serpent, the tip of its tail behind the mountain, its open mouth to the sea.

It is easy at such a thought to mount still higher over the small figure, to rise above the buzzard, and with circling sweep to scan that whole northland.

A thrill comes to Kenn as his eye takes in feature after feature, the shores of the Moray Firth, with all its villages and towns, every name charged with association, thick with the texture of life, Fraserburgh, Buckie, Burghead, Cromarty (the place of refuge), Tarbat Ness, Dornoch, Golspie, Brora, Helmsdale, and passing away nor'-east through Lybster to Wick.

At a glance Kenn can take in the whole steel-shimmering triangle of the Moray Firth. Each of its sides is barely seventy miles. For its size it is one of the finest breeding grounds of fish – and perhaps of men – to be found in any firth of the seven seas. Since the birth of his grandfather its story to Kenn is intricate with the doings of men and women, legendary or known to him. The rocks are quiet enough today. Even the headlands are stretched out in sleep. But Kenn smiles, knowing the rocks and the headlands, and that innocent shimmer of the quiet water like a virgin shield!

As he wheels slowly, the great plain of Caithness opens before his eyes and the smile that had been in them deepens with affection. This is the northland, the land of exquisite light. Lochs and earth and sea pass away to a remote horizon where a suave line of pastel foothills cannot be anything but cloud. Here the actual picture is like a picture in a supernatural mind and comes upon the human eye with the surprise that delights and transcends memory. Gradually the stillness of the far prospect grows unearthly. Light is silence. And nothing listens where all is of eternity.

Pride quickens the smile. This bare, grim, austere Caithness, treeless, windswept, rock-bound, hammered by the sea, hammered, too, by successive races of men, broch-builders and sea-rovers, Pict and Viking. Against the light, Kenn veils his eyes and wheeling round sees the Orkneys anchored in the blue seas with the watermark of white on their bows. Brave islands, he feels like saluting them with a shout.

Westward yet, and the granite peaks of Ben Laoghal, the magic mountain, beckon towards Cape Wrath and the Arctic. Westward still, and all the dark mountains of Sutherland march on Ben Mor Assynt, beyond which is the Atlantic and the Isles of the west.

Kenn completes the circle and his vision narrows on the winding strath beneath him, upon its skyey thread of water that links mountain to sea, west to east.

John o'Groats, Caithness (Highland)

168. John Hillaby, *Journey Through Britain* (1968)

The walk came to an end at a craggy-looking place called Duncansby Head, a mile or two beyond John o'Groats. There, from the cliff tops, I looked down on the outermost tip of Gaeldom, a flurry of water and black rock. I turned round and walked back to the hotel in the greenish twilight. I ate supper, alone, wrote up a few notes, and sat down on the edge of a small bed, flicking back through the pages of a diary filled with vigorous facts and names that already seemed rather strange and far-away.

ACKNOWLEDGEMENTS

We are grateful to the following authors, owners of copyright, publishers and literary agents who have kindly given permission for poems and passages of prose to appear in this anthology:

Methuen & Co for the extracts from *In Search of England* by H. V. Morton; and *The Call of England* by M. V. Morton.

John Murray Ltd for the extract from *Summoned By Bells* by John Betjeman.

The Estate of the late Henry Williamson and the publisher for the extracts from *Tarka the Otter, Tales of Moorland and Estuary* and *The Old Stag*.

Veronica Heath for the piece from *A Border Country* by Henry Tegner.

The Aycliffe Press Ltd for the extract from *Wild Harvest* by Hope Bourne.

Peters Fraser & Dunlop Group Ltd for the material from *In the Country* by Kenneth Allsop, and from *Brensham Village* by John Moore.

Michael Joseph Ltd for the extracts from both *How Green Was My Valley* by Richard Llewellyn (© 1939 by the Estate of Richard Llewellyn) and *Wetland: Life in the Somerset Levels* by Nicolson and Sutherland (© Text 1986 by Adam Nicolson).

Humphrey Phelps for the extract from his book *The Forest of Dean*.

Longman Group UK Ltd for the extract from *English Wild Life* by Eric Parker.

Penguin Books Ltd for the material from *Ring of Bright Water* by Gavin Maxwell.

The Estate of Richard Church for the extract from *A Window on a Hill* by Richard Church.

The Estate of Robert Gibbings for the extracts from *Coming Down the Wye* and *Sweet Thames Run Softly* by Robert Gibbing.

The Estate of C. Henry Warren for the extract from *England is a Village* by C. Henry Warren.

David Higham Associates for the extracts from *Akenfield* by Ronald Blythe, published by Penguin Books; from *It Shouldn't Happen to a Vet* by James Herriot, published by Michael Joseph; and from *Sailing Through Britain* by John Seymour, published by the Bodley Head.

HarperCollins Publishers for the extracts from *Along the Roman Roads* by G. M. Boumphrey, from *Nottinghamshire* by Alan Sillitoe, and from *The Wisdom of the Fields* by H. J. Massingham.

Oxford University Press for the extracts from *Lark Rise to Candleford* by Flora Thompson; and from 'A Tide in the Affairs' by Richard Mabey from *Places: An Anthology of Britain* edited by Ronald Blythe.

Commander M. E. Cheyne for the excerpts from *I Walked By Night* edited by Lilias Rider Haggard.

Random Century Group for the extracts from 'From a Train Window in Lincolnshire' from *A Song of Sunlight* by Phoebe Hesketh, published by Chatto & Windus; the excerpt from *Cider With Rosie* by Laurie Lee, published by the Hogarth Press; and the extract from *Corduroy* by Adrian Bell, published by the Bodley Head.

The Estate of H. E. Bates for the material from *Down the River* by H. E. Bates.

R. S. Thomas, 53 Gloucester Road, Kew, UK, for his poems 'The Chapel' and 'Good'.

Robert Hale Ltd for the extract from *Rambles in North Wales* by Roger A. Redfern.

Westmorland Gazette for the excerpts from *Pennine Way Companion* by Alfred B. Wainwright.

William Heinemann for the excerpts from *English Journey* by J. B. Priestley; from *Rivington* and *No Time for Cowards* by Phoebe Hesketh; and from *The Goat Wife* by A. A. MacGregor.

Victor Gollancz Ltd for the extracts from *Between Ribble and Lune* by David Pownall; *Vanishing Cornwall* by Daphne du Maurier; and *Dream Island* by Ronald Lockley.

B. T. Batsford Ltd for the extract from *The North Country* by Edmund Vale.

Martin Secker & Warburg for the extract from *The Hired Man* by Melvyn Bragg.

Chambers Publishers for the extract from *Walking in the Lake District* by H. H. Symonds.

Richie Bernard for his *Walks in the Ochils*.

The Estate of Betsy Whyte for the extract from *The Yellow on the Broom*.

Aberdeen University Press for the extract from *Hamish Brown's Scotland*.

Faber & Faber for the poem 'To the River Duddon' from *Five Rivers* by Norman Nicolson; and the extracts from *Highland River* by Neil Gunn, from *Country World* by Alison Uttley, from *Farmer's Glory* by A. G. Street, and from *The Horse in the Furrow* by George Ewart Evans.

Sheila Clouston for the poem 'The Hill Burns' by Nan Shepherd.

Constable Publishers for the extracts from *Journey Home* and *Journey Through Britain* by John Hillaby.

The Society of Authors as literary representative of the Estate of John Masefield for the extract from *Reynard the Fox* by John Masefield.

INDEX

(Numbers in italics refer to the number of the extract or poem.)